The Double Life of Books

The Double Life of Books

Making and Re-Making the Reader

Peter D. McDonald

EDINBURGH
University Press

Edinburgh University Press is one of the leading university presses in the UK. We publish academic books and journals in our selected subject areas across the humanities and social sciences, combining cutting-edge scholarship with high editorial and production values to produce academic works of lasting importance. For more information visit our website: edinburghuniversitypress.com

© Peter D. McDonald 2024, 2025

Edinburgh University Press Ltd
13 Infirmary Street
Edinburgh EH1 1LT

First published in hardback by Edinburgh University Press 2024

Typeset in 11/13 Adobe Sabon by
IDSUK (DataConnection) Ltd

A CIP record for this book is available from the British Library

ISBN 978 1 3995 2440 7 (hardback)
ISBN 978 1 3995 2441 4 (paperback)
ISBN 978 1 3995 2442 1 (webready PDF)
ISBN 978 1 3995 2443 8 (epub)

The right of Peter D. McDonald to be identified as the author of this work has been asserted in accordance with the Copyright, Designs and Patents Act 1988, and the Copyright and Related Rights Regulations 2003 (SI No. 2498).

Contents

List of Figures	vii
Preface: Two Voices	viii
Acknowledgements	xv

Part I: First Voice

1. 'The History of Sex': Orality, Literacy and the Living Brain — 3
2. 'The Lure of Literature': Books, Histories and the State — 20
3. 'Scant Cream': Sense, Nonsense and the Reader Remade — 37
4. My *Finnegans Wake*: Like HCE, Rhodes Must Fall — 53

Part II: Second Voice

Extra-Disciplinary: Questions of Method

5. Getting over Discipline Envy — 71
6. Ideas of the Book and Experiences of Literature: After Theory? — 80
7. Reclaiming the Future of Book History from an African Perspective — 100
8. Elton John, Libel and the Perils of Close Reading — 114
9. The Worldliness of Books — 128

Reading Envelopes: Four Examples

10. Republishing Yeats's 'The Lake Isle of Innisfree' in the 1890s — 151
11. Rereading Pound's 'In a Station of the Metro' — 182

12. Calder's Beckett 203

13. Once upon a Time in a Bookshop: *The Satanic Verses*
    Revisited 222

Bibliography 236
Index 247

Figures

1. 'Song of Myself' from 'Square Word Calligraphy' Series © Xu Bing Studio.   2
2. Robert Darnton's Communications Circuit (1982) adapted by Murray and Squires (2013).   5
3. Digital Publishing Communications Circuit (Murray and Squires: 2013).   6
4. Bilingual environmental print, Cape Town, South Africa.   18
5. A new model for the study of the book (Adams and Barker 1993: 14). © Adams and Barker 1993.   21
6. Conduits of transmission and survival for *Twentieth-century Short Stories*.   33
7. D. F. McKenzie's blank book.   45
8. Book designer's mock-up for the cover of *Also the Hills* (1944). Courtesy of Don McKenzie.   46
9. Annotated page from the fax dated 21 October 1988.   231

Preface: Two Voices

In 2008, I was asked to be part of a closing panel for the annual conference of the Society for the History of Authorship, Reading, and Publishing (SHARP), the leading scholarly body in the field now widely known as 'book history'. As the panel was intended to mark fifty years since the publication of Lucien Febvre and Henri-Jean Martin's field-defining *L'Apparition du livre* (1958), the contributors were asked 'to consider how the scholarly interest in print culture or the history of the book has developed since then' and 'to identify an individual, a group, a publication, a theme or an event from the past fifty years that has most significantly shaped your own work' (Sharp 2008: 29). Two of my co-panellists chose key figures in the fields of bibliography and textual criticism, Harold Love and W. W. Greg; one focused on the concept of 'Material Culture'; and another on a 1985 conference on the history of the book in Renaissance Europe held in Tours, France. I opted for the French writer-philosopher Maurice Blanchot (1907–2003). This is the text of my statement, which appeared alongside the four others on the conference programme:

> When did 'the book' arrive in my case, not as an historical phenomenon or as material artefact in the post, as it were, but as a challenging question in my own mind? Was it when I struggled to come to terms with the baffling novelty of J. M. Coetzee's *Foe*, which I first read in 1986? Was it when I had the privilege to be in D. F. McKenzie's bibliography classes three years later, and to see him magically lead his sometimes reluctant flock of students to date, describe and classify a blank book? Was it when I first responded to Pierre Bourdieu's inventive attempt to re-think the linkage between the material and symbolic aspects of cultural life? I do not know. What I do know is that my first sporadic forays into Maurice Blanchot's writings in the mid-1990s radically altered everything I had thought about the question of 'the book' up to that point.
>
> At one level, this was simply because Blanchot alerted me to the intellectual problem engendered by literature's dependence on

a range of institutions for its very existence, on the one hand, and what we might call its boundless capacity for evasion, on the other. Yes, various powerful guardians—publishers, booksellers, lawyers, librarians, bibliographers, editors, critics, teachers, etc.—categorise and label literary works, often to protect them as literature. But, yes again, these same works seem constantly to expose the limits, if not the perversity, of all such generally well-intentioned efforts. 'All that matters is the book, such as it is, far away from genres, outside the categories—prose, poetry, novel, chronicle—with which it refuses to align itself, and whose power to impose its place and determine its form it denies,' Blanchot commented in 1953 (Blanchot 1995: 141). This was in an essay calling for a new understanding of the task of reading and a new responsiveness to the generative fragility of literature as a category.

At another level, my reading of some of Blanchot's later essays opened a series of more fundamental quandaries about 'the book' itself, whether considered as a material object or as a cultural (perhaps even philosophical) idea. In an extended footnote criticising Jacques Scherer's misguided edition of some of Mallarmé's unpublished writings, for instance, Blanchot raised questions not just about the protocols and ethics of scholarly editing, but about 'all the forces—secret, personal, ideological, unexpected—that are exercised over our will to force us to write and publish what we do not want to.' 'What is this power?' he asked.

> It is neither the reader, nor society, nor the State, nor culture. To give it a name and realize it, in its very unreality, was also Mallarmé's problem. He called it the Book (Blanchot 2003: 265).

This takes us into a large, intricate and essentially metaphysical debate, the origins of which Blanchot traced back to the hubristic aspirations of the German Romantic poets. He could just as well have constructed a genealogy through the tradition of Romantic writing in English, which led up to W. B. Yeats and culminated in his desire to affirm his authority as a specifically Irish poet by creating what he called, following Mallarmé, his own 'sacred book' (Yeats 1922: 191, 196).

In the first instance, however, Blanchot's scepticism about the megalomaniacal, perhaps even fatal allure of 'the Book' took me back, via some of his other late writings, to the paradoxes surrounding the public presence of the writer as published author, to the question of literature's demanding singularity and to the specifically historiographical lessons of Blanchot's own admirably astringent refusals. This was, in part, because his insistence on the right of the writer to refuse 'the power and the glory' of celebrity authorship, whether offered by the state, the media or the publishing industry—all the modern institutions of 'the Book', we might say—was premised on the recognition that 'there is always, for authority, something suspicious and badly timed in the very act of publishing' and on his belief in the value of literature as an endlessly labile, illimitable and evasive cultural space, which is always oriented towards the future, or, as he put it, to the arrival of the as yet unfinished and, in principle, unfinishable 'book to come' (Blanchot 2003: 246). From Blanchot, in short, I learned that the celebrated phrase 'l'apparition du livre', 'the coming of the book', refers less to an historical event, datable in the case of Western Europe, as Febvre and Martin reminded us, to the 1450s, than to an indispensable principle of cultural life, which remains as pertinent today as it did fifty years ago.

Revisiting this statement over a decade later, my only major reservation concerns the passing remark about my first encounter with J. M. Coetzee's *Foe* in 1986. There is no doubting the impact of that experience, given *Foe*'s preoccupation with authorship, writing and the book trade. Yet many other books had as much, if not more, of an unsettling effect on me as a reader born just as the book, or what Marshall McLuhan called *The Gutenberg Galaxy* (1962), was losing its cultural centrality. As I began to reflect on the tenor of our discussions at the 2008 conference, however, it was not so much the arbitrariness of that choice that struck me. What concerned me more was the emphasis my statement and our wider discussions placed on the scholarly and theoretical questions Blanchot raised, relegating my experience as a so-called 'ordinary reader' to a background detail. Fair enough, perhaps, given the occasion and the brief, and yet for me it was impossible to quell the unease I began to feel about the gulf my statement and the conference exposed between the book understood as an object of academic *study*, on the one hand, and as an occasion of readerly *experience*, on the other.

The Double Life of Books confronts that gulf not so much to bridge it—there are no secure anchor points on either side—as to uncover the subterranean passages that have always belied the reality of the divide, connecting the two worlds of reading in idiosyncratic, sometimes secret ways. It does so by bringing two voices into play. The first belongs to the reader who delivered the Rosenbach Lectures at the University of Pennsylvania in 2022 as an exercise in materialist autobibliography (chapters 1–3). The series was entitled 'The Secret Life of Books'. These chapters develop the experiential back story alluded to in my reference to Coetzee's *Foe* in the conference statement, tracing a line from Dr Seuss's *The Cat in the Hat* (1957) to James Joyce's *Finnegans Wake* (1939). In addition, as exercises in autobibliography, they address a central challenge for the history of reading: the difficulty of capturing the elusive process of what the leading book historian Robert Darnton called 'inner appropriation' (Darnton 1996: 85). This voice also permeates chapter 4, which extends the discussion of the experiential impact of the *Wake* taking issue with overly clear-cut distinctions between so-called 'intrinsic' and 'extrinsic' approaches to reading. The second voice emerges in the final section of the book, which shifts genre from autobibliobiography to academic essay. This is the voice of the professional scholar who wrote the essays comprising chapters 5–13. These originally appeared in academic journals and book collections across a range of disciplines, including book history, literature and law and world literature. They now appear here in a revised form. By contrast, the first three chapters are largely unrevised, partly to retain the oral delivery of the lectures, partly to mark the difference in voice stylistically.

I focused on Blanchot for the SHARP conference because I was asked to identify an individual who had 'most significantly shaped my own work' as a professionalised academic with an interest in the history of media and reading. As I knew all along, however, what drew me to Blanchot in the first place was my own always evolving, never complete experience of one book in particular: *Finnegans Wake*. Joyce's last and most eccentric foray into literary writing is, after all, one of the best examples of a work (anti-Book?) that, as Blanchot put it, refuses to align itself with established genres and categories, denying the modern institutions of the book any power to 'impose its place and determine its form'. In its strategic incompleteness—the unstopped final sentence is 'A way a lone a last a loved a long the'—it is also a paradigm of Blanchot's unfinished and unfinishable 'book to come' (Joyce 1975: 628). Yet, as ever, it was not so much Blanchot who helped me come to terms with the *Wake*'s many eccentricities as the *Wake* that fuelled my interest in Blanchot's anti-scholastic reflections on the question of 'the book'. Once again illustrating the generative capacity of books themselves, and subverting the scholastic order of things, the experiential preceded and then directed the theoretical, not the other way around.

How is this possible given the *Wake*'s well-earned reputation as an iconically unreadable (and unread) book? It turns out that Joyce's last work is not just an extended 628-page puzzle designed to derail reading in its ordinary sense. It is also a compendium of reading lessons, addressed chiefly to the 'abcedminded'—that is, readers trained in the Latinate writing system and existentially immersed primarily in the English language and at least one of its many cultures (Joyce: 18). Moreover, to guide these readers through its meandering labyrinths of letters, it includes a pantheon of exemplary bad male readers, each of whom serves as an object lesson in how *not* to read. Two proved especially important for this book: the 'ornery josser' and the 'grave Brofèsor' (Joyce: 109, 124). As their names indicate, they come from opposite ends of the cultural spectrum and they cut very different figures, but, as the rhyme hints, they share more than their gender.

When it comes to the Brofèsor, Joyce's endlessly interlingual, polysemic and polyphonic play on the Latinate writing system allows *professors* (think English or Danish) simultaneously to be *Brotessers* (German), or bread-eaters, who in turn tend (at least in Joyce's book) to be devotees of the Catholic Eucharist, seeing (and consuming) Communion bread as the transubstantiated body of Christ. Joyce also associated Brofèsors of this kind with Neoplatonists, who think the 'everintermutuomergent' world of appearances can be resolved into one ultimate Idea or reality, and with followers of Saint Paul, who believe the 'letter killeth but the spirit giveth life' (Joyce: 55; Carroll 1997: 224). By contrast, the *Wake*, which is a sustained humanistic affirmation of earthly life—'ourth' in all its bodily specificity, finitude and imperfections—stands Paul, and all the traditions of interpretation he prefigured, whether legal, religious, philosophical or literary, on his head, insisting it is the singular, otherworldly spirit that killeth, and the endlessly generative letter that giveth life (Joyce: 18). So, for me, the *Wake*'s first injunction was deeply anti-scholastic: do everything you can to avoid becoming a 'grave Brofèsor'. This warning echoes throughout this book.

The 'ornery josser' is not as high-minded as the Brofèsor, but he too displays an unhealthy singlemindedness when it comes to reading 'a quite everydaylooking stamped addressed envelope' (Joyce: 109). Why? Because he focuses obsessively on the letter it contains, its contents or, even more narrowly, its supposed meaning, ignoring not only the envelope itself but 'the enveloping facts themselves circumstantiating it' (109). At one level, the josser is the bad reader who has always haunted book and media history: the literary critic, say, who attends exclusively to the 'words on the page', whether digital or print, or the intellectual historian who is interested only in books as vessels for the ideas they supposedly contain. As I show in chapter 8, the fictive josser found a real-life avatar in the figure of Elton John during one of his many libel cases. At another level, however, the josser serves as further warning to any institutionalised agent of the book, whether located in the university, the publishing industry or elsewhere. These intermediaries are the envelope-makers who, following Joyce's analogy, package and address the author's letter for readers, a process which, in the case of the Brofèsors, also brings various methods or circumstantiating disciplines and sub-disciplines into play. All these intersecting envelopes demand the forms of attention the josser avoids, but, to pursue the logic of Joyce's analogy and Blanchot's anti-scholasticism, they can never be determinative or definitive, since letters can always be re-addressed and put in new envelopes. This conviction also runs through this book, emerging most explicitly in the concluding section, called 'Reading Envelopes' (chapters 10–13).

By making the 'ornery josser' and the 'grave Brofèsor' a rhyming pair, non-identical twins with more in common than they would like to believe, Joyce invites us to be cautious about distinguishing too sharply between what the academic literary critic John Guillory calls 'lay' and 'professional' readers (Guillory 2022: 320). As Guillory notes, this binary shaped, indeed, deformed literary criticism from its very beginnings as an academic discipline. When it 'crystallized in its present form in the twentieth century, its professionalized reading practice was defined precisely by a deliberate cultivation of a difference from lay reading and even by the expression of antagonism toward that mode of reading' (327). By contrast, the 'lay' reader has been an important object of study for book historians ranging from Roger Chartier to Leah Price (323–24). To overcome the 'spectacular failure' of their own discipline, professionalised, university-based literary critics could do well, Guillory argues, not just to learn from book historians but to recognise 'the continuity between lay and professional reading' (342). Yet, with regret—'alas' he laments—he has 'no program for reconciling these practices' (342). *The Double Life of Books* does not pretend to fill the gap. Rather, taking its cue from Joyce, it addresses some of the less promising continuities between 'lay' and 'professional' reading, while bringing other, potentially more productive connections into view. By blending two voices and crossing two genres of writing, it offers not a 'program' for reconciling the 'professional' and the 'lay' but a way of keeping the *professorial* and the *experiential* in dialogue, opening lines of communication between the book as disciplinary or inter-disciplinary *object* of study and the book as extra-disciplinary *occasion* of readerly experience—hence *The Double Life*.

So much for the title. What about the subtitle? At the publisher's request, I toyed with *Making and Re-Making a Reader*. That appealed because it gives due prominence to my autobibliobiographical self and links the lectures to some of my own sources of inspiration, notably the broadly feminist tradition of biblio-memoir-criticism illustrated by Azar Nafisi's *Reading Lolita in Tehran* (2003), Rebecca Mead's *My Life in Middlemarch* (2014), Kirsty Gunn's *My Katherine Mansfield Project* (2016) and Jane Tompkins's *Reading through the Night* (2018). The closest I come to this is chapter 4, titled 'My *Finnegans Wake*'. Lauren Fournier reflects on the wider contexts and consequences of this tradition in *Autotheory as Feminist Practice in Art, Writing, and Criticism* (2021). Other points of reference were the music critic Carl Wilson's different, but no less self-reflexive, book about Celine Dion, *Let's Talk about Love: A Journey to the End of Taste* (2007), and the writer-musician Amit Chaudhuri's essay collection *The Origins of Dislike* (2018). In the end, however, I decided the indefinite article downplayed the double-voicedness of my own project and risked being too restrictive. Whereas, despite the counterintuitive grammar, *Making and Re-Making the Reader* allows for the many ways and guises in which the figure of the reader emerges across this volume: as biographical individual (chapters 1–4 and 8), as hypothetical construct (chapter 9), as market (chapters 7 and 12), as legal fiction (chapter 8) and as guiding but always debatable concept (*passim*).

Acknowledgements

I am grateful for permission to reprint in whole or part the following essays, all of which have been revised for this volume:

'Under the shadow of the Monument: on first looking into *Finnegans Wake*', *Irish Literature in a Global Perspective*, ed. Cóilín Parsons (Cambridge: Cambridge University Press, 2024).
'Seeing through the *Concept* of World Literature', *Journal of World Literature*, 4.1 (2019), 13–34.
'*Semper Aliquid Novi*: Reclaiming the Future of Book History from an African Perspective', *Book History*, 19 (2016), 384–98.
'Libellous Literature: Elton John and the Perils of Close Reading', *Literary Trials*, ed. Ralf Grüttermeier (London: Bloomsbury, 2016), 175–90.
'Calder's Beckett', *Publishing Samuel Beckett*, ed. Mark Nixon (London: British Library, 2011), 153–70.
'Sataniske vers I Sor-Afrika', *Dagbladet*, 26 September 2006, 51.
'Ideas of the Book and Histories of Literature: After Theory?', *PMLA*, 121.1 (January 2006), 214–28.
'Book History and Discipline Envy', *The European English Messenger*, XIII: 1 (Spring 2004), 51–56.
'Modernist Publishing: "Nomads and Mapmakers"', *A Concise Companion to Modernism*, ed. David Bradshaw (Oxford: Blackwells, 2003), 221–42.
'A Poem for all Seasons: Yeats, Meaning, and the Publishing History of "The Lake Isle of Innisfree" in the 1890s', *The Yearbook of English Studies*, 29 (1999), 202–30.

I am also indebted to the William Kentridge Studio for permission to use as the cover image an opening from *2nd Hand Reading* (2014), a multimedia project based on the 1936 edition of the *Oxford English Dictionary*; to the Xu Bing Studio for 'Song of Myself', which is part of his 'Square Word Calligraphy' series (figure 1); and to British Library Publishing for permission to use the image in figure 3, which first appeared in Thomas Adams and Nicolas Barker, *A Potencie of Life: Books in Society* (1993).

Special thanks to Bronwyn Brady for recounting her experience of the Initial Teaching Alphabet and for lending me her copies of the books we read as undergraduates; to the many others who helped revive and/or clarify my memories of reading at home, school and university, including Debbie Hall, Ian Jennings, Judie Stringer and Marius Vermaak; and to David McKnight, Lynne Farrington, Sean Quimby and Eric Dillalogue for inviting me to give the Rosenbach Lectures at the University of Pennsylvania in 2022. The YouTube recordings of the lectures, which are fully illustrated, can be accessed via: https://www.library.upenn.edu/event/secret-life-books.

Part I

First Voice

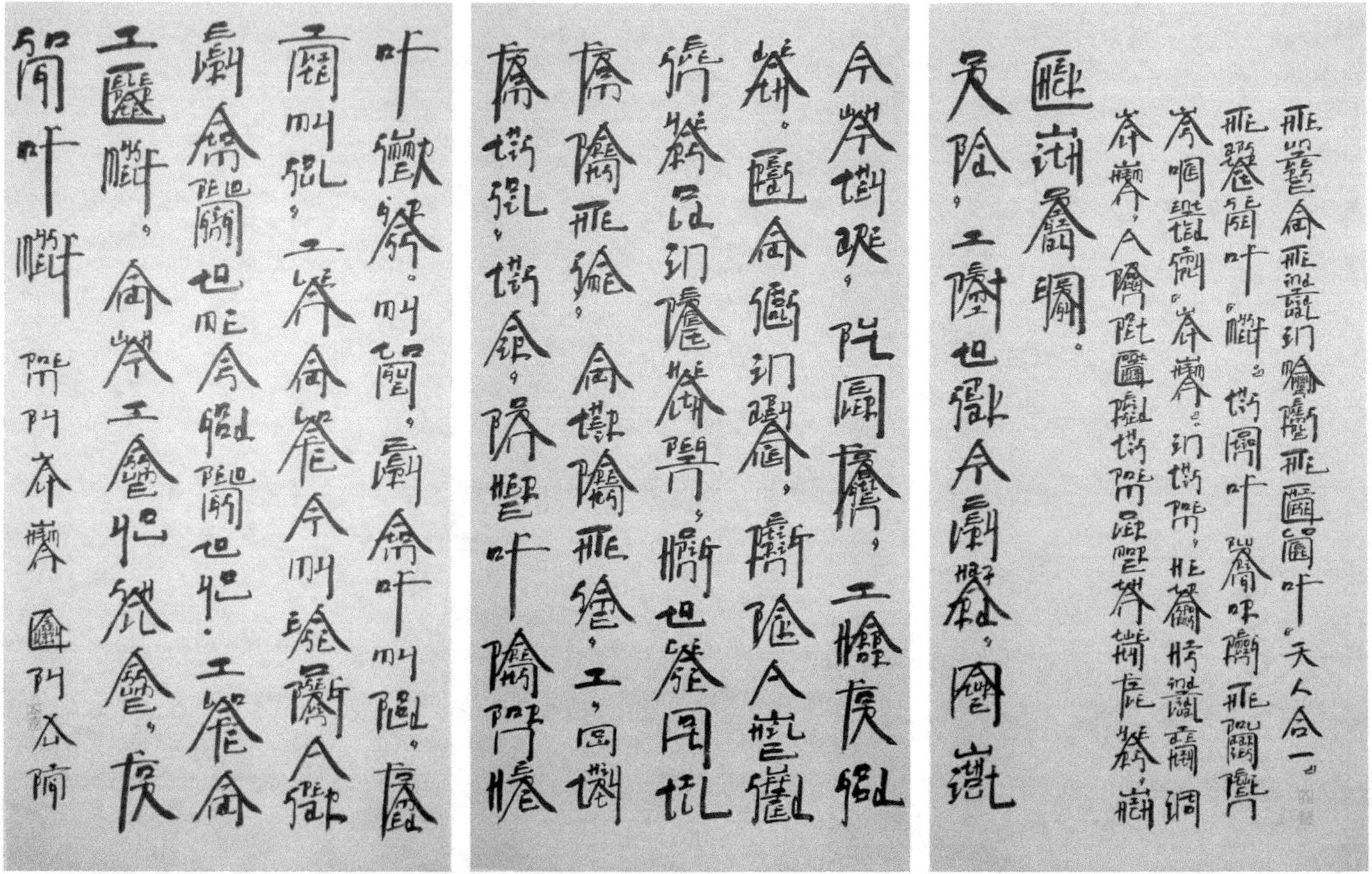

Figure 1 'Song of Myself' from 'Square Word Calligraphy' Series © Xu Bing Studio.

Chapter 1

'The History of Sex': Orality, Literacy and the Living Brain

I feel confident in saying that the other one, the one called Professor McDonald, is honoured to have been invited to give the Rosenbach Lectures for 2022. Established just over ninety years ago, this series commemorates an entrepreneurial scholar who dedicated his life and wealth to a great cause: collecting rare books and manuscripts, above all, some of the most celebrated European and American artefacts of literary writing ever produced. In fact, for me, 'Rosenbach' was at first the name not of a person, let alone a lecture series, but of a manuscript, now identified as EL4.J89ul 922 MS, the author of which was characteristically touchy when it surfaced for auction in January 1924, selling for $1,975. 'Rosy Brook he bought a book / Though he didn't know how to spell it,' James Joyce wrote archly to Harriet Shaw Weaver a few months later, 'Such is the lure of literature / To the lad who can buy and sell it' (Joyce 1957: 214).

For all the Wakean play on Rosenbach's name, this throwaway gibe does Joyce little credit. Yet one alliterative phrase—'the lure of literature'—got me thinking, first about the complex life of books as commodities of a special kind, and then about my own rather uncertain place in that life. For Dr A. S. W. Rosenbach, books and other textual artefacts had a clear value not simply as investment opportunities, as Joyce would have us believe, but as essential parts of a cultural heritage worth preserving for future generations. For the other one, the one I see listed in library catalogues under Peter D. McDonald, they are equally prized objects of study and, given his career as a salaried academic, the *sine qua non* of his professional life. But what about me, I found myself asking. Where exactly do I fit in all this?

If you have been following the debates within book history over the past four decades or so, then my *place* seems clear enough. I am the figure in the 'Readers' box on the left-hand side of the 'Communications Circuit' that the book historian Robert Darnton first proposed in 1982, soon after giving his own first Rosenbach Lectures (figure 2). Though competing with a host of others in the same box—purchasers, borrowers, clubs and libraries—my presence is not negligible, as the broken line completing the circuit intimates and as Darnton explains in his gendered way: 'The reader completes the circuit because he influences the author both before and after the act of composition' (Darnton 1990: 111).

As Darnton also acknowledges, however, 'models have a way of freezing human beings out of history', so knowing my place in the circuit does not take us very far (113). In fact, for Darnton, the chances of us getting much further are not good. 'The difficulty lies with reading itself,' he later noted, 'we hardly know what it is when it takes place under our nose' (Darnton 1996: 85). The philosopher Ludwig Wittgenstein agreed. 'The use of the word "reading" is, of course, extremely familiar to us in the circumstances of our ordinary life,' he remarked in *The Brown Book*, before adding in parenthesis '(it would be extremely difficult to describe these circumstances even roughly)' (Wittgenstein 1969: 119). Thinking mainly about how readers in the past made sense of the books they read, Darnton felt it might be possible to give a plausible account of reading's '*external* circumstances', say, via a history of libraries, printing or censorship. The real challenge, in his view, lies with the more elusive process of 'inner appropriation'—in fact, he thought this 'ultimate stage in the communications circuit,' as he now called it, 'may remain beyond the range of research' (1996: 85). Since this fugitive inner world is very much my world, it looks like I am fated, on Darnton's terms, to be something of a vain hope for book historians, a dream endlessly deferred.

Since Darnton made these observations in 1996, the digital revolution has changed the 'external circumstances' of reading, writing and their mutual entanglements forever. It has also changed my role, if not my place, in the circuit. On the revised Murray and Squires digital model (2013), I am now no longer a reader pure and simple (figure 3). I am a hybrid consumer-borrower-reviewer-content generator-crowd funder-subscriber. And in this new guise it seems I am no longer beyond the range of research. I leave traces everywhere. As a reader-reviewer, I not only generate trackable clicks and more substantive digital content in response to particular books. I promote them via

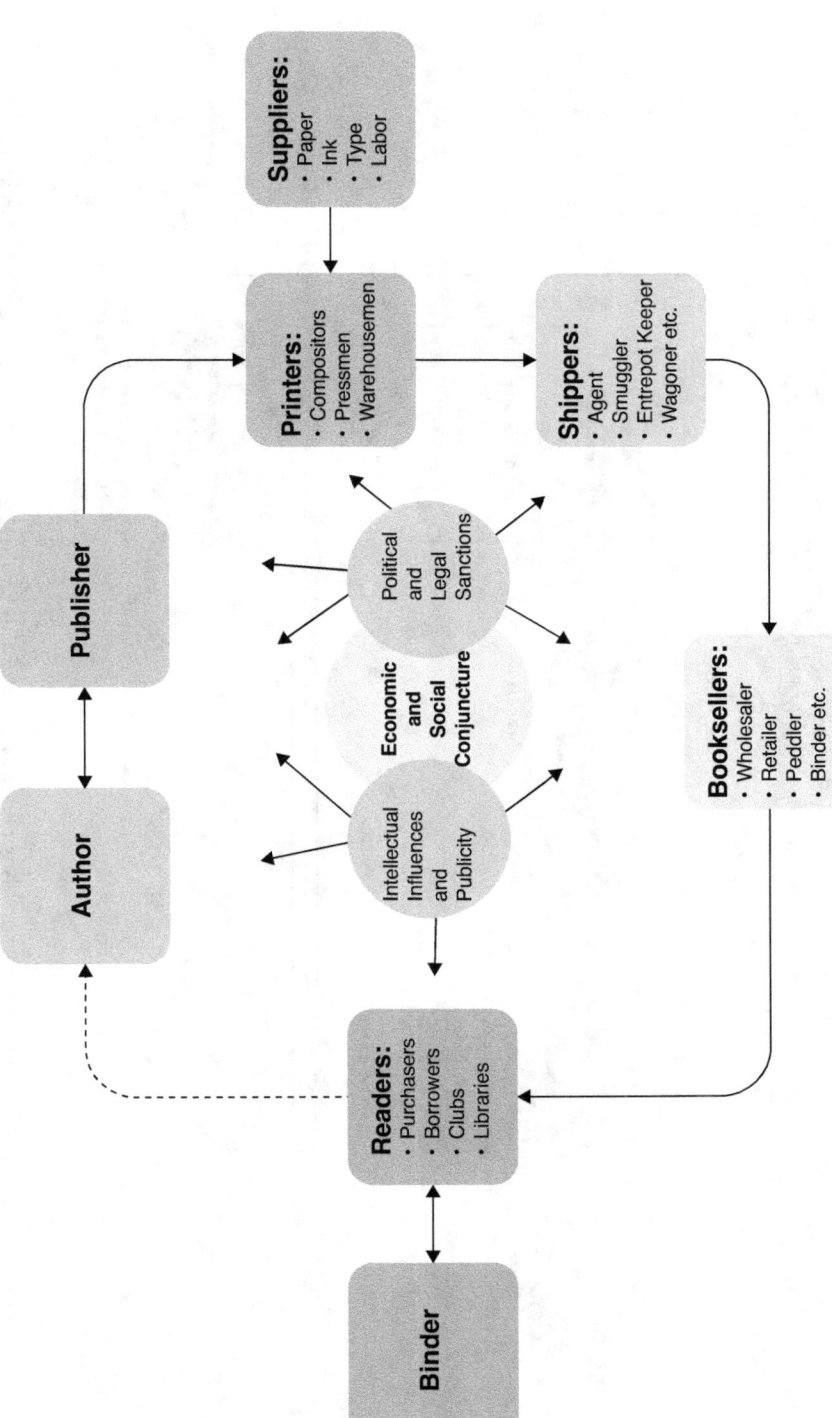

Figure 2 Robert Darnton's Communications Circuit (1982) adapted by Murray and Squires (2013). Available under a Creative Commons licence.

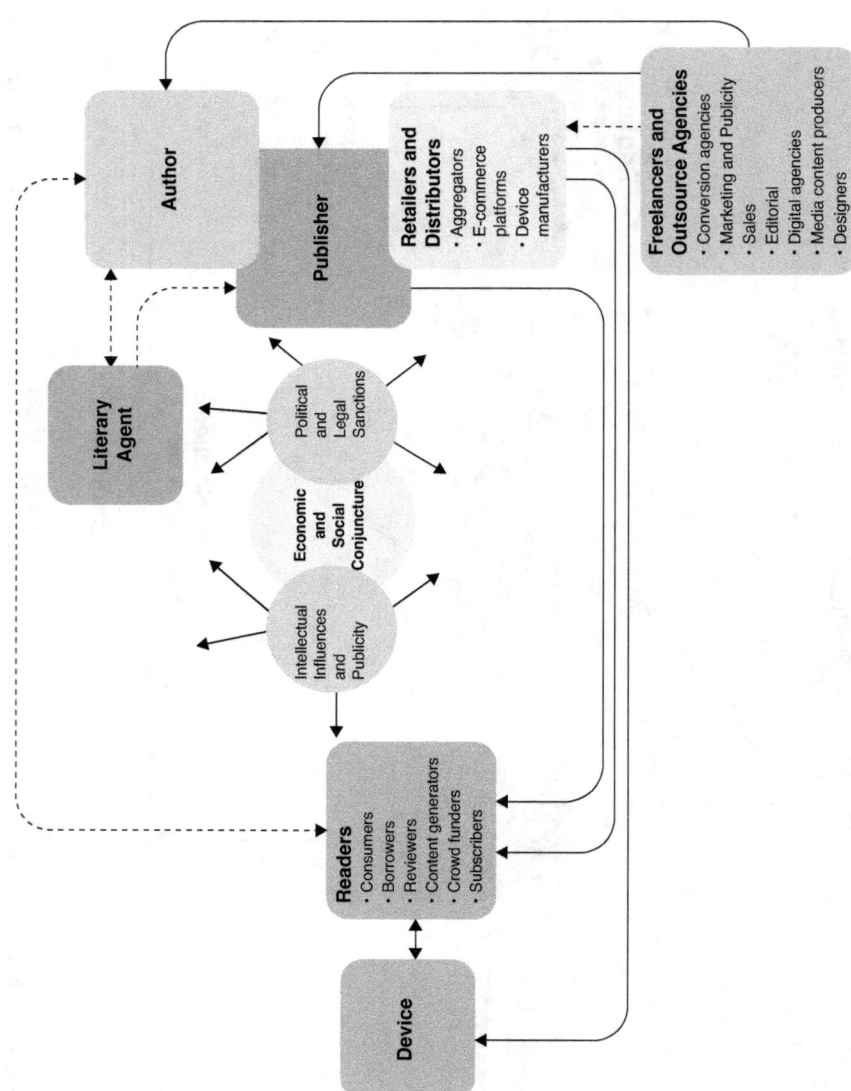

Figure 3 Digital Publishing Communications Circuit (Murray and Squires, 2013). Available under a Creative Commons licence.

social media, build reading communities and more, so much so that I have become an object of interest for multinational corporations and the surveillance state. Since 2007, CAPTCHA and Google have even used me as a free proof-reader for various digitising projects. As a reader-crowd funder, I could even be said to be filling the gaps in Darnton's dotted line, actively making authorship and publishing possible as a new kind of patron for subscription projects like the British crowd-funding publisher Unbound, launched in 2010, or the US-based Kickstarter, started in 2009.

But do all these digital traces really solve Darnton's evidential problem? Do they not simply stand it on its head? Far from being the print era's dream deferred, am I not, thanks to the oceanic excesses of the digital revolution, something more like a big data nightmare? Or, put otherwise and more urgently, am I really just the sum of my myriad clicks and likes, as Amazon's recommender algorithm would have it (to say nothing of the machinations of Cambridge Analytica)? The difficulty—and, as I shall argue over the course of these lectures, the ongoing challenge—lies with Darnton's pointed phrase 'inner appropriation'. There is no doubt that my numerous blog posts and opinionising tweets constitute a vast archive of outwardly expressive content. But does this really count as evidence for the more elusive inward history Darnton envisaged? The book historian Mary Hammond does not think so. Even in our pornographically saturated digital age, she notes, 'the history of reading, like the history of sex, is anything but an open book' (Price and Rubery 2015: 251). Once we see through the mirage of our politically or commercially exploitable algorithmic identities and big tech's ethically bankrupt dreams of total surveillance, reading as a process of 'inner appropriation' remains as elusive as ever.

And yet, as the linguist Michael J. Reddy powerfully reminded us a few years before Darnton proposed his 'communications circuit', this inner world is where culture, including the literary culture Dr Rosenbach wished to preserve, really lives. 'Libraries, with their books, and tapes, and films, and photographs' are not 'the real repositories of our culture', Reddy insisted in his 1979 essay 'The conduit metaphor', since 'there is no culture at all unless it is reconstructed carefully and painstakingly in the living brains of each new generation' (Ortony 1993: 187). His conclusion is perhaps even more apt for our digital age: 'We do not preserve ideas by building libraries and recording voices', or, we could now add, by loading everything onto the internet and feeding it into the vast data maw which is ChatGPT: 'The only way to preserve culture is to train people to rebuild it, to "regrow" it, as the word culture itself suggests, in the only place it can grow—within themselves' (187). I hope Reddy's words will keep echoing in your own 'living brains' throughout these lectures.

If we look back from the 1990s to the claims made by some of Darnton's more exuberant predecessors in the nascent fields of media and book history, then his caution about capturing the experience of reading as 'inner appropriation' looks even more creditable. Take that icon of the 1960s, Marshall McLuhan. Over-civilised 'Western man', hyper-visual creature of 'phonetic writing', benighted Finnegan 'mesmerised' by print, even 'schizophrenic'—these are just some of the epithets McLuhan marshalled to describe the ill-fated Euro-American reader in his flamboyant 1962 classic *The Gutenberg Galaxy*, which he subtitled *The Making of Typographic Man* (1962: 22, 263). Given everything McLuhan, like his mentor Harold Innis, owed to Oswald Spengler's *Decline of the West* (1926), he could have subtitled it: *The Decline of the Western Reader*.

It was from Spengler via Innis, after all, that McLuhan developed his governing idea of a prelapsarian village phonosphere, or what he also called, now drawing on Joseph Conrad's *Heart of Darkness*, the lost 'Africa within' (1962: 45). 'Our auditory predecessors were essentially gentle and complacent herbivores,' Jonathan Rée observes, wryly summarising Spengler's mythopoeic vision, whereas 'we ocular moderns' have become 'aggressive predators' (1999: 4). McLuhan agreed, blaming 'Western man's' initial predatory turn on the Greek invention of the 'phonetic alphabet', though tracing the ultimate 'fission of the senses', as he put it, to the era of mass print production which, in his view, signalled the triumph of the visual over the 'audile-tactile' (1962: 54–55). To make matters worse, the new technology also fuelled the rise of nationalism by driving the ascendancy and standardisation of vernacular languages in Europe. Hence McLuhan's Joyce-inspired vision of Typographic Man as a monstrous ocular nationalist, a one-eyed Cyclops bred of ink, paper and print.

Other leading figures in the emergent fields of media and book history looked back to Ancient Greece in equally colourful terms, while drawing a very different, far more triumphalist conclusion. Jack Goody, Ian Watt and, in certain moods, Walter Ong celebrated the advent of the Greek writing system because it formed the 'essential basis' for 'many characteristic cultural institutions of the Western tradition'—democracy in particular—and 'the distinctive features of Western thought' (Watt and Goody 1963: 320). Those are Watt and Goody's words. 'The completely phonetic alphabet,' Ong added, 'favors left hemisphere activity in the brain, and thus on neurophysiological grounds fosters abstract, analytic thought' (1982: 91). Too bad for Confucian philosophy and, indeed, the Chinese writing system, which Ong confidently predicted would be replaced by the 'roman alphabet' once Mandarin became the standard language of China (87).

Ong's position in these debates was in fact more ambiguous than this suggests, in part because an undercurrent of Spengler-Innis-McLuhanite catastrophism continued to run through his work. For one thing, in his effort to rescue orality from literacy's 'imperialist' gaze, as he put it in his 1982 primer *Orality & Literacy: The Technologizing of the Word*, Ong rehearsed the Spengler-McLuhan phonocentric fairy-tale, reconfiguring it as an existential story of the living and the dead (12). 'The oral word,' Ong notes at one point, 'never exists in a simply verbal context, as a written word does. Spoken words are always modifications of a total, existential situation, which always engages the body' (67). Later, referring to the description of pressed flowers in Robert Browning's poem *Pippa Passes*, he observes that 'the dead flower, once alive, is the psychic equivalent of the verbal [i.e. written] text' (81). Despite his efforts to rebalance the orality-literacy debate, this kind of language only bolstered the McLuhanite two-cultures vision Ong spent much of his time trying to undo.

Yet, as he immediately adds, there is a 'paradox' here, because the 'deadness of the text, its removal from the living human lifeworld, assures its endurance and its potential for being resurrected into limitless living contexts by a potentially infinite number of living readers' (81). The 'living reader': finally, I thought, someone with whom I might at last be able to identify, an unfrozen human being with a 'living brain'. But, once again, Ong's language, like McLuhan's, baffles. In this formulation, the ghostly written 'text', which Ong construes as the oral word's shadowy doppelgänger, appears to haunt the 'living human lifeworld', engaging actual, embodied readers fitfully at best—this is Reddy's conduit metaphor reworked as a Christian allegory of the incarnate soul. By contrast, Ong's 'living reader' seems more than human, possessing as she does an almost god-like power to raise the dead—no doubt, to pursue the logic of his underlying conduit metaphor, by performing the everyday miracle of incarnation we call 'reading aloud'.

So when it comes to the field of book history, the jury in the case of the missing reader is still out. For book historians, it seems either I have to reconcile myself to remaining forever absent, an elusive spectre of 'inner appropriation' never quite in Darnton's picture; or I must agree to being present on terms I find implausible, even alienating. Who, after all, would willingly self-identify as Goody's paragon of 'Western thought', McLuhan's one-eyed monster or Ong's oddly superhuman 'living reader'? What to do? Having reached an impasse among the book historians, I decided to direct my enquiries elsewhere.

Taking my cue from Reddy's 'living brain' and from Ong's forays *across* the other notorious two-cultures divide, I turned to contemporary neuroscience, where I was amazed to find myself fascinatingly, even copiously present. A marginal concern among a few pioneering outliers in Ong's day, it turns out I am now a vast and flourishing field of scientific research. You could even say I have become something of a celebrity. Where book historians fear to tread—recall Darnton on not knowing what goes on under our noses—a new generation of scientists has boldly hypothesised, experimented, imaged and analysed, shedding light not just on the reading brain's astonishing complexity but on some of its innermost secrets.

Recognising the wider public importance of their work, which touches on everything from dyslexia to the impact of digital media, some of this new generation have ventured beyond the lab, the journal and the conference circuit, addressing non-specialist audiences in trade books, TED Talks and other popular platforms. Over the past decade or so, Stanislas Dehaene, Daniel Willingham, Maryanne Wolf and others have led the way, highlighting the policy implications of their work, particularly in the field of education, as well as its practical consequences for parents, caregivers and teachers. True, their Kinsey report on reading as an act of 'inner appropriation' is still some way off, but by opening Mary Hammond's closed book they have initiated a wholesale reappraisal of the meaning and consequences of literacy, with implications for readers of all kinds, including the so-called 'ordinary' ones who are anything but.

Given the humanistic lineage I have sketched so far, I shall focus briefly on two basic tenets of this scientific endeavour. First, the neuroscientists have relegated what we could call Spengler, McLuhan, et al.'s sensory literalism to the dustbins of a pre-Copernican worldview. It is of course still the case that non-Braille readers like me access writing in all its forms and media primarily through our eyes, but we process those extraordinarily intricate visual stimuli with ever-changing, densely internetworked brains. Whether you take the most schematic outlines (Grainger 2009) or the most detailed magnetoencephalographic images (Cornelissen 2009), the idea that we literate moderns are essentially, let alone rapaciously or imperialistically, ocular simply does not add up. Partly for this reason, many contemporary neuroscientists have turned against 'whole language' or 'look-say' approaches to early learning, putting their collective weight behind phonics instead. Yet it is not just the visual and the auditory neural pathways that are inextricably linked. When it comes to the reading brain, interconnectedness is all. It encompasses the cognitive, the linguistic, the motor and the affective as well—and this is just in the uppermost cortical layer of the brain's reading network.

Second, the neuroscientists have reminded us of a deceptively simple fact: evolution did not make us readers. Here is Maryanne Wolf:

> The acquisition of literacy is one of the most important epigenetic achievements of *Homo sapiens*. To our knowledge, no other species ever acquired it. The act of learning to read added an entirely new circuit to our hominid brain's repertoire. The long developmental process of learning to read deeply and well changed the very structure of that circuit's connections, which rewired the brain, which transformed the nature of human thought. (2018: 1–2)

The extent to which Wolf's 'circuit' is 'entirely new' has been debated. For Stanislas Dehaene, it is possible that the 'visual word form area', otherwise known as the brain's 'letterbox', is in part an effect of 'neuronal recycling', whereby the more primordial pathways for vision and attention that evolution gave us—the ones enabling newborns to recognise their mother's faces, say, or hunter-gatherers to follow animal tracks—are repurposed for reading (2009: 144). Whether a modification or a new addition, one thing is clear: the 'letterbox' is inextricably bio-cultural. 'Inner appropriation', in other words, begins as culturally triggered neuronal transformation, with, as Wolf notes, radical consequences for 'human thought'.

There is something familiar about all this, especially the way Wolf's final sentence moves effortlessly from literacy to 're-wiring' to the transformed 'nature of human thought'. Is this not Ong and McLuhan all over again? Wolf raises this prospect herself. Later in the same book, which is centrally concerned with the effects of digital media on the brain, she references their work in passing, while upbraiding herself for coming to it rather late. 'Unlike scholars in the past such as Walter Ong and Marshall McLuhan,' she comments, 'I never focused on the influences of the medium (e.g. book versus screen) upon this malleable circuit's structure' (2018: 7). This is an important admission, reflecting the ongoing relevance of the pioneering work that emerged from McLuhan's stable in the 1960s. Yet, as I have already intimated, the Ong-McLuhan legacy doesn't bear much scrutiny from a contemporary neuroscientific point of view, and, when it comes to Wolf's own writing, it is the differences, not the debts, that stand out.

For one thing, given her guiding assumptions about the brain's dense interconnectedness, she never overplays the visual dimensions of literacy. In line with the contemporary neuroscientific consensus, she recognises that any cognitive transformation reading effects occurs within, and depends on, the phonological, semantic and other neural pathways laid down during the earlier, instinctive stages of language development. No matter how 'Westernised' our literate brains might be, we have never lost touch with 'the Africa within'. For another thing (and again in line with the consensus), Wolf does not indulge in the more magical aspects of McLuhan and Ong's thinking—notably their short-circuiting leaps from 'the phonetic alphabet' to 'Western thought' or from the mass production of print to ocular nationalism. Yes, the 'long developmental process of learning to read' involves deep immersion in a particular writing system as well as its many forms and media, but, for Wolf, a range of other environmental influences come into play as well. These include the social world into which each potential reader is born, the ways in which they are taught, the reading materials they encounter, and the unique passage they chart through the graphosphere's many galaxies over the course of their reading life.

A moment ago, I said I have become something of a celebrity in the field of contemporary neuroscience. That was, of course, a way of speaking. Thanks to this extraordinary body of work, we certainly know more about what is going on under our noses when we read, but what we know tends to be both generic and artificial. This is perhaps inevitable, given the methods, preoccupations and constraints of this kind of research. For the neuroscientists, the main object of study is *the* reading brain, at best differentiated by age (child/adult), writing system (English/Mandarin) or disability (dyslexia/hyperlexia). Moreover, when they design strictly controlled, repeatable experiments to, say, track the brain's lightning-flash impulses as it connects graphemes to phonemes, they tend to rely on simplified reading exercises, often using only words, pseudo-words or random letter strings. If they use any longer sequences of text, they generally require their obliging subjects to read a short passage on a screen while lying preternaturally still in an MRI scanner like a mummy in a sarcophagus. This is not reading as most of us know and experience it. As the great neurologist Oliver Sacks once put it, 'neuropsychology is admirable, but it excludes the psyche—it excludes the experiencing, active, living "I"' (1984: 164).

So, in a sense, I am as much of a problem for the scientists as I am for the book historians. Still, the insights neuroscience now affords into the bio-cultural processes of 'inner appropriation' have, in my view, changed the conversation about reading in fundamental ways. More than that, they have opened possibilities for a new cultural and historical investigation into the 'ultimate stage of the communications circuit' and, consequently, a new historiography of reading: since this will necessarily involve some element of life writing, we could call it a *materialist autobibliography*. I shall spend the rest of this lecture, and the next two, developing a series of notes towards such a writing project, but I hope one central tenet is by now already clear. Following the science, and *contra* Ong, the alternative historiography I am proposing recognises that, for literate societies, digital as well as pre-digital, writing is as much a part of the 'living human lifeworld' as speech. Moreover, given the neuroscientists' claims about the brain's interconnectedness and plasticity, literacy modifies 'a total, existential situation, which always engages the body'—again *contra* Ong, who associates this kind of modification exclusively with orality. The need to come to terms with embodied experience, for readers and writers alike, has acquired a new urgency today as well, given recent advances in machine learning and artificial intelligence, adding a further digital factor to Ong's mix of literacy and orality. You could even say that, for living brains like us, clarifying the difference between AI and B-CI (or artificial and bio-cultural intelligence) has become something of an existential imperative.

There is of course still that nagging question of evidence, which remains as challenging as ever. To address this, I will draw on an eclectic range of sources: institutional and publishers' archives, digital and print artefacts, published research, but also family folklore backed up by personal memory as well as correspondence with the editors of school anthologies, former teachers, fellow initiates into the secret life of books, and more. At times I may even turn to my professorial doppelgänger, though, for the most part, I shall keep him in the background where, I think, he belongs. He is, after all, a latecomer to my formative story. In my experience, he also tends to be otherwise occupied—typically, when I look into *his* world, I find myself eclipsed by the ethos, protocols and expectations of *his* professional community, relegated at best to the status of a slightly embarrassing secret sharer. So, you could think of this as a hijack lecture series, or the revenge of the repressed. One final point about evidence: I have called these 'sources', as if they are merely a means to an end or archives to be plundered. The opposite is closer to the truth. Like the 'external circumstances' to which they sometimes point, they are an integral part of my story, which is necessarily as individual as it is social, as internal as it is external, just as it is inescapably biological *and* cultural. This anti-dualism is central to the science, as we have already seen. It is also implicit in Darnton's economic metaphor of 'appropriation'. 'Appropriation', according to the OED, involves '*the making of* a thing private property', presumably something originally public, held in common, or shared—the English language, say, or a piece of writing, or a book (OED 2022).

In the time I have left today, I shall outline the first chapter of this bio-cultural story. From the very beginning, indeed with the question of *the beginning*, the science introduces complications. In my case, the first hitch can best be described via an ingenious experiment conducted in the 1980s, involving expectant mothers reading to their unborn children—one of the three stories used for the experiment happens to have been my own early favourite: Dr Seuss's 1957 classic *The Cat in the Hat*, which I was pleased to see is still prominently displayed in the Penn Bookstore (DeCasper 1986, see also Mampe 2009). For the purposes of this experiment, the mothers were asked to read their designated story aloud to their unborn baby twice a day during the final six weeks of their pregnancies—this meant they did so sixty-seven times on average before giving birth. The result? When tested three days after they were born, the *Cat in the Hat* babies turned out to be enthusiastic Dr Seuss fans. The mere idea of a newborn with a literary preference is remarkable, but, for the researchers, the challenge was to account for it. They were clear the plot, and even particular words, could be excluded; they had also designed the experiment in such a way as to rule out the sound of the mother's voice. What really attracted the babies in utero, they established, was the verbal music of the story itself, its intonation or melodic contour. Reverberating through the amniotic fluid, this set their ears and pattern-recognising brains ringing—McLuhan was right, at least in a developmental sense: we are primordially 'audile-tactile'.

What bearing does this have on my own bio-cultural story? For Tony DeCasper and Melanie Spence, the scientists responsible for this research, the experiment showed that the 'inner appropriation' of *specific* linguistic properties, prosody and melody in particular, begins before birth for babies with no congenital hearing difficulties. From inside the womb, these properties are inevitably auditory. As I was a late starter by these standards—I apparently began to express a preference for *The Cat in the Hat* aged around two—many other influencers outside the womb line up: my aspirational mother's belief in reading as a cognitively enriching cultural practice, the familiar sound of her accented voice, the affective and social benefits of jointly engaging in a shared activity, as well as the physicality of the book itself with all its alluringly surrealistic illustrations. *The Cat in the Hat* was thus deeply woven into the 'living human lifeworld' into which I was born not just as a 'thing' (Ong's word for the physical book) but as a repeated 'utterance' (again Ong's word) and mode of affective engagement (1982: 125). According to the science, it was this total bodily (not just aural) immersion that set the long developmental process of 'inner appropriation' in motion, shaping my malleable brain and giving me a neurological head start even as a pre-reader (see Sun, et al. 2023).

Yet even outside the womb, my experience of *The Cat in the Hat* as 'utterance' was key. At one level, this had nothing to do with the story as such. Like all the other printed words my mother read aloud—or 'resurrected', to recall Ong's theological metaphor—Dr Seuss's classic was simply a prized facet of the ambient oral culture through which I first encountered what we could call 'Book English'—the rather strange, always varied dialect found in printed books (see Castles, et al. 2018 and Montag, et al. 2015). Who, after all, speaks like this in real life?

> The sun did not shine.
> It was too wet to play.
> So we sat in the house
> All that cold, cold wet day. (1958: 1)

At another level, the story's specific soundscape was decisive, especially in neurological terms. For me, this no longer had simply to do with the melody of the words, the four-beat prosody of the lines, as was the case with the experimental babies in utero. Outside the womb it was that plus the specific verbal patterning of the rhymes, alliteration and assonance. All the phonetic repetitions with variation from 'cat' and 'hat' in the title to 'play' and 'day' in these opening lines—but also 'not', 'wet', 'sat' and 'that'—helped establish neural templates for the forty-six or so basic phonemes of spoken English via the essentially statistical and abstractive process of iterative listening. True, these simple, accentuated sound patterns were not peculiar to *The Cat in the Hat* or, indeed, to the many other early varieties of Book English I internalised—I had a good repertoire of nursery rhymes, for instance. They also featured prominently in the child-directed language adults tended to use when speaking to me, otherwise known as 'parentese' or 'motherese', another major influence on early language learning. These two stylised sub-varieties of spoken English, one essentially oral, the other book-based, complemented one another. Working in concert, they nurtured my brain's increasingly specialised phonological pathways, sharpening my capacity to segment the individual sounds of English, once again preparing the way for my initiation into the mysteries of its writing system.

Increasingly specialised is the key phrase here. As the neuroscientist Patricia Kuhl put it, we are all born audile 'citizens of the world' capable of hearing the sounds of many languages, but between the ages of six to twelve months the ambient oral culture begins to transform the cosmopolitan brains evolution gives us, gradually making limited first-language monolinguals like me ever more specialised citizens of a single phonosphere (2004: 833). That a printed book was among the agents of this neurological refashioning in my case is vital for the purposes of the argument I will be developing over the course of these lectures. Books, I will contend, are not simply conduits for ideas. They do things to us, including change our brains. In the first instance, this was of course the book as 'utterance' performed by my mother in her guise as Ong's 'living reader'. But, as my professorial research assistant discovered much later, the book as 'thing', or, more accurately, as commodity, contributed too. As it turns out, the effect *The Cat in the Hat*'s soundscape had on my brain was very much part of the author's or, initially, the publisher's plan.

Responding to a crisis about literacy in 1950s America, prompted by Rudolf Flesch's provocative pro-phonics polemic *Why Johnny Can't Read* (1955) and fuelled by the Cold War rivalry with the Soviet Union, William Spaulding, the director of the education division of the Boston publisher Houghton Mifflin, commissioned Theodor Geisel (aka Dr Seuss) to write a children's book, drawing on a specified list of 225 basic words, mostly short monosyllables—Geisel ended up using 223. The idea was not simply to produce a livelier and more engaging alternative to the *Dick and Jane* primers that had been a staple of US primary education since the 1930s. The publisher's plan was to push back against the dominant 'look-say' or 'whole word' pedagogic method, and, following Flesch's challenge and the successful Soviet lead, to promote phonics instead. *The Cat in the Hat* was the result. It was an instant success, at least among children and parents—teachers, committed to the old ways, were more resistant—giving it, as the historian Adrian Johns notes, 'a fair claim to be considered the most important poem published in the twentieth century' (Johns, 2023: 337). The literary critic Louis Menand put it more colourfully, describing Dr Seuss's instant hit as 'one of the Cold War's most potent unguided missiles' (2002). I prefer to think of it as a letter posted to my two-year-old brain's still non-existent letterbox in an unaddressed envelope. But, despite the horrors we are currently witnessing in Ukraine, let's run with Menand's Cold War metaphor.

In my case, the missile was not unguided. It followed an elaborate but traceable trajectory we can track backwards from the moment it entered my ears as a sequence of designedly iterative sounds, having just passed through my mother's eyes as an organised arrangement not of mere printed marks but of meaningful words. All this was possible because she bought the British edition first published in London in 1958 from the Central News Agency in Pinelands, Cape Town, after Collins, the British publisher, working within the essentially colonial book trade networks of the time, negotiated the rights with the American publisher to sell their own edition across the Commonwealth. Thus guided, the Geisel-Spaulding missile hit what we can safely call an unintended target over 12,000 km from its first launching site: my pre-reading brain. The consequence? As the ultimate stage of that hybrid oral-literate communications circuit, which extended from Boston and New York to Cape Town via London, one small neurological part of me will forever be a collateral fragment of the Cold War.

Unlike Louis Menand, I cannot claim Dr Seuss played a decisive part in the next turning point in my bio-cultural story. For Menand, *The Cat in the Hat*, or, more precisely, its second most frequent word—'and'—marked the magical, duck-rabbit moment he stepped across the threshold separating pre-readers from novice readers of the alphabetic, Latinate writing system. 'I knew the phonetic value of each letter,' he recalls:

> What I could not figure out was how you got from those three discreet sounds to the sound-blur 'and.' I remember the moment the switch was flipped, and 'a,' 'n,' 'd,' turned into 'and.' I said to myself, 'So that's how you do it.' It is the moment you awake to the realization that there is a world available through print. (2002)

My own grapheme-phoneme epiphany was more mundane but no less magical. For me, the duck-rabbit was not 'and' but 'stop', and the medium was not a book but a conspicuous instance of the environmental print to which my mother frequently drew my attention:

Figure 4 Bilingual environmental print, Cape Town, South Africa.

the stop sign at the bottom of our road—as it happens another product of the 1950s, at least in its standardised octagonal shape, white lettering, white border and red background (figure 4). Realising that the four letters mapped onto the four discreet sounds /s/, /t/, /o/ and /p/ and so spelt the word 'stop' certainly installed a rudimentary phonics 'letterbox' into my brain's evolving language pathways, making it possible for me to become a five-year-old novice reader. As a form of environmental print, however, the stop sign also made me start looking more closely at the densely written world in my immediate neighbourhood, which, as my mother regularly pointed out, included many other everyday inscriptions not just in English but in Afrikaans, though none in German or isiXhosa, the other languages I frequently heard spoken. As my letterbox expanded, decoding most of these bilingual public signs became easier, but comprehending others, like the 'Whites Only/Slegs Blankes' beach signs in apartheid South Africa, remained a life-long challenge.

Coda: All of us in this room are, I suspect, too far advanced as readers to give much thought to the life-changing, duck-rabbit moment when arrays of letters become words, but some contemporary thinkers, like the Chinese verbovisual artist Xu Bing, have found ways of allowing us to re-experience it. Revisit figure 1—hint: it begins 'Song of Myself' on the top left, reading down.

Chapter 2

'The Lure of Literature': Books, Histories and the State

I began my first lecture discussing Robert Darnton's doubts about our ability to investigate what he called the communication circuit's 'ultimate stage', the reader's 'inner appropriation' of books. Today, I'd like to start by considering a question at the opposite end of the inner-outer scale. From Thomas Adams and Nicolas Barker in 1993 to Sarah Brouillette in 2019, the difficulty many commentators have had with Darnton's model (see figure 2) is not that it freezes human beings and their inner reading lives out of history. Rather, it freezes history out of book history, or, more precisely, it consigns what Darnton called 'outside influences'—that is, the larger social, economic, political, intellectual and legal forces beyond the circuit—to a simplified Venn diagram at its centre, a lead Murray and Squires followed for their updated digital model in 2013 (figure 3).

To rectify this, Adams and Barker made two key changes (figure 5). They replaced Darnton's eight *agents* with five *events*, and they put the circuit inside 'the whole socio-economic conjuncture', identifying particular points at which its impact is likely to be most acute (Adams and Barker 1993: 14). So 'social behaviour and taste', for instance, have a special bearing on 'reception', 'commercial pressures' on 'distribution' and so on. My professorial research assistant contributed to these debates in the 1990s, pointing to the ways in which Pierre Bourdieu's structural sociology of fields offered other ways of refining Darnton's model (McDonald 1997). In her more recent critique, Brouillette was characteristically more severe. Besides accusing Darnton of Eurocentrism, she took issue with his model because it 'relegates to its margins the question of how the circuit's entire functioning relates "with other systems, economic, social, political, and cultural, in the surrounding environment"'. As such, it fails to deal adequately with material

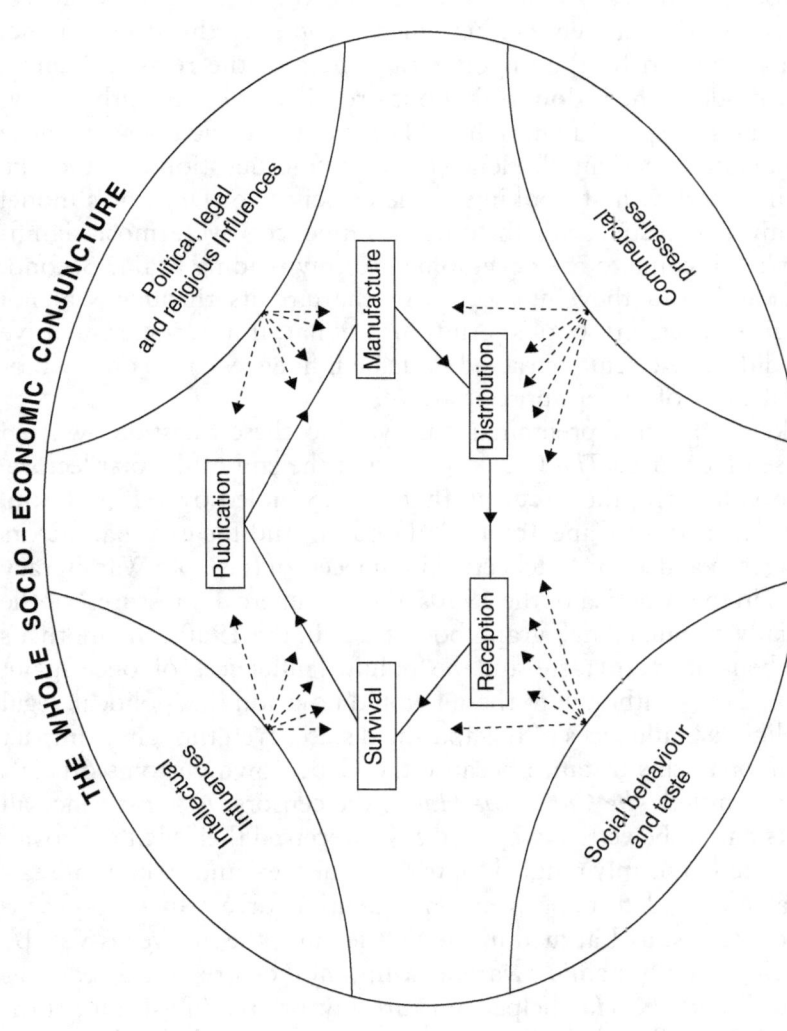

Figure 5 A new model for the study of the book (Adams and Barker 1993: 14). © Adams and Barker 1993.

realities and structures of power that have what she called 'determinative, consequential force' (Brouillette 2019: 79–80)

Like my professorial assistant, I share many of these questions about the conceptual and methodological limitations of the model Darnton himself revisited in the early 2000s (Darnton 2007). For the professor, one key concern centres on the 'determinative force' of those 'outside influences'. Yet when it comes to this central issue, he is as troubled by the ongoing vagueness of the revised Adams-Barker model as he is doubtful about Brouillette's confidently knowing, Marxist-inspired materialism. For me, the difficulties are more concrete and experiential. Hence the threefold question I would like to address today: first, looking at the criticisms of Darnton's model from my perspective, which 'outside influences' were most significant when it came to the development of my reading brain? Second, how exactly did they intersect with the circuits through which I first gained access to books? And third, what, if any, 'determinative force' did these circuit-refracted 'outside influences' have on my biocultural story of 'inner appropriation'?

I sketched a few preliminary answers to these questions when I discussed Dr Seuss's *The Cat in the Hat* at the end of the first lecture. As you will recall, the circuit in that case extended over 12,000 km, from New York to Cape Town via London. And the external factors shaping it included the 'intellectual influences' of the Cold War literacy debates in the America of the 1950s, the 'commercial pressures' of the essentially colonial Anglograph book trade in the 1960s, my mother's 'social behaviour and taste' and the 'political influences' of, once again, the Cold War—although to these I would now add the 'political, legal and religious' influences of the apartheid state, even though its impact was minor in this instance because the Cape Town customs officials never submitted *The Cat in the Hat* to the censors. At most, since all imports had to be vetted, we could say it received their tacit approval.

Did these multiply tangled 'outside influences' and structural realities have any 'determinative, consequential force'? In deeply neurological terms, as I argued in the first lecture, the answer is yes. By enhancing my phonemic awareness, my mother's repeated readings of *The Cat in the Hat* helped nurture my pre-reading brain, turning me from a linguistically open 'citizen of the global village' into a more neurologically attenuated denizen of the English-language. For Louis Menand, this made Dr Seuss's brilliantly inventive book 'one of the Cold War's most potent unguided missiles'—a colourful phrase containing an element of truth, though, as I argued, the 'missile' in my case was not unguided (Menand 2002).

Much the same colonial-era story could be told for most of my early encounters with books in the so-called 'private sphere' of the family household. Given the relatively modest scale of English-language publishing in the South Africa of the 1960s, roadmaps, local history, photography, bird and cookery books, not children's reading, dominated the local market. More or less everything else emanated from London—things were of course very different when it came to Afrikaans and African-language books. And with only a few notable exceptions, the well-worn London circuit continued to dominate the next major turn in my developmental story, which sees the scene shift from home to the schoolroom, and from books chosen chiefly by my mother to the officially prescribed reading materials that over the course of a decade or so saw me gradually turn from pre-reader to novice to orthographically competent ten-year-old decoder and then to increasingly fluent, even quasi-automatised teenage comprehender.

This extended initiation took me from the partly book-based phonosphere of my early years to the graphosphere proper. Much to my mother's dismay, it also brought home the reality that I was, like her and around 22 million others in 1970s South Africa, already part of a much larger but very different written world as well—though that is not how she would have described it at the time. Like the more familiar written world of the pre-digital era, this other one was made of paper, ink and print, but it was not authored in the ordinary sense, it did not remain confined between the covers of a book, or even in bookshops and libraries, and it had real 'determinative, consequential force'. I am of course talking about the entire political and statutory apparatus of the apartheid state. Like a monstrous, one-eyed Cyclops, this 'other system', to recall Brouillette's phrase, imposed its own forms of legibility, evicting communities, segregating beaches, prohibiting inter-racial sex, banning books, dividing, deforming and destroying lives. It also constituted one of the most potent 'outside influences' on the circuits through which my early reading brain developed.

There is perhaps nothing very surprising about this. As the political scientist and anthropologist James C. Scott has long argued, writing has always been an instrument and expression of state power—Scott himself has focused on the ancient states of Zomia in Southeast Asia (Scott 2009). Since at least the late nineteenth century, moreover, the modern state has actively and directly promoted mass literacy. Britain passed legislation to establish its first state-funded primary schools in 1870, for instance—an example the British Cape Colony followed—and by the 1930s the success of the Soviet Union's ambitious literacy programme was widely recognised, even envied. The same cannot be said of post-war South Africa. When the white supremacist National Party came to power in June 1948—six months before the *Universal Declaration of Human Rights* was published—it immediately set about re-making the already segregated colonial education system in its own atavistic image. This had particularly devastating consequences for Black children born after the 1950s, as the iconic 1976 Soweto student uprising revealed. The degraded and degrading system established under the so-called 'Bantu Education Act' of 1953 was designed not only to remodel or shut down the mission schools of the colonial era, but to eliminate the class of Black urban professionals they sometimes produced, creating a mass disenfranchised underclass instead. By contrast, the white schools, following the policy of what was officially called 'Christian National Education', were tasked with ensuring that 'the European' remained 'the torch-bearer in the vanguard of Western civilization in South Africa'—to use the official lexicon of the time (McDonald 2009: 24).

How exactly did this looming 'outside influence' impact the educational book circuits in which I participated from 1970? At one level, the answer is brutally material in Brouillette's sense: the system invested around ten times more resources in my education than it did in any of my Black compatriots. At another level, the answer is crudely ideological, again in Brouillette's sense. Besides bolstering white supremacy, apartheid education was designed to corral the entire population into separate, supposedly divinely ordained, *volke*—only the Afrikaans word will do—based on ethnicity, heritage and, above all, language. Hence the official hostility to dual-medium schools and the sprawling state bureaucracy—there were no fewer than eighteen separate education departments by the late 1980s. In my case, the bureaucratic conduit for the state's 'outside influence' was the Cape Education Department, part of the semi-autonomous Cape Provincial Administration, itself a remnant of the nineteenth-century British Cape Colony. Acting through a series of shadowy committees, which were guided by the broader policy of Christian National Education, the Cape Department drew up lists of approved books from which the individual schools under its authority made their own selections. So, if we go back to the Adams-Barker model, it was these committees, rather than 'commercial pressures', that had the greatest influence on the *distribution* of prescribed books. This is not to deny that publishers operating in the system, including the local representatives of British publishers, did all they could to promote their own commercial interests, given the lucrative nature of the schoolbook market, but they did so as lobbyists rather than decision-makers.

When it comes to understanding the effects of Adams and Barker's 'whole socio-economic conjuncture', these bureaucratic minutiae matter. They are, after all, what the schematic broken-line arrows in their diagram are intended to represent, and, to use the affectless academic parlance of book history, they detail exactly how 'political, legal and religious influences' *relate* to the circuit. From my perspective, these minutiae matter for a quirkier reason as well, one that brings us back to the post-war pedagogical debates about early reading. As a product of the Cape Education Department, I was, unlike my counterparts in the north of the country, not subjected to the Initial Teaching Alphabet (or ITA), a reading scheme James Pitman developed in the early 1960s to deal with English's notoriously opaque orthography—McLuhan includes an example in *The Gutenberg Galaxy*, describing it as a laudable attempt to 'restore more phonic character to our script' (1962: 47 and 49). Taking inspiration in part from his grandfather Isaac Pitman, who invented not just shorthand but phonotypy (a form of phonetic writing and printing), the grandson devised a rationalised set of graphemes, using a combination of standard Roman letters and special characters, each representing one of the forty-five main English phonemes. Though this made a kind of sense, it created an obvious problem: after developing a set of neural pathways for ITA, novice readers then had to create another for the standard 'heterotypic' orthography—to use Isaac Pitman's damning label (Pitman 1843). Not surprisingly, the experiment had a short life in the UK, but the (McLuhanite?) Transvaal Education Department in the north of South Africa, an outlier in many respects, stuck with it well into the 1970s.

The Cape Department, by contrast, followed the more mainstream trends across the Commonwealth and the US at the time, which meant a categorical no to ITA, a slightly less emphatic no to phonics, and a yes to the so-called 'whole word' and 'sentence' methods. Following this policy, my primary school adopted two early readers: *The Happy Venture Series*, the brainchild of the Australian educationalist, Fred Schonell, which the Edinburgh publisher Oliver and Boyd launched in 1939; and the *Ladybird Key Word Reading Scheme*, which the British remedial teacher William Murray developed with the Loughborough firm Wills & Hepworth in 1964. Neither scheme denied the value of phonics, but both were clear that the focus in the initial years (i.e. from age five to seven) had to be on what Schonell called 'the visual patterns of words' and Murray called 'sight words' (Schonell 1945: 12; Murray 1962: 4). 'Psychological research confirms the opinion that for many pupils the phonic method is too analytic,' Schonell explained, 'they do not really understand what they are doing, and not a few of them are mentally unable to associate sounds with symbols and then to analyse and blend these as they find them in words' (46). Besides, phonics was too 'artificial,' he argued, citing these surrealistic examples from Alfred Hayes's *Phonoscript Primer* (1922):

> The pig with a wig did a jig in the bog,
> The fox saw a hen in the pen. (Schonell: 14)

This turn against phonics, which left little room for Louis Menand's magical duck-rabbit moment with the word 'and' in *The Cat in the Hat* or mine with the stop sign at the bottom of our road, has now largely been reversed. So much so that, following the growing neuroscientific consensus, British legislators made teaching phonics in the early years a legal requirement in 2006. The major outlier is the United States, where, despite Dr Seuss's efforts in the 1950s and, indeed, George W. Bush's in the early 2000s, phonics remains contentious (see Smallwood, 2023 and Johns, 2023).

Yet, on its own terms, the graphocentric post-war orthodoxy was progressively child-centred and scientific. Designed to be as visually appealing to their intended readership as possible, the *Happy Venture* and the *Key Word* series used short one-line sentences, lengthening from one book to the next, and large modernist sans-serif type, which resembled 'as nearly as possible the print script' children might be acquainted with in their own writing, as Schonell put it (20). The bestselling fifty-six-page Ladybird books were a product of post-war paper restrictions—the format meant each book could be printed on a single, standard sheet of paper, minimising waste and cost—but this material constraint also had the happy consequence of creating a colourful, cheap pocket hardback, perfectly suited for child-sized hands. According to the publishers, the *Key Words* series, which was the most popular reading scheme in the UK by the mid-1970s, achieved a readership of 90 million (Johnson 2009).

Sequencing the words as 'visual patterns' was also carefully planned, moving in the case of the *Key Words* series from an initial twelve, to 100, 300 and then 1,000 over the course of thirty-six books, linking visual to speech and motor skills in a systematic way at each stage. This was all based on Murray's analysis of word frequency in children's book English, as the blurb explained:

> Research shows that twelve of these Key Words make up one quarter of all those we read and write. One hundred of them form half, and three hundred about three quarters, of the total number of words found in juvenile reading. *Reading skill is accelerated if these important words are learned early and in a pleasant way.* (Murray 1964: inside cover)

So, over the course of my first two school years from age six to eight, through an iterative process of seeing, saying and writing, these two series nurtured my brain's neural 'letterbox' with minimal recourse to phonics, adding new visual and motor pathways to the sound templates I brought from home, first for twelve 'sight words' and then building progressively to 300 and more. Recent research into what neuroscientists call 'embodied cognition' confirms the powerful link between the motor skills of handwriting and the fine visual pathways required for reading, raising questions about new generations of learners who first learn to write by typing on keyboards of various kinds (Kiefer 2012: 16).

So far, so graphocentric and neurological. Opposing the perceived artificiality of phonics complicated matters. What Schonell called 'the real experiences of the children' were essential to this (50). It underpinned the 'sentence method', which foregrounded 'meaningful material' rather than mere grapheme-phoneme patterns, and it justified the careful choice of illustrations, which were intended to portray 'the ideas of the printed material', providing further visual cues to aid word recognition (61). The more lavish full-colour illustrations in the *Key Words* series were intended 'to create a desirable attitude towards learning', but they too made the graphemes, words and sentences more meaningful by embedding them in an ostensibly recognisable world (Murray 1964). Perhaps unsurprisingly, for a series of books created mainly by middle-class, middle-aged white men, *the* world was a utopian, post-war English suburb, home to a happy, well-heeled white family of four: a housewife called Mummy, a bread-winner called Daddy, doll-loving girls called Jane or Dora, sporty boys called Dick or Peter and dogs called Nip or Pat. If this was recognisable to some, it was fantastical to most, even in the Britain of the 1960s. In the context of apartheid South Africa in the 1970s, it was nakedly ideological in Brouillette's sense: no doubt, for the proponents of Christian National Education, as my mother regularly claimed, it was reassuring to know that generations of white, English-speaking children were inwardly appropriating their letters from books that conjured up a vision of Englishness as idealised and monochromatic as the segregated, Anglophile suburbs in which they lived.

In Britain, this fantastical Ladybird vision came under attack on all fronts over the course of the 1970s, forcing Wills & Hepworth, who had by then been bought up by the larger educational firm Pearson, to rethink the illustrations, which gradually became more ethnically diverse and less crudely gendered, contributing to the ongoing global success of the *Key Words* series, even in late-apartheid South Africa. I missed these revisions as a novice reader of the early 1970s, but I did encounter a Ladybird image of Blackness in the next stage of my initiation into the English writing system. Independent, silent reading begins to propel our brain's development aged around ten, and it was at this point that I worked my way through the school library's holdings of the very popular Ladybird 'Adventure from History' series. I was especially drawn to the 'Great Civilization' books, covering, for example, Greece, Rome, China and the Inca Empire, and the ones about explorers, ranging from Marco Polo and Christopher Columbus to Captain Cook and David Livingstone. Because it featured a part of the world with which I had some familiarity, the latter left a particularly powerful impression. First published in 1960, Ladybird's *David Livingstone* was, like over half the books in the History series, written by the popular British playwright and *Punch* humourist Lawrence du Garde Peach, who took this writing commission on as a retirement project in his late sixties.

Following Livingstone's own *Missionary Travels and Researches in South Africa* (1857/99), from which he quoted directly, du Garde Peach began his Ladybird account with a motivational portrait of the Scottish village boy as a self-improving reader. The first illustration shows the ten-year-old Livingstone, who was then working a fourteen-hour day in a cotton mill, teaching himself Latin in the evenings. Unfortunately, though Livingstone himself detailed his later commitment to spreading literacy in southern Africa, du Garde Peach did not develop this theme, nor did he quote this observation from Livingstone's *Missionary Travels*:

> To all natives who have not acquired the art, the mode in which knowledge is conveyed through letters is unfathomable. It seems supernatural to them that we should distinguish things taking place in a book. (Livingstone 1899: 126)

Instead, du Garde Peach championed Livingstone as an intrepid 'missionary explorer' who braved lions and 'savage tribes', healed the sick, preached the 'Gospel of Peace', formed close inter-racial alliances, and heralded the abolition of the slave trade in 'darkest Africa' (du Garde 1960: 16, 30, 50). This impeccably heroic vision, which again sat comfortably with the basic tenets of Christian National Education, captured my ten-year-old imagination, though, as I started to question the history we were being taught at school, again with my mother's promptings, I too began to wonder if the 'knowledge' conveyed 'through letters' was not at times 'supernatural'.

Like many of his post-war European and American counterparts, the Australian educationalist Fred Schonell saw literacy in unquestionably progressive terms. While serving various 'personal needs', as he put it, it raised 'social awareness', ensuring that every 'well-read child' could become 'an effective adult member of a democratic community' (88, 91). For a more critical take on this post-war idealism, we need to look beyond the Euro-American world to figures such as the Tamil philosopher Ananda K. Coomaraswamy, who denounced what he called 'The Bugbear of Literacy'. 'Modern "education" imposed upon traditional cultures (e.g. Gaelic, Indian, Polynesian, American Indian),' he wrote in 1949, 'is only less deliberately, not less actually, destructive than the Nazi destruction of Polish libraries' (Coomaraswamy: 57). Yet, while Schonell was certainly among the post-war idealists, he was primarily a functionalist, who saw reading as 'only a means to an end'.

> Pupils learn to read, at first largely orally and later silently, in order to understand the printed word. The ultimate objective is to understand the ideas, to appreciate the story, or to follow instructions, or to enjoy the beauty of the words or the rhythm, or to gain information from the written words of the author. (87)

Teaching 'the mechanics of reading' is, in other words, all about turning diffident decoders into automatic comprehenders capable of looking through 'the printed word' to the things it supernaturally conveys—again recall Reddy's conduit metaphor: not just the meaning of the author's 'written words', but 'the ideas', 'the story', 'the instructions', 'the beauty' or the 'information'—or, as Livingstone put it in his Victorian idiom, 'knowledge'.

It certainly felt like a learned forgetfulness of writing or 'the printed word' as such was the ultimate purpose of my own decade-long school apprenticeship in reading. The object was to get information out of biology textbooks, to follow instructions for chemistry experiments and, when it came to literature, to understand 'the story', especially the plot, the characters and themes. Even poetry (which is no doubt what Schonell had in mind when he mentioned 'beauty' and 'rhythm') was simply a resource for learning advanced literacy skills: the basics of metre, versification, poetic kinds and figures of speech. This at least is how I found myself, aged seventeen, being taken in my final year of school through *Hamlet*, *Far from the Madding Crowd*, a poetry anthology and a short story collection. No doubt the Cape Education Department's shadowy book committee thought this canon of mainly English classics would facilitate the 'inner appropriation' of my racialised ethno-linguistic identity as a privileged white English-speaker, but there was little sense of this among my teachers, who, for the most part, treated everything in a pragmatic Schonellian spirit as so much scholastic grist for the final examination mill. Increasingly disaffected, I groused my way through all this in a teenage fashion, saved somewhat by my mother who, as usual, recommended alternative, extracurricular reading. Es'kia Mphahlele's autobiography *Down Second Avenue* (1959) and George Orwell's *Down and Out in Paris and London* (1933) proved especially eye-opening. Yet, among the prescribed books, three works, one from the short story collection, the other two from the poetry anthology, hooked me like a lure, albeit almost incidentally: Joseph Conrad's 'The Secret Sharer', Dylan Thomas's 'Do not go gentle into that good night' and e. e. cummings's 'r-p-o-p-h-e-s-s-a-g-r'.

Returning to these set books after four decades, what strikes me most is the disjunction between my memory of first encountering these three works in the 'total existential situation' of the time, to recall Walter Ong's phrase, and the way the prescribing committees, teachers and the anthologists themselves envisaged, perhaps even tried to influence, my 'inner appropriation' of them—again recall those arrows in the Adams-Barker model. For me, the classroom experience of 1982 was mainly one of puzzlement, even bewilderment. Why, I recall asking, did Conrad's respectable Captain-narrator decide to protect a fugitive who may have murdered a fellow crew member? And why did Conrad expend so much effort creating an atmosphere of uncertainty in his story only to leave everything hanging? We never know if a murder has indeed been committed or exactly why the Captain acts the way he does. I found all this baffling in part because I had also read my way through Agatha Christie and the Sherlock Holmes stories, which never left such crucial questions unanswered. Other stories in the collection, including D. H. Lawrence's 'The Odour of Chrysanthemums', Katherine Mansfield's 'The Daughters of the Late Colonel' and E. M. Forster's 'The Machine Stops' also made a strong impression. But 'The Secret Sharer' stood out. No doubt my analyst would have something to say about a white teenager in apartheid South Africa being lured by an unresolved story of criminal complicity—Conrad's great subject—but it is difficult to imagine that this was something the Cape book committee intended to encourage. Needless to say, criminal complicity was not part of the classroom discussion either. In answer to my questions about the Captain and the fugitive, I was told Conrad was working with a literary device called the *doppelgänger*.

For different reasons, puzzlement also dominated my response to the Thomas and cummings poems. With 'Do not go gentle', I remember getting the sonorous rhymes and the heady drama of the five-beat lines; I also understood the guiding metaphor about the night and noted the puns, alliteration and so on. What puzzled me were the repeated lines, beginning 'Do not go' and 'Rage, rage', which recur in a carefully patterned way. It is a villanelle, the teachers explained, a poetic form defined in part by its use of refrains. But why keep saying the same thing, I asked? After all, it's not as if we don't get the idea the first time. It's a villanelle, they said, and we moved on. The cummings was more obviously perplexing. What was I supposed to do with this? Look at it? Or somehow try to say it aloud, like the Thomas poem? The teachers pointed me to the editorial note describing it as a 'technical exercise', 'a poet's attempt to convey a simple experience he had had—watching a grasshopper leap', but this did little to resolve my puzzlement, and again we moved on (Malan 1969: 124). Yet, by that point, the lure had done its trick, and I found myself increasingly, if often querulously, drawn to these strange, sometimes bewildering 'printed words', which the culture casually called 'English literature' but which I struggled to understand, let alone inwardly appropriate, as an otherwise fairly competent teenage comprehender.

This at least is how the experience survives as memory. As I now realise, the editors of the anthologies had their own ideas about literature and reading, which were rather at odds with my inchoate feelings. Conrad's 'Secret Sharer' was one of six stories included in the bestselling *Twentieth-century Short Stories*, a self-consciously experimental school anthology first published in 1959 by the generally rather staid London educational firm George G. Harrap but edited by two progressive British schoolteachers, Douglas Barnes and R. F. Egford, on behalf of the London Association for the Teaching of

English (or LATE). With LATE, Barnes and Egford gave the collection its experimental edge.

Founded in 1947, LATE was a small, voluntary association committed to modernising the post-war English school curriculum following the 1944 British Education Act. Among other things, the act made secondary schooling free for all in England and Wales. Strongly influenced by George Rudé, the British Marxist historian (a background detail of which the Cape book committee was no doubt unaware), the group was determined to shake off the pedagogical ethos of the established 'grammar schools'—to use the British terminology—and to promote a more socially inclusive curriculum for the emerging 'comprehensives', as they would come to be called. This meant moving away from the traditional approach to language study, which was Latinate, technical and prescriptive, recognising that language has a complex social life outside the classroom and affirming the children's own non-standard dialects. The group also embraced new media such as film and television alongside literature, rejecting the Leavisite hostility to mass culture and the related idea of the 'Great Tradition'. Underpinning this framework were two essentially philosophical convictions: an acknowledgement of the diversity and primacy of the 'child's experience' and a belief in the shaping power of language, its capacity 'to deepen [experience], order it, and make it accessible'. 'It is a commonplace that language helps us to think,' LATE argued in a pamphlet entitled *The Aims of English Teaching* (1956), 'our formulation implies also that language similarly helps us to perceive and feel and act' (Gibbons 2014: 33). Hence the particular value the group placed on modern literature and the historical span of *Twentieth-century Short Stories*, LATE's first textbook: the earliest story dates from 1909, the latest from 1954 (figure 6).

This socially progressive philosophy explains Barnes and Egford's concern with what they called 'the reader's response'. 'The aim of literary study,' they insisted in the preface to *Twentieth-century Short Stories*, is not 'the recital of those deadening "facts from the story"'—code for grammar-school scholasticism—but 'sensitive reading': 'If read closely these stories will "lead into new places the flow of our sympathetic consciousness"' (Barnes 1982: 7–8). As a prefatory comment to a school anthology, this is not especially remarkable. The free-floating, unattributed quotation simply rehearses a standard defence of literary study as a means of fostering sympathy, one that has a long pedigree in European thought. Traced to its original context, however, the quotation is a little more surprising, especially for an anthology first published in 1959. It comes from *Lady Chatterley's*

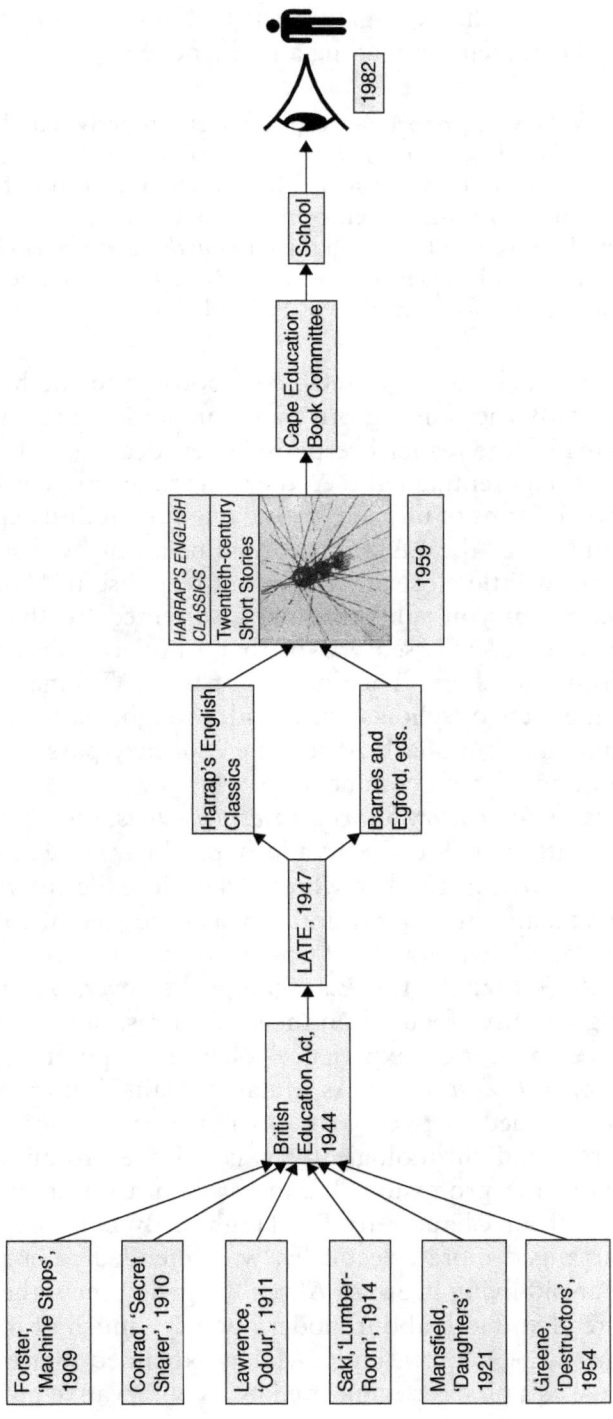

Figure 6 Conduits of transmission and survival for *Twentieth-century Short Stories*.

Lover, which, even in the expurgated British edition of 1932, includes this narratorial comment on reading and the novel:

> And here lies the vast importance of the novel, properly handled. It can inform and *lead into new places the flow of our sympathetic consciousness*, and it can lead our sympathy away in recoil from things gone dead. Therefore, the novel, properly handled, can reveal the most secret places of life: for it is in the *passional* secret places of life, above all, that the tide of sensitive awareness needs to ebb and flow, cleansing and freshening. (Lawrence 1932: 118)

If this brings us back to the secret life of books and the history of sex, it also casts Barnes and Egford's idea of 'sensitive reading' and their privileging of 'the reader's response' over 'deadening facts' in a rather different, Lawrentian light. At the same time, it opens the possibility that some forms of literary writing might revitalise experience not by ordering it, as the LATE group claimed, but by disordering it, which comes a little closer to my initial response to 'The Secret Sharer', especially if you substitute my disoriented 'reading brain' for 'experience' in LATE's sense. Not that I noticed any of this at the time. Did my teachers? They never got the LATE memo about the deadening effects of scholasticism and, though *Lady Chatterley* was finally unbanned in South Africa in 1980, they passed over the charged quotation without comment.

Unlike *Twentieth-century Short Stories*, *Inscapes*, the equally successful poetry anthology I read, was a local product. Edited by Robin Malan, a South African teacher who worked in exile in what was then called Swaziland (now Eswatini), it was produced in collaboration with the Cape Town branch of Oxford University Press and first published in 1969. Like the LATE anthology, however, *Inscapes* was a modernising initiative focused on the student response and organised around the concept of 'experience'—hence the pointed subtitle: *A Collection of Relevant Verse*. As Malan explained in the preface, the book was divided in two parts for a strategic reason. Part 1, which was organised chronologically, was designed to appease the traditionalists in the profession. It ran through a selection of prescribed staples from Chaucer to Ted Hughes. By contrast, Part 2, which was arranged more eclectically, was intended to engage the '16- or 17-year-old living in South Africa' by giving them the chance 'to discover, read and talk about modern poetry', much of it written after 1945 (Malan 1969: ix). Later, Malan explained that this two-part structure was a ploy recommended by a conservative publishers' reader as a way of getting the approval of the even more conservative book committees.

Why the focus on modern and contemporary poets? Relevance was not the only issue. 'The poet has, through writing the poem, become more aware of what these experiences really mean to him,' Malan commented in his gendered way, and so 'if the poem "works" for you,' he added, addressing the student reader, 'you will have been made more aware of some experience of life which you yourself have either had and not really thought about, or not had and are now capable of understanding more completely' (113). This was close to the LATE group's pedagogical philosophy. Like them, Malan put lived 'experience' first and understood poetic language as a means of giving it shape and significance, though, like Schonell, he also saw reading as a means to an end, the end, in this case, being the appreciation not of 'beauty' or 'rhythm' but of 'some experience of life'—Reddy's conduit metaphor comes to mind once again.

To clarify this guiding idea, Malan turned to Robert Graves's 1929 poem 'Warning to Children', which he placed as a manifesto-like statement at the beginning of the inspirational Part 2: 'The thing that strikes one more than anything else about the modern world is its kaleidoscopic variety, its contrasts, its contradictions—what Robert Graves calls in the first poem in this section of the anthology "the fewness, muchness, rareness, greatness of this endless only precious world"' (113). For Malan, this was the point of reading poetry, which he saw as an ever-changing kaleidoscope onto the lived experience of life's 'fewness, muchness, rareness', etc. That Graves's admonitory defence of poetry is also a forthright critique of empiricism appears not to have concerned him. Any child attempting to 'untie the string' of sensory experience in an empiricist fashion will, the visionary Graves insists, disappear into a solipsistic, infinitely regressive world of their own making (115).

Again, as a seventeen-year-old, I ignored all this editorialising, though, as I now see, Graves's critical reflection on our ways of knowing may have helped me deal with my bewilderment about the Thomas and the cummings, both of which appeared in the anthology's inspirational Part 2. What is perhaps most conspicuous about *Inscapes* now, however, is the narrow experiential range of Malan's own 'kaleidoscopic' vision in 1969. Besides the Thomas, the cummings and a selection of British and Commonwealth poets, Part 2 included Emily Dickinson, Walt Whitman, Robert Frost and Lawrence Ferlinghetti, as well as fourteen modern and contemporary South African poets, all white and all but one male. The only Black poet in the collection was the relatively obscure Jamaican H. D. Carberry. Again, as with the *Ladybird Key Words* series, I missed out on the shake-up that came four years after I completed my schooling. In 1986, Malan, a close follower of the South African poetry scene, persuaded a cautious Oxford University Press to publish *New Inscapes*, which added more contemporary poets from around the world and a wide selection of Black South African poets, including many leading figures of the 1970s Black Consciousness generation. Despite OUP's worries, the ever-more kaleidoscopic *New Inscapes* sold better than its predecessor (270,000 copies against 205,000), and it was prescribed across all the racialised education departments, white, mixed-race and Asian, the only exception being the one controlling Black education (Malan 2005: 15). A decade later, following the first democratic elections in 1994, Malan overhauled the anthology completely, reissuing it, again with OUP, as the more encompassing *Worldscapes: A Collection of Verse* (1997)—by the way, cummings's grasshopper did not survive the edit, but Thomas's 'Do not go gentle' did. In the final lecture, I return to the conduit metaphor underlying Malan's changing kaleidoscope and David Livingstone's equally beguiling claim about the 'knowledge' *conveyed* 'through letters'.

Chapter 3

'Scant Cream': Sense, Nonsense and the Reader Remade

In the second lecture, I quoted this passage from David Livingstone's *Missionary Travels and Researches in South Africa* describing the Makololo perception of books and reading. A sub-group of the Sotho-Tswana people, the Makololo were among Livingstone's main local allies during his travels through southern Africa in the early 1850s.

> To all natives who have not acquired the art, the mode in which knowledge is conveyed through letters is unfathomable. It seems supernatural to them that we should distinguish things taking place in a book. (Livingstone 1899: 126)

As I suggested, this formulation—in particular, Livingstone's alluring verb 'conveyed', a good illustration of Reddy's all-pervasive conduit metaphor—spoke to my own experience of acquiring the art of reading at school. It also prefigured the educationalist Fred Schonell's functionalist view of literacy. 'The ultimate objective' of learning to read, Schonell wrote in 1945, is to develop a fluent, even automatic understanding not just of the meanings but of the 'ideas', 'instructions' or 'information' books convey, treating the medium of 'the printed word' as a transparent window (87). The editors of the literary anthologies I read in my final school year agreed, though, in their view that, rather than convey 'knowledge', poems and short stories, like so many fragments of coloured glass, kaleidoscopically refract what they called 'experience'.

Despite my puzzlement about some forms of literature, I happily internalised this way of thinking during my school years. Learning to read, as I saw it, was like learning to ride a bicycle: once you successfully join up your brain's phonological, semantic and graphological pathways through hours of practice, you forget about the basic skills and go places, which is, after all, the point. But, as I entered the next phase of my initiation into the arts of reading, now as an undergraduate in the South Africa of the early 1980s, I began to hit bumps in the road; that is, I started to encounter kinds of writing that unsettled everything I had inwardly appropriated about reading up to that point. Many books contributed to this, but the fortuitous alignment of Bertrand Russell's *The Problems of Philosophy* (1912), Virginia Woolf's *To the Lighthouse* (1927), Chinua Achebe's *Things Fall Apart* (1958) and J. M. Coetzee's *Dusklands* (1974) proved transformative.

Seen in terms of Darnton's 'communication circuit', this idiosyncratic constellation did not represent much of a change from my school days. Reflecting the old colonial patterns of production and circulation, all four books reached me as paperbacks printed in and exported from Britain to South Africa. The only oddity was that the bestselling *Things Fall Apart*, the founding title of the generation-defining Heinemann African Writers series launched in 1962, was *published* not just in London but in Ibadan and Nairobi; whereas the lesser known *Dusklands* was *published* in Johannesburg by Ravan Press, the leading anti-apartheid publisher of the 1970s and 1980s. As my professorial research assistant later discovered, Ravan, who gave Coetzee his first break with the 1974 hardback edition of *Dusklands*, had done a deal with his London publisher Secker & Warburg over the 1982 paperback. So, like *Things Fall Apart*, there was a discrepancy between the place of printing and the site of publication. Not that I paid attention to these bibliographical and circumstantial niceties at the time; nor was I encouraged to, since the focus of my undergraduate training was very much 'the linguistic text', not the 'bibliographical code', to use Jerome McGann's distinction (McGann 1991: 13).

Seen in terms of Adams and Barker's 'whole socio-economic conjuncture', however, this four-book constellation did signal one important shift. Unlike the prescribed books I read at school, all of which came, as we saw in the second lecture, with the approval of the Cape Education Department, a branch of the apartheid state, these four books were selected by the faculty in the Departments of English and Philosophy at my undergraduate university (see chapter 4). In terms of the Adams-Barker model, it was their 'intellectual influences', rather than any commercial or narrowly ideological pressures, which had the greatest impact on distribution. How far these influences can be separated from questions of politics or taste is debateable. All I need to say for now is that Russell's *Problems of Philosophy* was more than an introductory textbook. It was a flagbearer for my undergraduate philosophy course, which offered a traditional, Russell-inspired introduction to the history of 'Western philosophical thought', running from the Ancient Greeks to late twentieth-century language philosophy. The English curriculum, by contrast, was more attuned to an African context. Following a series of heated scholarly debates about the canon, whiteness, Britishness and Westerness in the 1970s, it had already diversified by the time I arrived in 1983—hence the inclusion of, among others, Achebe and Coetzee. Though the faculty curriculum-makers may not have been instruments of the state, they were not exactly free-floating guardians of the 'Republic of Letters' either. Suffice it to say, they were, like me and all my fellow students in the slowly desegregating South African universities of the 1980s, enmeshed in a state-funded higher education system and censorship apparatus, caught between ruthless repression and a failing strategy of co-optive reform.

For my philosophy teachers, *The Problems of Philosophy* was an accessible introduction to the Western tradition. For Russell, it was an experiment in popular writing. First published in 1912, *Problems* was commissioned by the London publisher Williams & Norgate for their new Home University Library of Modern Knowledge. A direct response to the 1902 Secondary Education Act, which promoted the growth of secondary schools in England and Wales, the Home University Library reflected the democratising ideals of the time, though neither Russell nor his commissioning editor, the Oxford Professor of Greek Gilbert Murray, received the memo about the new egalitarian ethos. 'You have got a message for the shop-assistant about philosophy,' Murray wrote with mock-levity to Russell, who, in turn, referred to his book as a 'Shilling Shocker'—in fact its initial cost was 2 shillings and 6 pence (Wilson 1987: 190). As the Home University Library sold over a million copies in its first two years, there were no doubt some self-improving shop assistants among its first readers, but *Problems* quickly became an undergraduate staple. By the time I came to read it in 1983, it had migrated to the Oxford Paperback University Series (or OPUS), which was launched in 1966. This series, like its precursor, the Home University, was billed as presenting 'learning to the layman', though, again like its precursor, it sold largely to an undergraduate readership.

From its disorienting opening to its utopian conclusion, I found Russell's 'Shocker' compelling reading.

> I believe that, if any other normal person comes into my room, he will see the same chairs and tables and books and papers as I see, and

that the table which I see is the same as the table which I feel pressing against my arm. All this seems to be so evident as to be hardly worth stating, except in answer to a man who doubts whether I know anything. (Russell 1967: 1)

So Russell begins, shattering all my convictions about the everyday sensory world around me, while treating maleness as self-evidently as I had until then treated books and tables.

Thus contemplation enlarges not only the objects of our thoughts, but also the objects of our actions and our affections: it makes us citizens of the universe, not only of one walled city at war with all the rest. In this citizenship of the universe consists man's true freedom, and his liberation from the thraldom of narrow hopes and fears. (93)

So, Russell concludes, explaining the value of philosophy as the 'unalloyed desire' not just for 'truth' but for 'justice' and 'universal love', a visionary appeal I found irresistible in the South Africa of the 1980s. What proved especially generative, however, was the distinction Russell drew between 'knowledge by acquaintance' and 'knowledge by description'. The former, as I initially understood it in my shop-assistant way, included my knowledge of Cape Town, my mother and the present, the latter my knowledge of Philadelphia, Hamlet and the past—Russell's distinction, which has to do with knowing directly via what he called 'sense data' and indirectly via concepts/language/representations, is rather more nuanced, I later realised.

As an inheritor of the British empirical tradition, Russell understood these two ways of knowing to be interdependent, a point his few passing remarks on reading clarify. Note, for instance, the parenthesis he adds after these thoughts on Julius Caesar:

When, for example, we make a statement about Julius Caesar, it is plain that Julius Caesar himself is not before our minds, since we are not acquainted with him. We have in mind some description of Julius Caesar: 'the man who was assassinated on the Ides of March', 'the founder of the Roman Empire', or, perhaps, merely 'the man whose name was *Julius Caesar*'. (In this last description, *Julius Caesar* is a noise or shape with which we are acquainted.) (32)

In a later passage, he considers the dependence of description on acquaintance in relation to the 'beliefs produced by reading' newspapers.

> If the newspapers announce the death of the King, we are fairly well justified in believing that the King is dead, since this is the sort of announcement which would not be made if it were false. And we are quite amply justified in believing that the newspaper asserts that the King is dead. But here the intuitive knowledge upon which our belief is based is knowledge of the existence of sense-data derived from looking at the print which gives the news. This knowledge scarcely rises into consciousness, except in a person who cannot read easily. A child may be aware of the shapes of the letters, and pass gradually and painfully to a realization of their meaning. But anybody accustomed to reading passes at once to what the letters mean, and is not aware, except on reflection, that he has derived this knowledge from the sense-data called seeing the printed letters. (77)

This is Russell's philosophically elaborated version of Reddy's conduit metaphor and of Livingstone's observation about the knowledge *conveyed* through letters. It also rehearses Schonell's functionalist understanding of reading as a means to an end—the end, in this case, being not just 'meaning' but truthful propositions (e.g. 'the King is dead').

What about the beliefs produced by reading novels or philosophy books, I began to wonder? This is when the worries set it. For all his commitment to interdependency, Russell placed a special premium on description. This is not just because he thought description in all its modes radically enlarges what we know by acquaintance, a view I found inspiring, but because some descriptive modes give access to the 'universals' he valued most as an analytical philosopher, a view I found implausibly cerebral. On this issue Russell sounds more like Plato than like Hume:

> the free intellect will value more the abstract and universal knowledge into which the accidents of private history do not enter, than the knowledge brought by the senses, and dependent, as such knowledge must be, upon an exclusive and personal point of view and a body whose sense-organs distort as much as they reveal. (93)

This reflected Russell's professional interest in formal logic and mathematics, which, for all his claims, are no less dependent on forms of notation with which we need to be acquainted—think only of '$p \lor q$' or various representations of the number 7/VII/七. As I read more, I realised that this bias underpinned Russell's search for a 'logically perfect language' that might transcend not just the 'body whose sense-organs distort' but ordinary language in all its many changing forms, media and varieties, providing, in effect, a transparent window on to the supersensory realm of 'abstract and universal knowledge' (Russell 2010: 18).

These doubts about Russell were not self-generated, nor did they emerge from my philosophical studies. They came from writers my university, like the culture more generally, categorised as literary. Virginia Woolf sowed the first seed by opening my eyes to the novel's very different way of thinking about knowledge and the body. Not only did she create characters like *To the Lighthouse*'s Mr Ramsay, an academic philosopher, based partly on her father, who embodies something like the Russell tradition, personal quirks, warts and all. Woolf also relativised this approach to knowledge, making it one all-too-human perspective among others. The first inkling we get of Mr Ramsay's philosophical work, for instance, is via the self-doubting young painter Lily Briscoe, who hears about it from his oldest son, Andrew. 'Subject and object and the nature of reality,' Andrew tells her, adding 'Think of a kitchen table . . . when you're not there' (Woolf 1977: 26). What follows is a multi-layered commentary on this way of thinking, blending Lily's own awed attempt to understand it and the more knowing narrator's ironised take on analytic philosophy and its abstractions.

> Naturally, if one's days were passed in this seeing of angular essences, this reducing of lovely evenings, with all their flamingo clouds and blue and silver to a white deal four-legged table (and it was a mark of the finest minds to do so), naturally one could not be judged like an ordinary person. (26)

Mr Ramsay not only represents a particular outlook on knowledge, however. He is also a shifting *object* of knowledge, not least for his wife, eight children and the reader. Russell would no doubt consider Woolf's interest in the interplay of embodied perspectives a matter of 'temperament'. Unlike Mr Ramsay or her father, who austerely concerned themselves with what Russell called the supersensory 'world of being', which is 'unchangeable, rigid, exact', she was drawn, like Lily, to the sensory 'world of existence', which is 'fleeting, vague, without sharp boundaries' (Russell 1967: 57). The more likely explanation, I began to think, is that Woolf approached the problems of philosophy as a novelist.

Achebe sowed more doubts by raising other questions about descriptive knowledge via his own, very different novel. In this case, everything turned on the five sentences with which *Things Fall Apart* ends:

The story of this man who had killed a messenger and hanged himself would make interesting reading. One could almost write a whole chapter on him. Perhaps not a whole chapter but a reasonable paragraph, at any rate. There was so much else to include, and one must be firm in cutting out details. He had already chosen the title of the book, after much thought: *The Pacification of the Primitive Tribes of the Lower Niger*. (Achebe 1985: 147–48)

Again, as with Woolf, we have an ironised commentary on an embodied perspective—at this point we are seeing things through the eyes of an officer of the colonial state, the unnamed District Commissioner—but Achebe also uses this device to introduce a series of self-reflexive questions about writing, knowledge and power. Unlike Woolf, who implicitly puts the novel in dialogue with essayistic philosophical writing and symbolic logic, Achebe explicitly pits *Things Fall Apart* against a fictionalised colonial historiography of the 1890s, the period in which the novel is set, asking his twentieth-century readers to weigh one form of 'knowledge by description' against another: the District Commissioner's 'reasonable paragraph' against his own twenty-five-chapter novel, a summary judgement against a fully realised fictional world, colonial against decolonial ways of knowing—the latter combining a European literary, linguistic and print inheritance with forms of pre-colonial orature, English with Igbo. By representing literacy itself as one of the forces of disruption in the fictional world, Achebe links his questions about writing and knowledge thematically as well—literacy divides Okonkwo, the tragic central figure, from his son, for instance.

With Achebe and Woolf I felt I was on reasonably secure ground: using the knowledge of printed English letters I had internalised by acquaintance, I could see that, as novelists, they were questioning the descriptive knowledge other forms of writing *make* but claim simply to *convey*. With Coetzee's *Dusklands*, I was at sea. In the first place, I could make no sense of the baffling paratextual apparatus, particularly when it came to the second section, called 'The Narrative of Jacobus Coetzee'. Was this a series of actual documents about an eighteenth-century Dutch frontiersman, edited by one S. J. Coetzee and translated from the Dutch and Afrikaans by J. M. Coetzee, as the title page indicates? Or was it all an elaborate literary hoax, written in English by J. M. Coetzee, the owner of the copyright to the book called *Dusklands*? The main narrative, which includes some outright contradictions, only made matters worse. At one point, for instance, Jacobus Coetzee's comically faithful 'Hottentot' manservant

Jan Klawer both drowns and does not drown while crossing a river (Coetzee 1982: 94). Some early reviewers thought this was a proofing error. I could not help thinking back to Russell's claims about readers credibly believing the King is dead based on what they read in newspapers.

Not knowing what to make of it, I put *Dusklands* aside, opting to write a rambling essay on E. M. Forster's *A Passage to India* (1924) instead. But, like an unfinished puzzle, Coetzee's literary debut kept luring me back. Eventually, on a third, entirely extracurricular reading, a switch flipped: maybe, I thought, Coetzee was asking Achebe's questions about literacy, knowledge and power in his own way. Like *Things Fall Apart*, 'The Narrative of Jacobus Coetzee' makes a turn at the very end when Jacobus signs his formal deposition with an X, revealing that he is, like Achebe's Okonkwo, illiterate. Yet, as ever with this kind of writing, there is a difference. Whereas Achebe's final move self-reflexively affirms the power of the African novel, setting his fictional account of Okonkwo's tragic fate against the District Commissioner's dubious but invented colonial history, Coetzee's concluding X highlights the dubious workings and reworkings to which Jacobus's absurd, sometimes contradictory 'narrative' has been subjected by an equally dubious entourage of writers, scholars, editors and translators, all called Coetzee. As it happens, the deposition, which features as an appendix to the narrative, is a largely accurate but also edited and manipulated translation of the actual Dutch document the historical Jacobus Coetsé Jansz signed with an X on 18 November 1760. What, I began to ask, did all this mean not just for the 'knowledge by description' magically *conveyed* through letters but for literacy itself, to say nothing of my own position as a reader, would-be scholar and product of a dominant literate culture?

This question set the terms for the next stage in my initiation into the art of reading, which sees the scene shift from South Africa to England in the late 1980s, and from undergraduate classes on literature and philosophy to the eminent New Zealand scholar D. F. McKenzie's graduate seminar on bibliography in 1989. Squaring up to his somewhat sceptical audience at the first meeting, McKenzie began by passing a blank book around the room, insisting we each take time to acquaint ourselves with its various sense data, to use Russell's lexicon: its texture, paper quality, weight, binding, colour, size and smell (figure 7). Like a bibliographical Sherlock Holmes, he then started asking a series of pointed questions. What genre of writing did we think the book was destined to support? When did we think it was published? What was its likely market or readership? And so on. Within a few minutes, we

Figure 7 D. F. McKenzie's blank book.

all surprised ourselves by getting the answers pretty much right. It was, we guessed, most probably a mass-market novel of the mid-twentieth century. In fact, it was the printers' mock-up for the British edition of the bestselling American writer Frances Parkinson Keyes's thirteenth novel, *Also the Hills* (1944, figure 8).

McKenzie's canny point was, of course, to show us that we were all already new-style bibliographers of the 1980s, responsive, almost despite ourselves, to the 'sociology of texts' and to the material book not as mere conduit but as 'expressive form' (McKenzie 1999). In retrospect, the timing of this lesson could not have been more poignant. Though Kindle's ebook was still some way off, the World Wide Web had just been invented, and so, unbeknown to any of us creatures of print, revolution was in the air. For me, McKenzie's unwittingly epochal lesson had a transformative effect not so much because I saw a future in the history of the book as an academic field—I left that to my professorial research assistant. What struck me were the implications his Holmesian gambit had for the philosophy I had been reading as an undergraduate. Most notably, all those sense data made me rethink Russell's sensory 'knowledge by acquaintance'. Going against

Figure 8 Book designer's mock-up for the cover of *Also the Hills* (1944). Courtesy of Don McKenzie.

my undergraduate training, which only reinforced my Russell-like fixation on 'printed letters', or McGann's 'linguistic text', as conduits for meaning, McKenzie revealed how literacy fosters, and unconsciously depends on, a rich bodily understanding of the book as a complex constellation not of raw sense data but of meaning- and value-making material signs. By troubling the ancient philosophical distinction between *noumena* and *phenomena*, or what Kant later called the *intelligible* and the *sensible*, this raised further questions about Russell's residual Platonism. Like *To the Lighthouse*, *Things Fall Apart* and *Dusklands*, McKenzie-style bibliography, I began to think, represented another powerful challenge to my internalised habits of reading and to 'Western philosophical thought' in the Russell tradition.

Yet McKenzie's blank book also left me with a problem. Out of curiosity, I called up *Also the Hills* in the Bodleian Library a few days after the seminar, partly to see the finished product, but mainly to find out something about the novel for which the mock-up had been made. It was an unexpectedly edifying experience, and not only because I discovered that the final version was produced on cheaper paper in compliance with the 'war economy standard'—this was 1944 after all.

Also the Hills turned out to be an understandably patriotic but also rather high-coloured romance about the disruptive effects of the Second World War on a well-to-do New England family, which includes sentences such as the following:

> They had been sleighing ever since, and that was three hours ago: now the frostiness of the air had become part of Judith's glowing skin, and Dexter was conscious of its freshness as his lips moved over her face. But her mouth was still miraculously warm, and it grew warmer as his kisses gained in intensity. She did not draw away from him, either, this time. (Keyes 1944: 10)

Another passage, from a scene later in the novel when we find Judith serving as a military nurse in North Africa, stood out for different reasons:

> There seemed to be nothing she could do in the way of more personal service at the moment, so she conscientiously began to check her other patients. But involuntarily she returned to Peter MacDonald, bending over him with a solicitude which no matter how hard she tried, she could not feel towards any of the others. She straightened up to see the chief nurse standing beside her, and hastened to rise herself, words coming with a rush. (370)

To give you an idea of the novel's dramatic plotting, Peter MacDonald, a rather dashing war correspondent, is the former lover of Judith's sister, Jenness, who commits suicide after turning to a life of crime.

So, what exactly was the problem? Essentially, McKenzie's seminar opened my eyes, or rather all my senses, to the strange phenomenology of reading. As his gambit with the blank book revealed, we were, as graduates who took some pride in our reading abilities, both oddly indifferent to the book as expressive form and yet, when nudged, fairly adept interpreters of the bibliographical code. Somehow, during our initiation into the complex print culture of the pre-internet era, we had acquired a rudimentary ability to treat the sensible, the tactile quality of the paper say, as intelligible. Yet this went hand in hand with a certain learned obliviousness—again, recall Reddy's conduit metaphor. Consequently, when I read *Also the Hills* in the Bodleian after the seminar, I could not help noticing how quickly the material reality not just of the book but of the printed letters faded from view. It felt like I was reading Keyes's novel, rather than looking at Eyre & Spottiswoode's book, focusing on the story, as if it were some kind of supersensory *noumenon*. The *phenomena* of the individual letters, then words, sentences, paragraphs and chapters, to say nothing of the type and paper, out of which the book was composed, seemed simply to disappear. This was no doubt partly an effect of the printers' skill at producing a clean, effortlessly 'readable' text. Yet, I now began to suspect, it must also have something to do with how my eyes had been educated, how literacy had transformed my brain, making it a high-speed device not just for scanning print but for turning it, as if by magic, into a window onto the intelligible. Losing myself in the world of the book, it seemed, meant losing any sense of my body and the book in the world. Again, recall Russell on the way practised newspaper readers focus on meaning, forgetting the 'printed letters' before their eyes.

From then on, McKenzie's compelling bibliophilosophical lesson coloured everything I read. It also encouraged me to return to another, rather different book, which I had been squinting at warily since my second year as an undergraduate and which, I now realised, raised bibliophilosophical questions of its own. As a physical object, this other book was as clearly printed and well designed as *Also the Hills*. Beyond that all comparisons fail. For one thing, it has clusters of printed letters like these:

bi tso fb rok engl a ssan dspl itch ina

For another, it includes passages like the following:

Yard inquiries pointed out → that they ad bîn "provoked" ay Λ fork, of à grave Brofèsor; àth é's Brèak—fast—table; ;acùtely profèššionally *piquéd*, to=introdùce a notion of time [ùpon à plane (?) sù ' ' fàç'e'] by pùnct! ingh oles (sic) in iSpace?! (Joyce 1975: 124)

No prizes for guessing these come from *Finnegans Wake* (1939), Joyce's last and most extreme foray into literary writing.

Again, as with Coetzee's *Dusklands*, the *Wake* left me feeling at sea, but, after McKenzie's seminar and my experience with *Also the Hills* in the Bodleian, I began to pay more attention to the way it relentlessly refuses the bodily forgetfulness Keyes's novel induced and which so much of my school and undergraduate training as a reader had also encouraged. Reading, the *Wake* insists on every unscannable page, is not an unworldly encounter with a spirit medium. It is a learned bodily practice involving a complex meeting between a materially inscribed writing system, a finite living brain and a well-trained eye, at least for the sighted. The first example ('bi tso . . .' above) I now realised is a solvable visual puzzle designed to highlight that great Irish scribal invention: white space as a means of word separation. Arranged differently, the letters read: 'bits of broken glass and split china'. The second is more enigmatic, though the random punctuation marks from English and other European writing systems, the diacritics most commonly associated with French and Czech, the capital letters and italics, and the symbols from IPA, logic and mathematics, all foreground the visual dimensions of literacy by, once again, interfering with the brain's ability to scan printed letters. For good measure, though risking further obscurity, Joyce underscored the point by adding an oblique reference to Dr Rosenbach's avatar, the Irish palaeographer and book collector Sir Edward Sullivan. Based on the prevalence of square rather than round punctuation marks, Sullivan suggested that *The Book of Kells*, Ireland's most treasured ancient manuscript, itself a testament to writing as a graphic art, dated from the tenth century—he attempted that is 'to=introdùce a notion of time . . . by pùnct! ingh oles (sic) in iSpace?!'.

Yet the *Wake* insisted I do more than unforget the history and peculiarities of writing, understood not as a shadow of speech but as a graphic medium in its own right. Take the word 'iSpace' from the second example. Given his openness to an unpredictable future, Joyce would no doubt be delighted that this now seems to us like an uncanny prefiguration of the typographic logo a large fruit-associated tech company first introduced with the iMac in 1998. What struck me a few years earlier, however, was its generative potential as an idiosyncratic, multi-sensory duck-rabbit grapheme. Heard, rather than seen, it morphs into 'eye-space', itself an inventive description of the printed page; then again, after my professorial assistant picked up some knowledge of Italian and its orthography, I realised it could also be a translation of *ispazio*, now the name of an Italian blog about

Apple products, but once an old way of writing *spazio*. So, like many of the *Wake*'s improbable duck-rabbit graphemes, 'iSpace' did not just interfere with the workings of my reading brain by tampering with the quasi-phonetic Latinate writing system and the book English I first learnt from Dr Seuss's *The Cat in the Hat*. It put additional pressure on the classic distinction between the sensible and the intelligible, extending McKenzie's bibliophilosophical lessons and raising more questions about the everyday phenomenology of reading.

Admittedly, the stakes in these two transformative reading lessons were rather different. With McKenzie, if I failed to address his central challenge, all I risked were accusations of bibliographical illiteracy. With Joyce, I was in danger of becoming one of the *Wake*'s many bad male readers, possibly the violently pedantic 'grave Brofèsor' or perhaps the 'ornery josser, flatchested fortyish, faintly flatulent' who cannot read 'a quite everydaylooking stamped addressed envelope' in the appropriate Wakean way (109, 124). Typically, the 'josser' ignores the expressive 'outer husk' (not just the material form of the envelope but 'the enveloping facts themselves circumstantiating it') because he obsessively desires the contents—not just the letter the envelope contains, but its 'literal sense or even the psychological content' (109). Ratcheting up the *Wake*'s critique of a philosophically dubious fixation on a disembodied, supersensory, perhaps even fundamentalist idea of the intelligible—what Samuel Beckett sardonically called 'the scant cream of sense'—Joyce then shifts the analogy, comparing the 'josser' to 'some fellow' who, on being introduced to 'a lady' for the first time, immediately envisions 'her plump and plain in her natural altogether' (109; Beckett 1929: 13). Again, Russell's preoccupation with print as a conduit for knowledge and his search for a transparent, 'logically perfect language' came to mind. Was Russell just a high-minded version of Joyce's predatory 'fellow', I began to wonder?

Like *To the Lighthouse*, the *Wake* is clearly in dialogue with philosophy, but, as ever, there is a difference. Whereas Woolf engaged with a certain tradition of philosophy as a novelist, Joyce created an uncategorisable artefact of writing, every printed letter and page of which takes issue not only with some of the supersensory aspirations of Western philosophical thought but with 'knowledge by description' in all its forms and varieties. In the *Wake* no fetishised 'idol worts' are safe, whether philosophical, religious, political, literary or something else. Here, for instance, is Shaun, one of its archetypal bad male readers, denouncing his feckless, subversive twin brother Shem by declaring the supremacy and indubitable truthfulness of his one and only orthodox philopoliticoreligious book:

my trifolium librotto, the authordux Book of Lief, would, if given to daylight, (I hold a most incredible faith about it) far exceed what that bogus bolshy of a shame, my soamheis brother, Gaoy Fecks, is conversant with in audible black and prink. (425)

This makes the *Wake* look like an exercise in radical scepticism, a 'black and prink' machine for reducing every fetishised idea of the intelligible to 'scant cream'—not just sense, as Beckett claimed, but sound and any light 'printed letters' seem magically to convey: ideas, experience, knowledge and more. Yet, if the *Wake* critiques bookishly monomaniacal orthodoxies of all kinds, it does so by being a humane and creative answer to its own challenge: a generative stream of heterodox graphemes, dedicated, as its vast population of bad readers intimates, to bringing a new, more grounded and worldly kind of reader into being.

So what might these remade *Wake* readers be like? One thing is clear: they would not be as determinedly gendered as Shaun and his avatars. Equally, unlike the predatory 'fellow', these good finneganites would bring a McKenzie-like attention to the fragile physical realities of every artefact of writing from the materials on which it relies for support, whether papyrus, bamboo, paper or recordable binary code, to the technologies through which it is transmitted, whether manuscript or print, analogue or digital. I like to think this attunement to physical documents would endear these readers to Dr Rosenbach. Then again, unlike the 'josser', they would be alive to the 'enveloping facts' circumstantiating each documentary encounter, including all the agents in Darnton's 'communications circuit', all the forces at play in Adams and Barker's 'whole socio-economic conjuncture', and, for that matter, Ong's entire 'living human lifeworld', which for Joyce is as much a place of writing in all its changing forms as of speech in all its mutating varieties. Above all, they would recognise that when it comes to reading, as with listening, there is no escaping the finite 'body whose sense-organs distort as much as they reveal', to recall Russell's formulation. The reason? For Joyce, all 'knowledge by description', including Russell's most abstract 'universals', depends not just on corruptible forms of writing and speech but on the living brains of readers and listeners who, for better or worse, actively collaborate in its production. Why for better or worse? Because, unlike Shaun, who believes in the single truth his author-centred 'Book of Lief' conveys, the *Wake*'s remade readers acknowledge that, as all-too-human collaborators rather than mere receivers, what they bring is not just the promise of further revelation but the risks of more distortion.

By this stage, it will come as no surprise that when my professorial or Brofèsorial doppelgänger was invited to give these lectures, I could not resist the temptation to set him a research project of my own. Once he had alerted me to Darnton's comments on the challenge of investigating reading as 'inner appropriation', the nature and scope of this autobibliobiographic exercise became clear. Yet it was, in the first instance, my evolving experience of the *Wake* that made me point him towards the latest scientific research into the reading brain, and then to dig into the public and private accidents of the long, unfinished history of my own development as a reader, beginning with Dr Seuss's *The Cat in the Hat* as spoken in my mother's voice. This history involved many books, as the Brofèsor discovered, but it also involved the many intermediaries and institutions who took it upon themselves to teach me how to read. For most, this was a functional business, along the lines Fred Schonell advocated: reading as a basic skill, the ultimate purpose of which is to enable us to look through writing to the 'ideas', 'instructions' or 'information' it conveys. This was true even for the editors of the literary anthologies I read in my final school year, who encouraged me to see poems and short stories as kaleidoscopic windows onto 'experience'. As an undergraduate, I discovered that Bertrand Russell gave all this a sophisticated philosophical gloss at the turn of the last century, not just when he described the facts readers gain from newspapers but when he attempted to ground 'universal knowledge' in a transparently 'perfect language'. Yet, as the Brofèsor grudgingly began to accept, and as I secretly knew all along, the most influential and generative instructors were really books themselves. This was especially true of those like *To the Lighthouse*, *Things Fall Apart*, *Dusklands* and *Finnegans Wake*, each of which insisted, secretly and in its own way, that I unlearn everything I had inwardly appropriated about reading, provoking me to become another kind of reader altogether.

Chapter 4

My *Finnegans Wake*: Like HCE, Rhodes Must Fall

Writing about *Finnegans Wake* has always been beyond me, though I have once written with it. The notoriously idiosyncratic project to which Joyce devoted himself during the tumultuous interwar years plays a central part in my book *Artefacts of Writing* (2017), setting the terms, alongside Rabindranath Tagore's extraordinary oeuvre, for a way of thinking about languages, heritages, communities and the state. 'Though many reading experiences, rather than any fixed set of norms or methodological principles, let alone any general theory of criticism, have shaped and continue to shape my evolving engagement with literary writing,' I wrote in the introduction, 'repeated, often bewildering encounters over a number of years with James Joyce's *Finnegans Wake* (1939) proved pivotal for this book' (McDonald 2017: 23). The reason? In the process of re-making me as a reader, a process I described in the previous chapter, the *Wake* changed how I thought about the foundations of the sovereign, self-determining modern state—hence the title of the central chapter on Joyce in *Artefacts*, which comes from a throwaway remark he made about the United States in a letter to his son on 4 July 1935: 'Independence, Dependence, Interdependence Day' (Joyce 1966: 369–70). My changing and change-making experience of the *Wake* was only part of the story, however. No less influential were the circumstances in which I first encountered it. Though this became clearer to me only after I finished *Artefacts*, I should have known better. After all, as the *Wake* itself insists, there is no secure distinction between what is supposedly 'intrinsic' to reading and what is 'extrinsic' to it. Or, to be more precise and to use one of its own guiding figures: while we can take a letter out of its envelope, we cannot read it in a properly Wakean way if we ignore its mode of delivery and 'the enveloping facts themselves circumstantiating it' (Joyce 1975: 127).

I could say the intrinsic experience of reading *A Portrait of the Artist as a Young Man* (1916) steered me to the *Wake*, but, once again, that is not the whole story, because I did not stumble on Joyce's first foray into long-form fiction by chance or as an isolated artefact. I initially encountered *Portrait* on a 'World Novel in English' course as a second-year undergraduate in 1984, where it appeared alongside Joseph Conrad's *Heart of Darkness* (1899), E. M. Forster's *A Passage to India* (1924), William Faulkner's *Light in August* (1932), Saul Bellow's *Herzog* (1964), Chinua Achebe's *Arrow of God* (1964), J. M. Coetzee's *Dusklands* (1974) and V. S. Naipaul's *A Bend in the River* (1979). As I read them over the year, each of these books cast new light on the others, creating different patterns and connections like a shifting kaleidoscope. With *Portrait*, *Heart of Darkness*—or rather the *Heart of Darkness* debate Achebe provoked in the 1970s, and Naipaul complicated—had the most powerful refraction effect. At issue was not just the canonical status of Conrad's novella, or the conflict of interpretations, but questions about the ownership of the English language, its literary forms and the heritages with which it was associated in the era of decolonisation. On the one hand, there was Achebe, in his guise as a writer-critic, denouncing Conrad as a 'bloody racist' in his now-classic essay 'An Image of Africa' (1977: 788). On the other, there was Naipaul, the creative practitioner, reworking Conrad's novella in *A Bend in the River* to tell his own African story. Reading outside the very masculinist list of prescribed books, I found Nadine Gordimer coincidently doing the same as Naipaul in *Burger's Daughter* (1979).

All this alerted me to *Portrait*'s own questions about language, ownership and empire. 'His language, so familiar and so foreign, will always be for me an acquired speech', Joyce has the undergraduate Stephen think during his scholastic exchange about art and language with the English dean of studies: 'I have not made or accepted its words. My voice holds them at bay. My soul frets in the shadow of his language' (Joyce 200: 159). He and the dean have just been arguing about 'tundish', which Stephen tries to claim as an Irish word for 'funnel'. Later, he realises he is wrong, noting in his diary entry for 13 April: 'I looked it up and find it English and good old blunt English too. Damn the dean of studies and his funnel! What did he come here for to teach us his own language or to learn it from us. Damn him one way or the other!' (212). Complicating this anti-colonial animus, Stephen's next entry records his apprehensions about an 'old man' from the west of Ireland whom he represents as an atavistic adversary in his own inner drama, casting himself as the high poet-priest of modernity. A figure out of a nativist Gaelic League imaginary (or Yeats's Celtic Twilight?), the cabin-dwelling old man nonetheless switches casually between English and Irish.

What struck me most about *Portrait*, particularly when compared to the other novels on my second-year course, is the way Stephen's evolving and always fraught relationship with English shapes the narrative itself, making the language question much more than a thematic concern. This shaping impetus runs from the first sentence and the oral story Stephen's father tells him as a small child ('Once upon a time and a very good time it was there was a moocow') to the last, which centres on the high-minded Hellenism of Stephen's final written diary entry ('*April 27*. Old father, old artificer, stand me now and ever in good stead') (5, 213). So, for the Joyce of *Portrait*, the English language in its various spoken idioms and written forms was more than a contestable colonial inheritance or an elective literary medium. It was a central subject and structuring device.

With my curiosity piqued, I ferreted out Joyce's other books in the university library. For some reason, *Finnegans Wake* came to hand first. The library had the 1946 Faber and Faber hardback, a reprint of the first edition which includes a list of 'Corrections of Misprints' at the end. Opening it for the first time on that day in 1984 was for me about as far from Keats's experience of first looking into George Chapman's seventeenth-century translation of Homer as it is possible to get. A 'new planet' the *Wake* might have been, but I did not feel like an awestruck 'watcher of the skies', even less like 'stout Cortez', and not just because Keats mixed up his Spanish conquistadors. To me, planet-*Wake* seemed utterly airless, alien and bewildering. I barely got past the first page. True, I could 'read' the Latinate script and the printed characters. I could even recognise many familiar-looking English words, despite all the verbal shenanigans (Sir Tristram's 'penisolate war' stood out). I also got the idea that someone (Finnegan?) had had a fall a bit like Humpty Dumpty ('the pftjschute of Finnegan, erse solid man, that the humptyhillhead of humself') (3). But for the rest I was at sea without a compass.

All I had were questions. Why was Joyce messing with the basic rules of English punctuation? No apostrophe in the title, no capital for 'riverrun', and then this one-hundred-letter parenthetical monster: '(bababadalgharaghtakamminarronnkonnbronntonnerronntuonnthunntrovarrhounawnskawntoohoohoordenenthurnuk!)'(3). The paragraphing was somewhat reassuring, but, if Joyce was mainly a novelist, why was there no dialogue? I knew from *Portrait* that he did not like quotation marks, but, if this was a novel, as the slabs of prose seemed to suggest, then who was the narrator and where did one character begin and another end? Asking for a plot was obviously asking for trouble. In the face of all this, the errata at the end of the library edition seemed like an exercise in absurdist pedantry. Was any sane reader really going to care that 'Quáouauh!' on page 4 should read 'Quaouauh!' or that 'Mac Dyke' on page 8 should be printed 'MacDyke' (Joyce 1946: 629)? After half an hour, I returned the book to the shelf and went back to an essay I was trying to write about E. M. Forster's *A Passage to India*. Yet, for all my befuddlement (or because of it?), I was hooked, and so I found myself returning to the *Wake* again and again in the years ahead, lured by the most basic question: why did Joyce, a writer I admired even more after reading *Ulysses* (1922), spend the last seventeen years of his writing life on such a seemingly deranged and deranging project?

* * *

The first glimmerings of an answer came about a year later, when I returned to the library and to that opaque first page, now armed with William York Tindall's *A Reader's Guide to Finnegans Wake* (1969), which opens with these faintly encouraging words: '*Finnegans Wake* is about anybody, anywhere, anytime' (Tindall 1969: 3).

From Tindall I learned that the *Wake*'s second paragraph details some of the many invasions and migrations that had shaped, and were still shaping, the history of Ireland ('the scraggy isthmus of Europe Minor'): from the ancient Celts, some of whom immigrated from Brittany, to the modern Irish, many of whom emigrated to the United States—hence the play on 'North Armorica' and 'doublin', which is also a city on the Oconee River in Georgia, US (3). Underpinning all this, Tindall intimated, was something like a Joyceanic philosophy of history. These specifically Irish migrations reflected the workings of two very different but always crosscutting world-historical forces—Tindall called them 'principles'—each of which is potentially creative and destructive: a free-flowing, circulatory 'feminine' force, associated chiefly with the river Liffey ('riverrun') and Anna Livia Plurabelle (ALP); and a master-building, rising-and-falling (tumescent-detumescent?) 'masculine' one, linked most immediately to Dublin's Howth Castle and Humphrey Chimpden Earwicker (HCE) (Tindall: 30). When Tindall then connected this characteristically visceral philosophy to Joyce's word play a switch flipped. I was particularly taken by his comments on 'penisolate', which he describes as a 'radiant word' because it 'carries Wellington's Peninsular War, the Wellington

Monument, the lonely penis, and the lonely pen'—the Anglo-Irish Duke of Wellington (1769–1852) is one of HCE's many masculinist avatars (Tindall: 31). Moreover, Tindall added, all the crazy punning and mixing of languages itself bore witness to humanity's never-ending, often violent interactions: for example, '"Passencore," not yet in French, vies with German "wielderfight" (*wiederfechten*)'—literally 'fight again' (31). With Tindall's help I realised that the Joyce of the *Wake*, who was evidently more of the ALP than the HCE persuasion, is emphatically not the Stephen of *Portrait*. Far from fretting 'in the shadow' of the dean's English, Joyce used his last literary wager to ramp up *Ulysses*'s linguistic experimentalism, wresting the language from its erstwhile colonial owners and re-foreignising it for his own idiosyncratic (and to me still largely mysterious) purposes.

Though Tindall opened my eyes to the *Wake*'s densely textured Irishness, I continued to feel the lure of his 'anybody, anywhere, anytime' claim, which he supports with this edited quotation: 'Every those personal place objects ... where soevers' (Joyce 1975: 598). For the most part, this only compounded my puzzlement, though, as an undergraduate studying English and Philosophy in the mid-1980s in what was then called Grahamstown, South Africa, at what is still called Rhodes University, Tindall's promissory first sentence did get me thinking. There were, after all, some points of intersection between my immediate circumstances and the world of the *Wake*: the long shadow of the British empire being the most obvious. Grahamstown was founded in 1812 as a military outpost on the eastern frontier of the British Cape Colony, which was itself established to secure the sea route to the east during the 'penisolate' Napoleonic Wars. A product of the same history, albeit in a later phase, the university, which dates from 1904, took its name from its first benefactor, the mining tycoon, arch imperialist and former premier of the Cape, Cecil John Rhodes (1854–1902)—for CJR read HCE. Though the 'enveloping facts' of this long history were everywhere to be seen in the 1980s, they were overshadowed by the more urgently 'circumstantiating' present, which saw apartheid enter its darkest final years.

Yet there was one point at which the colonial past and the late-colonial present converged: a vast local icon called the 1820 Settlers National Monument, an odd amalgam of the Wellington Monument, Howth Castle and the 'Willingdone Museyroom' where the *Wake* begins (Joyce 1975: 8). A short walk from the university library, the monument occupies a commanding position on a hill overlooking the city—unlike Howth Castle, which is less imposingly situated. It is, in fact, adjacent to Fort Selwyn, a stone redoubt the British had located on the same spot for military purposes in the 1830s—hence Gunfire Hill. In keeping with this history, the monument itself was used to house a searchlight trained on the city's Black neighbourhoods during the militarised crackdowns the apartheid government imposed in the mid-1980s. Enough to make any soul do more than fret. In my case, the building's looming extrinsic presence had another, no less inward effect as well. Memories of the shadow it cast over my first efforts to look into, or simply at, the *Wake* fuelled my compulsion to return to Joyce's eccentric last work time and again in the years ahead.

* * *

Memorialising the arrival of four thousand British colonists at the Cape in 1820 was nothing new. Since the half-century in 1870, each milestone had been lavishly marked by a series of commemorative events. Then, in the centenary year, the first major physical memorial was erected in the city's high street—replaced by a granite trilithon (another HCE emblem) in the 1950s—and a specially dedicated museum, focusing on the military history, followed in 1965. The monument was of a different order, however, not just because it was grander but because it was intended to be a living memorial. Modelled on the monolithic modernist design the American architect Louis Kahn developed in the 1950s, the vast 20,000-square-metre, seven-level building, which was opened to great ceremony in 1974, includes a 1,000-seat theatre, a 200-seat cinema as well as art galleries and conference facilities. Since its inception, it has also been the venue for an annual festival of the arts. As its first publicity officer (Thelma Neville) explained in an article about the opening, the ship-like concrete, brick and glass structure—'proudly dominating the landscape'—was intended to embody the iconic function:

> As the use of the building had to be related to the contributions made by the British pioneers, the main functions are designed to concentrate on perpetuating the heritage bequeathed by the 1820 Settlers—the English language and the democratic traditions they brought with them—by means of an auditorium to be used mainly for English-language festivals and a conference centre that points to the democratic practice of debate and discussion. (Neville 1974: 12)

A plaque in the entrance, which pointedly speaks for the settler lineage in the possessive first-person plural, still makes the same point:

the 'facilities are open to all, to enjoy and enlarge *our* heritage of language and culture and to perpetuate *our* traditions of tolerance and freedom of speech'. As the publicity officer added, in another telling formulation, 'it is perpetuating more than a language. It is an ethos; a characteristic spirit; a heritage; an endowment' (13).

Three conspicuously displayed (and less noticeably modified) quotations in the cavernous main foyer, one etched in stone around a central fountain, the other two rendered in large, brushed-steel letters on the concrete walls at the entrance, reiterate the message in more poetic terms. 'That all might have life and have it more abundantly', the fountain inscription reads, adapting Jesus's parable of the good shepherd from the King James version of John 10:10. 'We must take root and grow or die where we stand', the writing on the first wall at the entrance declares, turning a past-tense observation the English missionary Henry Dugmore (1810–1896) made in *The Reminiscences of an Albany Settler* into a present-tense injunction—Dugmore's recollections of his arrival as a nine-year-old member of an original settler group began as a lecture on the occasion of the half-century celebrations in 1870. Finally, a side wall at the entrance carries four lines from the end of 'The Emigrant's Cabin', a 305-line 'conversation poem' by the Scottish writer, free-speech campaigner and abolitionist, Thomas Pringle (1789–1834), who was a leading figure in the settler community during his brief six-year residence in the Cape:

> Nor wild Romance nor Pride allured me here:
> Duty and Destiny with equal voice
> Constrained my steps: I had no other choice . . .
> Something for Africa to do or say.

This comprises lines 137–39 of the poem, plus line 230, all spoken in the Pringle voice. 'Thomas Pringle' lives on as the name of one of the building's primary venues as well. The cinema and main theatre are also named: the former after the writer, feminist and anti-war campaigner Olive Schreiner (1855–1920); the latter after the poet, academic and leading proponent of the monument Guy Butler (1918–2001). There is some acknowledgement of local Xhosa heritage too, but only via a single figure who also exemplifies the success of missionary evangelism. The art gallery is named after Ntsikana (1780–1821), the first Xhosa prophet to propagate Christian beliefs.

For the monument's founders, the talismanic settler names and quotations did more than express what they considered the 'characteristic spirit' of the British legacy. Like the plaque declaring the facilities 'open to all', they elevated their project above the brutally repressive realities of apartheid. 'Inscribed in the flagstones of the floor of the impressive memorial foyer, around a perpetually bubbling fountain, are the words from St John's gospel' testifying to the monument's 'openness and hospitality', the chair of the 1820 Foundation (then Jan Breitenbach) explained in 1991 (Neville 1991: 105). He was echoing his predecessors, who from the start had insisted 'this is no sectional or bombastic memorial' (103). The 'enveloping facts themselves circumstantiating' the construction of the building suggested otherwise. Two will suffice. First, a coincidence: the monumental tribute to '*our* traditions of freedom of speech' opened the year the white-only, Westminster-style Parliament, another settler inheritance, passed the Publications Act, 1974, inaugurating a new, more repressive phase in the history of apartheid censorship. Second, an enabling condition: far from disdaining, or simply ignoring, the latest drive to commemorate the 1820 settlers, the state actively supported it from the start, in the end covering 80 per cent of the final construction cost (R3.2 million of the R4 million total, around R200 million in today's values) (Neville 1991: 64, 93). Indeed, for the state, the monument was something of a propaganda coup—the publicity officer's promotional piece about the opening was, accordingly, given a six-page, illustrated spread in *S. A. Panorama* (1956–1993), a state-run periodical designed to boost South Africa's image at home and abroad. Evidently, any threat the founders' claims about openness, tolerance and free expression posed was outweighed by the endorsement their project gave to the state's own racialised ethnolinguistic vision of South Africa as an essentially Anglo-Afrikaner polity, comprising an association of divinely ordained, separate *volke*, each with its own language and ethnic heritage. 'No group had made a bigger contribution to the character of South Africa today', *Panorama* reported the state president (then J. J. Fouché) saying at the opening in 1974, before adding, again in his words, that the vast new building was not only a monument 'of which English-speaking South Africans could be proud but a symbol of pride and hope for all South Africa' (Neville 1974: 11).

* * *

Finnegans Wake challenges this kind of thinking at every level and takes issue with the monument's founding assumptions at every turn. Working out exactly how and why was a tortuous process, but the following passage pointed the way—it is, in fact, the first of the *Wake*'s many explicit reading lessons:

> (Stoop) if you are abcedminded, to this claybook, what curios of signs (please stoop), in this allaphbed! Can you rede (since We and Thou had it out already) its world? It is the same told of all. Many. Miscegenations on miscegenations. (Joyce 1975: 18)

I found the last sentence, which had a special resonance in the South Africa of the 1980s, particularly illuminating, because it hints at a cultural, even political rationale for Joyce's practice of creative re-foreignisation, which the passage also illustrates. By adding words like 'rede' (German and Anglo-Saxon for 'speech') and 'abeceda' (Czech or Slovak, also possibly Anglo-Saxon 'abecede', for 'alphabet') to the already interlingual English ('please' from French, 'signs' from Latin/French, 'world' from Old Frisian/Anglo-Saxon), Joyce layered his own inventive 'miscegenations' (itself a Latinate coinage) on the many 'miscegenations' of ordinary English, simultaneously claiming the language for himself and disabling any ideas of linguistic purity or ethnic ownership. As Seamus Heaney intimated, this spoke to many writers living with the colonial legacy of British-English in the mid-1980s. 'The English language belongs to us,' declares the defiantly angular Joyce of the *Wake*, who appears like *Hamlet*'s ghost to the self-doubting Heaney-figure in section XII of *Station Island* (1984). 'Keep at a tangent,' he then says, and 'fill the element / with signatures on your own frequency' (Heaney 1998: 268). As if in concert, Salman Rushdie took similar instruction from the *Wake* with world-shattering consequences in *The Satanic Verses* (1988) (McDonald 2017: 243–60). At around the same time—in 1984 and 1986, respectively—two leading contemporary writers in South Africa, Es'kia Mphahlele and Njabulo Ndebele, addressed the national English Academy, a white-led organisation with close ties to the monument. Their subject? The future of English as a decolonised, Black *lingua franca* in South Africa, beyond what Ndebele called the academy's 'prescriptive open-mindedness' (Ndebele 1991: 103; see also Mphahlele 2002: 344–60). The phrase applies equally to the idea of linguistic guardianship for which the monument stood. At that point, Mphahlele, who returned to South Africa in 1977 from two decades in exile, was the most eminent Black educationalist in the country—he founded the African Literature department at the University of the Witwatersrand in 1983. Ndebele, then teaching English at the National University of Lesotho, would go on to succeed him as head of the Witwatersrand department in 1991.

Yet, as I slowly came to realise, Joyce was doing more than targeting colonialist delusions about the English language. He was raising equally testing questions about his own primary medium: the Latinate English writing system. Though this critical feature of his project was staring at me from every page—for one thing, I had simply to read 'if you are abcedminded' literally—it took some time for me to see it, or, rather, to unlearn how I had been taught *not* to see it in the process of learning to read. By a curious trick of the literate brain, becoming 'abcedminded', as Joyce's word play implies, makes us absent-minded about the medium of alphabetical writing as such. From its unpunctuated title to its non-final word ('the'), the *Wake* is a counter-lesson in basic literacy designed not only to interfere with, and compound, the vagaries of the sound-based though notoriously untransparent English writing system but to foreground the promise and perils of writing as an endlessly proliferating, infinitely malleable and always corruptible artefact of human devising. 'Countlessness of livestories have netherfallen by this plage,' Mutt tells Jute in their non-dialogue on a dump just before the 'stoop' passage, 'flick as flowflakes, litters from aloft, like a waast wizzard all of whirlworlds' (17). He is contemplating the long, palimpsestic history of human interaction caught in the decomposing 'humus' runes of 'ourth', but could be referring to the litter-like frailty of the many 'claybooks' that come under Joyce's compendiously eclectic scrutiny: from the contested textual history of the Irish *Book of Kells* (900 CE) to fakeries like the Scottish poet James Macpherson's *Poems of Ossian* (1760), and from the Constitution of the Irish Free State to the Bible and the Quran. Like ALP's unreadably but emblematically defaced and recirculating letter, all form part of the mouldering 'museomound' which is, at once, the *Wake* itself and the ultimate site of humanity's worldly, earth-written heritage—etymologically 'mound' evokes the Latin 'mundus', the French 'monde' and the Germanic 'midden', all of which connect to the Germanic 'world' we are invited to 'rede' (8).

Reread in Joyce's desacralising, forensically humanistic terms, the monument's talismanic quotations begin to look rather different. 'We must take root and grow or die where we stood', as Dugmore originally had it in his 1870 memoir-lecture, recalling the moment he and his settler group found themselves alone in the 'wilderness' of the Cape frontier. 'But we were standing *on our own ground*,' he then added, 'and it was the first time many could say so' (Dugmore 1871: 9). This excised sentence, which follows directly from the present-tense injunction quoted on the monument's entrance wall, raises the question of land ownership, the most contested and as yet unresolved legacy of the settler era. It also casts a shadow over the words from John 10:10 around the fountain, which raise other, no less troubling questions when seen in their original context or envelope. While the inscription implicitly figures the settlers and their descendants as the good shepherds of Jesus's parable and so as Jesus himself, the original verse has Jesus contrasting himself to the 'thieves and robbers' (the false messiahs) who came before him: 'The thief cometh not, but for to steal, and to kill, and to destroy: I am come that they might have life, and that they might have *it* more abundantly' (Carroll 1997: 130). A further (repressed?) parallel with the Dutch, later Afrikaner, colonists as the 'thieves and robbers' now begins to look plausible—or is the implied distinction between the settlers and the terroristic military forces who preceded them? As the *Wake* cryptically has it, the 'polyhedron of scripture' is indeed a 'proteiform graph' (107). The lines from Pringle's 'The Emigrant's Cabin' create other complications, in part because the Pringle voice does not just say 'Duty and Destiny' vaguely instructed him to do or say 'something for Africa'. On the one hand, they compelled him to do 'something for the sad Natives of the soil, / by stern oppression doomed to scorn and toil', even if 'but one mite of Europe's debt to pay' (Pringle 1989: 29–31). This is the Pringle who would also write 'Makanna's Gathering', which begins: 'Wake! Amakósa, wake! / And arm yourselves for war' (35). The poem is a tribute to the Xhosa philosopher-warrior-prophet and Robben Island prisoner Makhanda (*c.*1780–1820), a more challenging figure than Ntsikana, who was defeated by the British at the Battle of Grahamstown in 1819. On the other hand, the same 'Duty and Destiny' directed Pringle to devise various 'schemes for civilizing savage men' (29). This Pringle would also conclude his *Narrative of a Residence in South Africa* (1835) with the words: 'Let us enter upon a new and nobler career of conquest. Let us subdue savage Africa by JUSTICE, by KINDNESS, by the talisman of CHRISTIAN TRUTH' (Pringle 1835: 341).

Yet the *Wake* is more than a commentary on the perils of conjuring a legacy from edited and selected writings. By undoing the English writing system from within in the way it does, it subverts the monument's *raison d'être* as a living memorial dedicated to 'perpetuating' the 'characteristic spirit' of the English language. To think of English as the expression of an unchanging 'ethos' or as the bearer of an inherently democratic ethnic 'heritage'—to use the publicity officer's formulations—is, for Joyce, to subscribe to a linguistic version of Christian 'infusionism', the doctrine of the soul as 'a divine emanation, infused into the body at conception or birth', which amounts, in Joyce's book, to little more than 'kapnimancy', a play on 'capnomancy' or 'divination by smoke' (117, and *OED*). This kind of thinking takes political, or politico-theological forms too, as Joyce recognised—the preamble to the Irish Constitution being one conspicuous example with which the *Wake* engages (McDonald 2017: 17–19, 144). By toying with the polyphonic and polysemic potential of the grapheme at every opportunity, each of the *Wake*'s 628 pages represents an obsessively orchestrated affront to infusionism in all its permutations and iterations.

Take just one example: the word 'rede' in the 'stoop' passage. To Anglograph eyes it might *look* like a misspelling of 'read' (itself Germanic in origin), modelled, say, on a verb like 'cede', an oddity that would not arise if the passage were heard rather than seen—to standardised British-English ears 'rede' would simply be a homophone of 'read' (/riːd/ in IPA). For a reader with knowledge of German, however, it would *look* like the word for 'speech' (also 'talk' or 'conversation'), which transcribes as /ˈreːdə/ in IPA. Unlike 'penisolate', Tindall's 'radiant word', which works more like a conventional if densely packed English portmanteau, 'rede', as an interlingual Latinate grapheme, refuses to incarnate any one language, meaning or sound, opening itself up to many readers and phonetic renderings while at the same time revealing the hazy, shape-shifting mirage that hovers between writing and speech. Hence the ditty Joyce composed as a sales pitch for his London publishers: 'Buy a book in brown paper / From Faber and Faber / To see Annie Liffey trip, tumble and caper. / Sevensinns in her singthings, / Plurabelle on her prose, / Seashell ebb music wayriver she flows' (Joyce 1930).

* * *

The unwrapped 1946 Faber edition is still on the shelves of the university library, but 'the enveloping facts themselves circumstantiating it' have changed decisively since 1984. A decade later, South Africa became a unitary, secular state and a constitutional democracy with eleven official languages, Afrikaans, English and isiXhosa among them, and a statutory commitment to promoting fourteen others, including Arabic, German, Hindi and Nama. More locally, following a protracted, twenty-year debate, Grahamstown formally became Makhanda (Pringle's 'Makanna') in 2018. In an official statement about the name change, Nathi Mthethwa, the South African Minister of Arts and Culture, explained:

It is the Truth & Reconciliation Commission [1996–2003] that recommended that the renaming of geographic features be a form of 'symbolic reparation' to address an unjust past. These reparations include changing the names of geographical places. Surely, we cannot prove ourselves committed (as government) to fully achieve these reparations if we retain names such as 'Grahamstown'—named after Colonel John Graham [1778–1821]—whose name is captured in history as being the most brutal and most vicious of the British commanders on that frontier, whose campaigns were executed with—in his own words—'A proper degree of terror'? At the time, British authorities praised Graham for 'breaking the back of the natives.' The battles he waged were not only against soldiers, everyone—including women, children and the elderly would not be spared. Even post-battle, he and his soldiers would employ the 'scorched earth policy' against those he had already brought violence and misery against, by burning their fields and killing their cattle; starving them into submission, before killing them. This is the man that 'Grahamstown' has been named after. (Mthethwa, 2018)

Three years earlier, Rhodes University also began reconsidering the HCE figure after which it was named in response not to the TRC but to the Rhodes Must Fall campaign, which led to the removal of Cecil John Rhodes's statue from the University of Cape Town in April 2015. After a two-year process, it was however decided to retain the name, largely on financial and pragmatic grounds. 'It cannot be disputed,' the university council nonetheless acknowledged, 'that Cecil John Rhodes was an arch-imperialist and white supremacist who treated people of this region as sub-human' (Council, 2017).

At the time of writing (2023), the vast building on the hill overlooking today's Makhanda is still called the 1820 Settlers National Monument but, starting in October 2015, its governing council too initiated a public consultation about its name and future. Though the RMF campaign was very much in the air, the council took its cue from the preamble to the 1996 Constitution:

We, the people of South Africa,
Recognise the injustices of our past;
Honour those who suffered for justice and freedom in our land;
Respect those who have worked to build and develop our country; and
Believe that South Africa belongs to all who live in it, united in our diversity. (Constitution, 1996)

As the briefing document for the consultation noted, 'the ethos and operations of the Monument should be based on this broader statement of commitment, rather than solely the values and ideals of the British Settlers who arrived in this area in the 1820s' (Foundation 2015). Since the process, which was due to end in October 2019, is still ongoing, there is scope for an unlikely thought experiment: imagining a post-monument future consistent not only with the Constitution—the preamble as well as the language provisions—but with *Finnegans Wake*. Whatever else this de-monumentalising initiative might involve, two guiding commitments would be clear. First, rejecting the infusionist assumptions on which the monument was founded—all the talk of 'perpetuating' a 'characteristic spirit'—it would acknowledge that, when it comes to the future of any heritage, there can be no otherworldly guarantees. This is not just because infusionism is capnomancy but because, as Joyce's philosophy of history has it, all the unjust heritages or 'Museyrooms' master-building HCE-figures construct must eventually fall. Second, replacing the symbol of the 'perpetually bubbling', single-source fountain with an ALP-inspired river of many origins and none, this initiative would call for the building to be rededicated, perhaps naming it simply iZiko laseMakhanda lezobuGcisa (the Makhanda Centre for the Arts). Its purpose? To serve the Eastern Cape's many languages and heritages, to redress the injustices of the past, and to uphold the promise of linguistic and cultural survival through intercultural engagement and creative exchange or, in Joyce's coinage, 'MUTUOMORPHOMUTATION' (1975: 281).

To signal this new start, the quotations from Pringle and Dugmore would have to be moved from the main entrance to a more modest location elsewhere in the building, where they could be remounted with an explanatory plaque giving the details of their original provenance or envelopes. What to put in their place? For the side wall where the Pringle quotation was originally situated, imagine an easily changeable display—words painted by local graffiti artists, perhaps, or inscribed by light as if written on water—with two initial quotations:

> What kind of makeshift shelter is this? (Wicomb 2020: 7)

This comes from the opening of Zoë Wicomb's *Still Life* (2020), an inventively fictive, ingeniously multivoiced reassessment of Pringle and his legacy. Alongside it on the same wall:

> More and more he is convinced that English is an unfit medium for the truth of South Africa. (Coetzee 1999: 117)

This is one of the rare moments in J. M. Coetzee's *Disgrace* (1999) when the central protagonist, David Lurie, glimpses a world beyond his own prescripted, often prescriptive, linguistic, literary and philosophical horizons.

Finally, on the forward-facing entrance wall where the Dugmore quotation once stood, picture the following two quotations in brushed steel and, ideally, in the original isiXhosa with translations captioned alongside. Here is the first:

> you entered with bible in hand,
> 'Receive the great book
> and spurn your lore and customs.'
> minister turned into soldier,
> he raised his rifle and blasted his cannon,
> Rharhabe's mountain roared,
> dust arose and the land was aflame. (Opland/Manisi 2012: 300)

This is a transcribed and translated extract from an oral performance David Yali-Manisi (1926–1999), the leading isiXhosa *imbongi* (ceremonial oral poet) of his generation, gave at the monument in July 1977. As the mode of address shows, Manisi was knowingly confronting the upholders of the Settler tradition, the descendants of the historical 'you' to whom he directed his words. Rharhabe (c.1722–87) was a key figure in the Xhosa royal lineage and founder of a prominent sub-clan who took his name. Here is the second:

> It comes from the sea; it is a tribe that looks as though it regularly attacks other tribes. Their language is so complicated, no one understands it. As for fighting, they are powerful people who fight using the heavens; the heavens thunder once, smoke and fire explode, and then something falls in the distance. (Mqhayi 2018: 72–3)

This is from S. E. K. Mqhayi's isiXhosa classic *Ityala Lamawele* (*The Lawsuit of the Twins*, 1914). Mqhayi (1875–1945), a prominent writer, journalist and language activist, was also Manisi's most eminent predecessor in the *imbongi* tradition. Looking back more than a century, he describes the arrival of the British, their strange language and mysteriously lethal weaponry through the eyes of early nineteenth-century Xhosa royal messengers. If his subject recalls the ancient Irish *Lebor Gabála Érenn* (*The Book of Invasions*), one of Joyce's many sources for the *Wake*, Mqhayi's inventively estranging language prefigures the opening of *Portrait*, where the young Stephen, who does not yet have the concept or word 'spectacles', sees his father 'through a glass' (Joyce 2000: 5). In its various iterations, *Ityala* is many things: a compilation of isiXhosa poetry and customary law, a biography of major historical figures, including Makhanda and Ntsikana, a reflection on the 'pandemonium of nations and tribes' the advent of the British wrought and a creatively intercultural engagement with the King James Bible and the Latinate writing system (Mqhayi: 70). It is also a fictive parable about the traditions of democratic deliberation among the amaXhosa in the precolonial era, written, as Mqhayi put it in his 1914 preface, to encourage 'young Xhosa males and females to look carefully at precisely what will disappear when these wise and distinguished expressions and customs of their origin vanish completely' (3).

Part II

Second Voice

Extra-Disciplinary: Questions of Method

Chapter 5

Getting over Discipline Envy

The title of this chapter alludes to Marjorie Garber's *Academic Instincts* (2001), an engaging reflection on *Homo academicus* at the turn of the millennium. Garber uses the phrase 'discipline envy' in her second chapter, where she re-examines debates among literary scholars of the 1980s and 1990s—she was then and remains a Professor of English at Harvard—about the function and merits of interdisciplinary studies.

> Like envy itself, 'discipline envy' is a mechanism—a structure. And it's the structure, not the hierarchy of disciplines, that endures. The prestige and power of individual disciplines vary over time. New disciplines develop; others fade away. Envy, or desire, or emulation, the fantasy of becoming that more complete thing, is what repeats. (Garber 2001: 67)

For Garber, recognising the existence of this recurrent structure makes it possible to rethink the received view of the relationships among academic disciplines, one that understands things in terms of turf wars and territorial rivalry. Against this view, she points out that, driven by a sense of lack or deficiency in their own discipline, academics also covet territories they take to be more glamorous, more rigorous or more serious than their own. 'Over this century alone my own discipline of literary studies,' Garber notes, 'has yearned to be, or to model itself on: linguistics, anthropology and ethnography; social science, natural science, psychoanalysis, sociology, history, and various strands of philosophy, from aesthetics to ethics' (65–66). If the territorial imperative has, in other words, constituted literary studies since its inception, it has also been shaped by the equal but opposite energy of discipline envy.

Garber's own position on these competing disciplinary desires is clear and emphatic: though wary of the longing for unity, the 'fantasy of becoming that more complete thing', discipline envy manifests, she welcomes the openness to interdisciplinary affiliations it affords, and suspects the self-imposed purism bred of the territorial imperative. At the end of her essay, she notes:

> If the humanities have a future, and I fervently believe they do, it will be a . . . future that involves going back to the past, and inhabiting [a] predisciplinary interdisciplinary moment. Not to do away with history or historicizing or context or culture, but rather to do the opposite: to see that Freud was righter than he knew when he imagined the human mind as being like the city of Rome, layer built upon layer, each cohabiting with, not replacing the past. Our task as scholars is to reimagine the boundaries of what we have come to believe are disciplines and to have the courage to rethink them. For as a member of any discipline comes to realize sooner or later, it's hard to know where discipline envy, like inspiration, will strike next. (95–96)

It should be said that she reaches this admirable conclusion only after considering the many prominent nay-sayers within literary studies, those, like Helen Vendler, Edward Said and Stanley Fish, who had spoken out vigorously against interdisciplinary, not to mention extra- or pre-disciplinary work, either because, as Fish put it in 1989, 'it is so very hard to do', or because it lacks rigour, tends to be driven by fads, or—and here we see the territorial imperative reasserting itself—because it pollutes the pure interests of authentic literary studies (Fish 1989: 12–22). This was the burden of Helen Vendler's call in 1980 for literary scholars to keep 'our own separateness from other disciplines', echoing the long purist tradition associated with American New Criticism (Vendler 1981: 349). Couched as thoughtful prudence, this is clearly a healthy outlook. The trouble starts only if caution modulates into a principled hostility to interdisciplinary work as such, not least because, in my view, more damage has been done to literary studies by those calling for its splendid isolation (as, for instance, the flagship discipline in the humanities) than by those eager to engage in productive dialogues across or between or outside disciplines.

I do not propose to focus here on literary studies and its disciplinary discontents, though I shall return to them briefly later. Rather, I want to consider a related but different set of concerns within a relative newcomer in the humanities, the field or sub-field, now commonly known in the English-speaking world as 'book history'. But I have started with a brief account of Garber's analysis of discipline envy in literary studies because it is relevant to some of the questions book history raised as an emergent field, albeit in a different way. If envy in literary studies is an expression of a desire to appropriate the vocabulary, methods or prestige of another discipline, in the context of book history it refers to a more primal need to acquire the professional status of a discipline as such. This difference is no doubt in part an effect of relative standing of the two fields. Though the origins of book history can be traced back well into the nineteenth century, particularly if we think of the British bibliographic tradition, it is none the less fair to say that it began to emerge as a new force in the humanities in the 1960s and 1970s, and to seek to define its identity as a 'discipline' in the 1980s and 1990s. Book history's envy is, then, the expression of an insurgent's uneasy mix of insecurity and ambition.

This created some confusion at the heart of the enterprise, for one rather obvious reason. At its best, book history is an interdisciplinary mode of inquiry not a 'discipline', an intersection not a place, as many of its champions have always insisted. Writing in 1999, the British-based bibliographer D. F. McKenzie, one of the leaders in the field, called it 'a form of inquiry relevant to the history of every text-dependent discipline' (McKenzie 1999: 1). More strikingly, Robert Darnton, the American historian, concluded his pre-internet manifesto-essay of 1982, entitled 'What is the History of Books?', in the imperative mode: 'By its very nature . . . the history of books must be international in scale and interdisciplinary in method' (Darnton 1990: 135). Yet it is here, I would argue, in Darnton's seminal essay, that the beginnings of the confusion can be detected.

Well aware of the long and complex genealogy of book history as a scholarly pursuit—he looks as far back as the Renaissance, and emphasises the importance of developments in the nineteenth century—Darnton none the less focused on the new co-ordination of activities among an international group of historians, literary scholars, bibliographers, sociologists and librarians in the 1960s and 1970s. Their increasingly shared sense of common enterprise, centring on problems relating to the 'process of communication', gave the new field a 'distinct scholarly identity' (107). And gradually, through conferences, lectures and then journals and research centres, a professional status as well. '"*Histoire du livre*" in France, "*Geschichte des Buchwesens*" in Germany, "history of books" or "of the book" in English-speaking countries—its name varies from place to place, but everywhere it is being recognized as an important new discipline.' It 'has developed so rapidly during the last few years,' Darnton went on, 'that it seems likely to win a place alongside fields like the history of science and the history of art in the canon of scholarly disciplines' (107).

In fact, Darnton's overt aim in this manifesto-essay was to help this process of canonisation along: to give the history of the book a semblance of unity, that is, the stability and coherence of a scholarly discipline. He wanted to ask and answer the question 'What is the history of books?' (a question that presupposes or wishfully posits a unifying centre) and, in so doing, bring some order to the 'rich and varied' field or, as he put it more colourfully, to 'get some distance from interdisciplinarity run riot'—a telling phrase, coming as it does from a historian of the French Revolution (110). Shifting into an equally revealing trope—the male scholar as intrepid explorer fighting through the jungle—he noted with alarm that book history looked in 1982 'less like a field than a tropical rain forest'.

> The explorer can hardly make his way across it. At every step he becomes entangled in a luxuriant undergrowth of journal articles and disorientated by the crisscrossing of disciplines—analytical bibliography pointing in this direction, the sociology of knowledge in that, while history, English, and comparative literature stake out overlapping territories. (110)

To civilise this unseemly riot/jungle, Darnton proposed his influential 'communications circuit', which was intended to give 'some holistic view of the book as a means of communication' and to prevent book history from becoming 'fragmented into esoteric specializations cut off from each other by arcane techniques and mutual misunderstanding' (111, figure 2). As a guide for the perplexed, and a strategy for taking stock of developments in the field and providing a larger perspective on a series of disparate activities, this was clearly a valuable, timely and important intervention (for another take on the circuit, see chapter 2). As a means of imposing some stabilising unity on various productively related lines of inquiry, its intellectual effects, however, were, in my view, regrettable, not least because of the way things began to develop after 1982.

It might seem that all this is just a semantic fuss about nothing, that I am making too much of Darnton's perhaps rather casual use of the words 'discipline' and 'interdisciplinary'. If we simply substituted the phrase 'mode of inquiry'—the formulation I prefer—for 'discipline', which, it could be said, is just a little scholarly hype, then the apparent confusion in the essay, and in book history, would disappear. There may be something to this, but, from the vantage point of the present, it does look as if Darnton's slippery use of terms in 1982 was a sign of things to come. After all, over the next two decades book history began to look more and more like a discipline. The first major publication in the field, the multi-volume *Histoire de l'edition française*, appeared in the course of the 1980s, opening up space for the array of national histories of the book in Britain, America, Canada, Scotland, Australia, etc.; the Society for the History of Authorship, Reading and Publishing (SHARP), now the main professional forum for book historians, was founded in 1991; the flagship journal *Book History* was launched in 1998, a major addition to the eighty-odd journals that currently welcome work in the field; and, in the course of the 2000s, building on earlier developments, new centres of the book, from Edinburgh to Lyon, continued to be created. Moreover, at the turn of the millennium, in what is perhaps the ultimate badge of professional accreditation, Routledge published *The Book History Reader* (2002, 2nd edition 2006), the first introduction to what the blurb called 'book history studies'. *The Blackwell Companion to the History of the Book* followed in 2007 (2nd edition 2019), and soon after came the *Oxford Companion* (2010) and the *Cambridge Companion* (2014).

These are, of course, encouraging developments from a professional point of view. They have put book history on the map; they have helped invent a tradition of sorts; and they have created various important contexts in which scholars can meet, establish networks, discuss and promote research. As such they are real gains. Yet such professionalisation can entail costs, particularly if, amid all the hype, book history loses its identity as a genuinely interdisciplinary mode of inquiry. Some eminent book historians clearly did not feel this was a danger. Indeed, they sought not simply to consolidate its professionalisation but to encourage its institutionalisation as a fully fledged discipline with all the attendant departmental structures, stages of accreditation and goals of self-replication. In 2001, Jonathan Rose, for instance, professor of history at Drew University in New York, founding president of SHARP, and co-editor of the *Blackwell Companion*, proposed that book history finally become a self-standing taught subject called 'book studies'. He outlined his mission in a speech to the American Printing History Association:

> Over the past ten years SHARP has concentrated its energies on building the basic apparatus of institutionalized book history scholarship, getting courses and conferences and journals up and running.

> Now that that has been accomplished, let us move on to conquer new worlds. And I have a specific and highly ambitious proposal to place on the table . . . In this new decade, we should work together to create new academic programs in Book Studies. (Rose 2001)

Rose's language and tone—all that talk about 'conquering new worlds'—was perhaps understandable. This is a founding president setting out his vision, which, after an unpromising start, did indeed herald a new turn in the years ahead. Though the early graduate courses in 'book history studies' were slow to recruit—'my own program at Drew University,' Rose admitted, 'has generated hundreds of inquiries, yet it enrolled no students at all in 1999 (its first year of operation) and only two in 2000'—the pace accelerated in the new decade and the SHARP website now lists just under thirty graduate programmes in Europe and North America alone.

Yet Rose's world-conquering vision raised more questions than it answered not just because it too was burdened by discipline envy but because it was driven by envy's more familiar twin: a rivalrous territorial anxiety, in this case about literary studies 'after theory' (see chapter 6). Warming to his theme, Rose observed:

> If we build programs in Book Studies, that larger community of book-loving students will come. At one time they would have naturally gravitated to English departments, but nowadays they are likely to find there a mix of opaque theory, dismal ideology, and few real job prospects other than teaching composition as a perpetual adjunct. For these students, we should create an alternative route of literary studies, one which offers fresh horizons for innovative scholarship, practical applications in art and business, and the possibility of earning a decent living. (Rose 2001)

Valid though some of these sentiments were—no one can deny that job prospects have only worsened over the past two decades—this kind of talk was always unlikely to lure literary students into book studies departments. Much the same could be said for Rose's academic version of Whig history: 'Once upon a time, professors studied literary *works*. Then, for the past 25 years or so, they studied *texts*. Now, we should redirect our attention to *books*.' As I noted in the introduction, Blanchot, who can all too easily be seen as an exemplar of the kind of theory Rose decried, had offered a very different, far more challenging perspective on the question the book as early as the 1950s.

No less off-putting was the odd blend of infusionism and materialist fundamentalism that underpinned Rose's advocacy.

> The problem with focusing on texts is that no one can read a text—not until it is incarnated in the material form of a book. It is perfectly legitimate to ask how literature has shaped history and made revolutions, how it has socially constructed race, class, and gender, this, that, and the other. But we cannot begin to answer any of these questions until we know how books (not texts) have been created and reproduced, how books have been disseminated and read, how books have been preserved and destroyed. (Rose 2001)

This is Rose's version of the bad reader as Joyce's 'ornery josser' who fixates on the letter at the expense of the envelope, now recast as the bad theorist in a disciplinary polemic about book history versus literary studies. Again, this could be seen as more hype coming from a single, very enthusiastic book historian, but, unfortunately, as the prospectus to *Book History*, the SHARP-sponsored journal, indicated, such rhetoric was from the start an official part of the newly professionalised discipline's self-image. Presented as 'a new journal for a new kind of history', which they date from 1979, the editors, Rose himself and Ezra Greenspan, declared in 1998 that 'with the exhaustion of literary theory, younger professors of literature are finding that book history provides a more rigorous and empirical approach to such issues as reader response, canon formation and the politics of literary criticism' (Rose 1998: x).

Underlying these formulations is not simply discipline envy of a special kind, but a more familiar reassertion of the territorial imperative. Book history is billed as the latest thing—from work to text to book—and the tone implies that it is superior to all other things, especially politicised, theory-ravaged literary studies. We are back with the ideology of splendid isolation which, I predict, will do as much damage to book history in the long term as it did to literary studies, not least if it fosters a new disciplinary frontier mentality. True, at a time when individuals and institutions were investing heavily in the subject, it might have been necessary, as Bill Bell, the founder of the Centre for the History of the Book in Edinburgh, wryly suggested in 2001, 'to behave, at least for the time being, as if a coherent and definable field exists' (Bell 2001: 3). Such fictions have their uses, not least when making applications to funding bodies for resources, but only if they remain just that—useful fictions. When mistaken for reality, especially by book historians themselves, they only invite trouble, as was already clear at the time to the author of an early field review entitled 'History of the Book: An Undisciplined Discipline?' (Clegg 2001).

For book history to flourish it could, in my view, do well to abandon the territorialist hype of its early years—all that masculinist talk of civilising the jungle, conquering new worlds and riot control—and the kind of discipline envy that fuels such inflated language. In the interests of avoiding misunderstanding, those with a stake in the field should also place a moratorium on the use of the word 'discipline'. To pre-empt confusions of this kind I would suggest replacing it with a less neat but more pliable phrase like 'interdisciplinary mode of inquiry'. I prefer this not only because it contains the word 'interdisciplinary' but because it insists on the idea of book history as a mode. Whereas the word 'discipline' tends to encourage nominalisation, thinking in terms of nouns, territorial metaphorics and questions of the 'What is book history?' kind, 'mode' encourages adverbial thinking; adverbs not only modify verbs, they discourage spatialisation and encourage questions like 'What do book historians do?' In this sense, book history can be thought of as a way of modifying any number of activities in a range of disciplines, or, indeed, outside any scholarly territories. On this analysis, it becomes possible to do, say, the history of ideas book historically, or to write a feminist literary history book historically, or to develop cross-disciplinary connections among linguists, bibliographers and sociologists book historically. And you can do this while respecting the complex traditions out of which these various fields emerged, and the detailed local knowledges at their command. Thinking adverbially, the possible modifications book history could effect within, between and outside disciplines are in principle endless, but it would, of course, still produce those modifications in a particular way by, for instance, encouraging scholars to consider the value of archival resources, ask questions about the politics and economics of publishing, or the technologies of text production, and give due weight to material considerations of all kinds, which, despite the apparent immateriality of the digital age, have not gone away.

In more practical terms, thinking and speaking about the subject as an interdisciplinary mode would make it possible for scholars, no matter what their official discipline, to introduce book history into every aspect of their academic life, whether in teaching, administration or research, without feeling they must stake out a territory and put up signs about trespassing. The strategy would be one of world permeation, rather than isolationism, or, worse still, world domination. In this way, the subject could continue to draw on the diverse range of traditional disciplines out of which it originally emerged—bibliography, history, sociology, library and literary studies—while also changing and evolving links with newer interdisciplinary areas, including film and media studies, cultural studies, digital humanities and older formations like 'theory'. Ideally it would, at the same time, never lose touch with the always changing, never predictable, extra- or pre-disciplinary *experience* of the book as material artefact and idea. Understood and promoted in this way, book history may well have a promising future, allowing those already invested in the field to welcome newcomers, scholars, students and, who knows, so-called 'ordinary readers' too, by saying: ask not what you can do for book history, ask what book history can do for you.

Chapter 6

Ideas of the Book and Experiences of Literature: After Theory?

At the turn of the millennium, books with the alluring, though far from transparent, phrase 'after theory' in their title were very much in vogue. Thomas Docherty got there early with his *After Theory* (1990), and then, following in quick succession as if driven by millennial fever, came David Kastan's *Shakespeare After Theory* (1999), Valentine Cunningham's *Reading After Theory* (2002), Terry Eagleton's *After Theory* (2003) and the more astutely interrogative collection of interviews *life. after. theory* (Payne 2003). *Theory after 'Theory'* (2011), a collection of essays edited by Jane Elliott and Derek Attridge, followed a little later, paying homage to what the editors called theory's 'ongoing wake' (Attridge 2011: 1). If you add to this Raman Selden's characterisation of the period from the mid-1960s to the mid-1990s as 'the age of *theory*', then it looked like literary studies in the English-reading world had undergone another major, indeed epochal, paradigm shift rivalling the 'linguistic turn' of the late 1960s (Selden 1995: 1).

True, the savviest proponents of the 'after theory' narrative always recognised its risks. Eagleton, for instance, who was among the most authoritative and certainly the most popular, began his own book with a pre-emptive warning: 'Those to whom the title of this book suggests that "theory" is now over, and that we can all relievedly return to an age of pre-theoretical innocence, are in for a disappointment' (Eagleton 2003: 1). Being 'after theory' was for him at once more banal and more profound than that. At one level it simply meant that the 'golden age of cultural theory is long past' (1). The 'pioneering works' of Lacan, Lévi-Strauss, Althusser, Barthes and Foucault are 'several decades behind us', as are the 'path-breaking early writings' of Williams, Irigaray, Bourdieu, Kristeva, Derrida,

Cixous, Habermas, Jameson and Said (1). At another more dramatic level, however, it represented a defining moment in a larger story of post-revolutionary betrayal. This implication was central not only to Eagleton's analysis in *After Theory* but to his re-invention of himself in the mid-1990s as the champion turned sardonic commentator on contemporary theory. In that new guise he had been after theory, in a more prosecutorial sense, for nearly a decade.

Like his earlier collection *The Illusions of Postmodernism* (1996), *After Theory* pursued several popular *doxas* of the time—an untroubled relativism, an exaggerated culturalism, an apparent indifference to politics or ethics, etc.—but, unlike its predecessor, it was also intended to be more directly and explicitly forward thinking, even inspirational.

> If [cultural theory] is to engage with an ambitious global history, it must have answerable resources of its own, equal in depth and scope to the situation it confronts. It cannot afford simply to keep recounting the same narratives of class, race and gender, indispensable as these topics are. It needs to chance its arm, break out of a rather stifling orthodoxy and explore new topics. (Eagleton 2002: 222)

So reads his conclusion. Viewed in isolation like this it is difficult not to see his point or to feel the uplift. The trouble is, these rousing sentiments made sense only as part of Eagleton's larger story about the betrayal of the 1960s revolution. Once-challenging new ideas, like the ones he championed in the 1980s, had become debased orthodoxies rehearsed by a culpably disengaged generation of linguistic turners. Whereas the past had pioneers, the millennial present had room only for mimics: pure Lacanians, at best, or a more modest group of applied Lacanians. 'Those who can, think up feminism or structuralism;' wrote Eagleton, 'those who can't, apply such insights to *Moby-Dick* or *The Cat in the Hat*' (2). To be 'after theory', then, was for Eagleton to be in a minor period, an age of borrowed silver perhaps, characterised by an ethical malaise and a dismal sense of belatedness.

For all its wistfulness about the heady days long gone, this was, on the face of it, a plausible way of thinking about the state(s) of literary studies at the turn of the millennium. It was difficult not to feel that the admirable, and always theoretically motivated, warnings against becoming Barthesians or Derrideans, issued most persuasively by Barthes and Derrida, had gone largely unheeded (see Barthes 2000: 457–78, and Derrida 1994: 63–94). At the same time, as Toril Moi argued, Wittgenstein's disparaging comment about philosophy leaving 'everything as it is' seemed to have even more relevance to work then still being done in the name of 'theory' (Payne, 2003: 145). Yet the assumptions underlying Eagleton's characteristically novelistic style of analysis—not least his epochal model of history—begged too many questions ever to be convincing. They also, of course, opened the possibility of an entirely different way of reading the situation, since, as Eagleton, the storyteller, himself noted in 1996, 'there is always . . . more than one story to tell' (*Literary*, 1996: 206).

If literary studies had become dominated by a routine academicism 'after theory', were they, therefore, in a phase that can be defined only negatively as minor? From a more distanced perspective today, would it not be more productive, and accurate, to think of the situation as coming not 'after theory', but after theory's own successful bid for hegemony? Viewed in this way, the period from the mid-1960s to the mid-1990s would make sense less as a rise and fall, epochal or betrayal narrative and more as a particularly disputatious episode—calling it the 'age of the theory wars' is perhaps overdramatic—which brought radical and necessary change but which also left a less fortunate legacy, including the strangely extended meaning of 'theory' itself, a parochial term which made little sense outside literature departments in the Anglograph world, and the potentially disabling memory of an overheated debate. That the sometimes Brexit-like debate was intense and divisive is, of course, unsurprising. Important questions to do with what Eagleton termed 'our guiding assumptions' were at stake; moreover, revolutions tend to require, and not simply to create, fierce polarisations (2003: 2). Difficulties arise only when a once expedient culture of factional advocacy, with its simple for or against logic, slogans and caricatured positions, outlives its usefulness.

Reconfiguring the 'after theory' story along these lines would have some distinct advantages. For one thing, it would enable us to abandon the more dubious models of history implicit in the standard narrative. For another, it would allow us to enjoy the benefits of not having to keep fighting old battles. Though small sects of stubborn liberal humanists, touchingly innocent positivists, dogmatic historicists or 1950s moralists (i.e. the monsters against whom theory established its own hegemony) may live on in the remote hinterlands, they are, thanks to the knights-errant of the theory struggle—among them Eagleton himself—now largely silent, or at least ineffective, spectres. More importantly, if the millennial turn is understood as a period in which the terms of the theory struggle began to look increasingly anachronistic, not as a minor coda to a golden age, then it becomes possible to think beyond the less welcome legacies of 'the age of theory' and to imagine new ways forward.

* * *

As Eagleton emphasised in *Literary Theory: An Introduction* (1983), one of theory's most productive clearings centred on the question of literature itself. Starting in post-war France, according to Eagleton's Euro-American story, notably in the writings of Blanchot, Barthes and Derrida and then extending to the Anglo-American world in the early 1970s, especially via the journal *New Literary History*, doubts about the viability of literature, as a stable or even valid category, gradually came to form the basis of a new consensus. This grew largely out of a reaction against various post-war studies—Sartre's *Qu'est-ce que la littérature?* (1948), Wellek and Warren's *Theory of Literature* (1949) and Northrop Frye's *Anatomy of Criticism* (1957) are especially noteworthy—which, it was argued, reinforced long-held beliefs in the possibility and desirability of treating literature as a clearly demarcatable object, possessing a definable essence. This project, which could be traced back to classical poetics, was, the critics claimed, at best ill-founded or at worst impossible. On the one hand, they noted that the *literary* (however it might be defined) is never restricted to what might conventionally be called *literature*; while, on the other, they pointed out that one of the peculiarities of *literature* (on certain definitions) is that it is always disturbing or overturning established ideas of the *literary*. The great Indian poet-philosopher, Rabindranath Tagore, in fact prefigured this view in the late nineteenth century, notably in his essay 'Literature' (1889), which begins pointedly: 'The essence of literature does not allow itself to be trapped within a definition' (Tagore, 2001: 49). The Euro-American intellectual world caught up with him just under a century later.

The fact that these problems at the level of description also frequently presupposed or felt the impact of powerfully normative uses of *Literature* as an honorific only complicated matters. *Literature*, in this sense, did not simply *refer* to a putatively distinct object, distinguishable in some stable way from, say, pornography or philosophy; it *constituted* the Literary as an especially privileged public discourse located within or even at the apex of a cultural hierarchy. Behind this lay the accumulated interests and valuations of various individuals, groups and institutions as well as the long, always fraught history of *Literature's* struggle to defend its often imperilled sense of cultural distinction (as against, for example, journalism, cinema and other new media, political writing or less acceptably 'literary' works). From this new recognition of the instability of the category a very different set of methodological protocols followed. In place of a quasi-scientific search for essences there developed a new preoccupation with the socio-political, historical and institutional conditions that made the category of the literary possible. Instead of repeating or contesting assertions taking the general form 'This is literature', enquiry now focused on radically situated statements of the form 'X said: "This is literature"', where the demonstrative was understood performatively. It is worth noting that this new self-consciousness about the varied uses and effects of the category, which presupposed a sharper sense of its cultural and historical specificity, was largely (though not exclusively) a consequence of the much-maligned 'linguistic turn'.

Though the high points of this debate are familiar enough, they are worth briefly revisiting, partly to recall the diversity of philosophical and critical traditions that influenced it, but mainly to challenge some of the often too settled positions that developed within it, particularly considering the recent so-called 'post-critical' turn. Disturbing these positions will also allow us to re-orient the debate by identifying some unexpected points of intersection between the apparently opposed enterprises of theory and book history. To say that the post-war era produced a new theoretical consensus is only partly true. If the instability of the category of the literary was widely accepted from the mid-1970s, there was not much agreement on what this meant or how it might be understood. In particular, a marked, though by no means absolute, division developed on how X (as in 'X said: "This is literature"') could or should be theorised, a division which reflected wider and deeper differences within the growing traditions of what was generally called 'anti-essentialist' thought—I prefer 'anti-scholastic' as a qualifier because it covers both the usual location (the university) and the most common mode (definitional anxiety) associated with this kind of thinking.

The first view, which I shall call *sceptical anti-scholasticism*, focused on the idea that the literary could, in principle, emerge anywhere, not simply in what was conventionally considered literature. It emphasised the role various guardians played in recognising and protecting the literary, presupposing a model of discourse as an uncharted space, any parts of which could be annexed as literature, depending on who was doing the defining and which descriptive criteria and/or normative imperatives were at work. One of the most emphatic proponents of this position, in its American neo-pragmatist form, was Stanley Fish, who remarked, in a classic formulation of 1980, that 'literature . . . is the product of a way of reading, of a community agreement about what will count as literature, which leads the members of the community to pay a certain kind of attention and thereby to *create* literature' (Fish 1980: 97). Since it was, for Fish, no longer possible to appeal to some 'once and for all specification of essentialist literary and non-literary properties', the most one could say, in answer to the fundamental question 'What is literature?', was that a particular community in a certain time and place—that is, his idea of X—deemed this or that to be literature (98). For Fish this put all the power in the hands of what he called the 'interpretive community', a collectivity that was as indispensable to his argument as it was vague in its historical and theoretical implications. Once it had enabled him to make the break with scholastic essentialism, in his case associated primarily with the American New Critics of the 1940s, and avoid the pitfalls of a collapse into subjectivism (the New Critic's 'affective fallacy'), he was content to leave it as an undefined postulate.

Other sceptical anti-scholastics developed richer and thicker versions of X. In his bestselling 1983 primer, reissued in a twenty-fifth-anniversary edition in 2008, Eagleton, for instance, gave Fish's neo-pragmatist arguments a distinctly (English) Marxist turn by focusing on the performative powers of certain historically determinable, often antagonistic 'social groups', rather than a generalised, internally consensual 'interpretive community'. After rehearsing the standard anti-objectivist arguments—'literature', as he put it, 'does not exist in the sense that insects do'—he noted that

> the value-judgements by which it is constituted are historically variable, but . . . these value-judgements themselves have a close relation to social ideologies. They refer in the end not simply to private taste, but to the assumptions by which certain social groups exercise and maintain power over others. (Eagleton 1996: 14)

Though the term 'social groups' was designedly unspecific—they could have been mapped along professional, generational, ethnic, religious, sexual, gender or other lines—Eagleton's subsequent analysis of the rise of English as a university subject in England privileged a class analysis. In his version, then, X was class ideology, as evidenced, he claimed, in the different ideas of literature associated with the 'upper-class chauvinism' of Victorians, like Matthew Arnold, and

F. R. Leavis's 'petty-bourgeois version' of the 1930s and 1940s (33). (Here we see Eagleton in his earlier guise as the champion of those 'narratives of class, race and gender' he would go on to decry as 'stifling orthodoxies' in the late 1990s.)

By far the most persuasive and theoretically sophisticated version of the sceptical anti-scholastic position was, however, articulated by the French sociologist Pierre Bourdieu. Like Eagleton, he focused on the classificatory powers of particular 'social groups'. Yet whereas, for Eagleton, these groups had their being in what might be termed the general social formation, Bourdieu's post-Marxist groups belonged most immediately to the 'peculiar universe', the 'Republic of Letters', which he called the 'literary field' (Bourdieu 1993: 181). These were, in the first instance, the various literary specialists and institutions—publishers, critics, academics; magazines, reviews, prizes, etc.—who made reputations and were the 'true' producers of the 'value of the work' (76). Crucially, for Bourdieu, their performative 'power to consecrate' had to be analysed structurally and diachronically—this was part of the Marxist inheritance he did not reject—not individually and synchronically (78). Far from being some charismatic gift, the authority to 'create literature', as Fish put it, depended on each cultural broker's accumulated 'symbolic capital', which was determined by his or her (or its) relative position in the literary field—e.g. newcomer or established, serious or commercial, dominant or marginal (76). The X operative in Bourdieu's analysis was, in other words, not class ideology or the interpretive community, but the dynamically and hierarchically structured field as a whole.

> The quasi-magical potency of the signature [e.g. the publisher's imprint, the author's name or the critic's review] is nothing other than the power, bestowed on certain individuals, to mobilize the symbolic energy produced by the functioning of the whole field. (81)

While Bourdieu ignored neither the influence of Eagleton's wider 'social ideologies', nor the economic order that supposedly shaped them, their effects were, in his view, always 'refracted' through the laws, struggles and history *specific* to the literary field, which was a social 'microcosm' in itself (181–82). Always eager to downplay the 'slightly perverse pleasure of disenchantment' associated with this kind of analysis—in this he was always less triumphalist than Fish and Eagleton—Bourdieu nonetheless recognised that his refusal of the 'Platonic temptation to produce essences' demystified the 'social alchemy' by means of which certain texts were recognised as literature and others not (190–91).

Sceptical anti-scholasticism, which I shall argue remains indispensable, had several salutary effects. By focusing on the various forces that produced and regulated literature as a category, it did not simply challenge scholastic essentialism and bring history back into the equation. It also contributed to what Barthes called in 1977 the desacralisation of literature, which had by then made institutions 'impotent to defend and impose it as the implicit model of the human' (Barthes 2000: 475). This was partly because the relatively rarefied debates, at the level of theory, coincided, and sometimes overlapped, with several broader socio-political developments that were given new impetus in the 1970s and 1980s, which also centred on the conflicting interests at stake in various definitions of literature. In the Euro-American world, the cultural critique pioneered in the Marxist tradition, and then taken forward in the name of feminism and multiculturalism, challenged strongly normative ideas of literature as a repository of universal human values, provoking heated debates over the canon. A comparable socio-political critique was at the same time being worked out in decolonial contexts, as writers and critics from the ex-colonies embraced, re-invented and contested concepts of literature inherited from the European lettered tradition.

For Barthes, who was temperamentally incapable of being a doomsayer, this process of desacralisation, which he called a 'moment of gentle apocalypse', came as something of a welcome relief (Barthes 2000: 476). It meant that the 'angels and dragons', the erstwhile defenders of literature's sacrosanct public authority, had thankfully departed, making it possible to return to the literary as if to 'a country free by default' (476). 'It is not . . . that literature is destroyed;' he noted, 'rather *it is no longer protected*, so that this is the moment to deal with it' (475–76). Not everyone was so sanguine. For some, these critical developments were anything but a 'gentle apocalypse'. Among the more resolute gainsayers was Harold Bloom, who, in his vehemently elegiac *The Western Canon* (1994), attacked what he called, echoing the Nietzsche of *The Genealogy of Morals*, the 'School of Resentment'—a ragbag assortment of Marxists, feminists, New Historicists and Cultural Studies critiquers—for whom the aesthetic, not just literature, was an object of suspicion (Bloom 1994: 23). Against all those who sought to reduce 'the aesthetic to ideology, or at best metaphysics' he urged a 'stubborn resistance whose single aim is to preserve poetry [or literature] as fully and purely as possible' (18). The tensions between Barthes's equanimity and Bloom's vehemence lived on in the 'post-critical' debates that followed the publication of Rita Felski's *The Limits of Critique* (2015).

What Felski largely ignored, however, was that the most credible and astute analysis of both the broad socio-political challenge to the canon, and the narrower theoretical demystification of the literary, came from within the anti-scholastic tradition itself. The *affirmative anti-scholastics*, as I shall call them, who prefigured the era of 'post-critique', shared some of Bloom's ideals but followed a very different set of protocols. Like Bloom, they recognised that once the socio-political interests at stake in any definition of the literary became the focus of attention, then not only the stability but also the validity of the category came into question. Scepticism always risked becoming prejudicial suspicion or programmatic critique. Unlike Bloom, however, they did not mount their defence by appealing to ideas of 'aesthetic strength' (Bloom 1994: 29). If they continued to affirm the literary, they did so by emphasising its paradoxically welcome and positive weakness as a category.

Why the paradox? Unlike the sceptical anti-scholastics, who tended to locate all the performative authority on the side of the interpretive community, class ideology or the literary field, they figured X in the formulation 'X said: "This is literature"' as innovative writing itself, a move which, as we shall see, was not without risks of its own. At the same time—and this is where the paradox lay—they were anti-scholastic not because they believed the literary could, in principle, turn up anywhere, but because they acknowledged that in performing its distinctive literariness, a particular artefact of innovative writing might simultaneously disturb or subvert *a priori* ideas of the literary.

These two affirmative anti-scholastic tenets began to take shape in France in the late 1940s and early 1950s. The first—the insistence on writing's own claims—can be discerned in Barthes's *Le Degré zéro de l'ecriture* (1953). Though still committed to certain Marxist assumptions at that early stage in his career—apparent, for instance, in his claim that 'the ideological unity of the bourgeoisie gave rise to a single mode of writing'—Barthes's emphasis, as this phrasing suggests, was already on writing's own capacity to 'signify something other than its content and its individual form, something which defines its limits and imposes [or posits] it as Literature' (Barthes 2001: 1–2). Writing, as he put it later in *Mythologies* (1957), was 'the signifier of the literary myth' (Barthes 1973: 146). Given his reference to class ideology, it would be easy to mistake this for an earlier version of Eagleton's sceptical anti-scholasticism. Barthes's perspective is, however, noticeably different. Whereas Eagleton tended to see class ideology as a force shaping the way *readers* classified certain texts as literature, Barthes saw it manifest in the changing ways in which *writing* ritualistically displayed 'Signs of Literature' (2001: 2). This key difference within anti-scholastic thought was brought out more sharply and, at times, more problematically by Blanchot in essays from the late 1940s and most systematically in *L'Espace littéraire* (1955). His insistence on what he called the 'work's demand' spoke directly against the neo-idealist tendencies of the sceptics, as is evident in his very different understanding of readers and reading:

> What most threatens reading is this: the reader's reality, his personality, his immodesty, his stubborn insistence upon remaining himself in the face of what he reads—a man who knows in general how to read. (Blanchot 1982: 198)

Here you need only to recall Fish's confidence in the interpretive community's readerly power to 'create literature' to see the gulf between the two positions.

Blanchot articulated the affirmative anti-scholastics' acceptance of writing's own demands most emphatically. He also gave the most exigent account of their further commitment to its endlessly disruptive potential. Though, as Derrida remarked in 1965, some of his formulations from this period—particularly his anti-reductive affirmation of various writers' *exemplary* uniqueness—sounded dangerously like a 'return to essentiality', others reflected his struggle to define an alternative anti-essentialism (Derrida 1978: 216).

> To read a poem [or any work announcing itself as literature] is not to read yet another poem; it is not even to enter, via this poem, into the essence of poetry. The reading of a poem is the poem itself, affirming itself in the reading as a work. It is the poem giving birth, in the space held open by the reader, to the reading that welcomes it. (Blanchot 1982: 198)

It could be argued that this formulation, which still focuses primarily on the work's assertion of its own identity, remains vulnerable to being read as residually scholastic. This, as we shall see, is one of the perils of pure affirmation. Yet the stress Blanchot placed in this passage on the reader's need to accommodate the otherness of *each* text, to acknowledge the singular ways in which it asserted its literariness, not only underscored the contrast between his thinking and that of sceptics like Eagleton, Fish and Bourdieu. It also set him apart from the Barthes of *Le Degré zéro*. For Barthes, the 'literary myth' each text signified was a product of its era, understood in (Sartrean) Marxist terms as a particular epoch in the history of the (French) class struggle. The 'formal history' he traced—from the eighteenth-century French classics, through the nineteenth-century realist novel, to the degree zero of the *nouveau roman*—would, he felt, 'manifest, in its far from obscure way, a link with the deeper levels of History' (2001: 2). For Blanchot, literature's inexhaustible capacity to exceed our categories, its demanding singularity, made any such epochal unities or hopes of a grand historical synthesis untenable. His Beckettian 'Signs of Literature'—Beckettian because of their negative status as impossibly singular signs—pointed only to a fragile 'space', not an object, essence or epoch, which always risked being misread or even unreadable; recall my remarks about *Finnegans Wake* in the introduction and see also my re-formulation of what Blanchot called 'creative criticism' (McDonald 2020).

Fish and Blanchot could be set up as the representatives, *in extremis*, of sceptical and affirmative anti-scholasticism, respectively. The breezily consensual neo-pragmatism of the former is about as cogent an answer as you could get to the latter's engagement with the idiosyncratic space he associated with the bewitching Song of the Sirens, and *vice versa*. Setting up the debate in these terms, as I have so far done, runs the risk of simply reinforcing the fault lines that run through it, however, by implying that these two positions are opposed or even incompatible. Yet, as Derrida's writings powerfully demonstrate, it is possible, indeed necessary, to espouse both simultaneously, not least to avoid their respective pitfalls. This doubleness, which characterises much of Derrida's radical rethinking of the phenomenological tradition, is particularly evident in his 1982 essay 'Before the Law'. Echoing the affirmative anti-scholastic position, he argued there that 'for the literary work as such to emerge', a piece of writing would need to have neither a particular content nor a distinctive form (Derrida 1992: 213). It would, however, have to use certain 'framing' devices (e.g. titles and other paratexts) and 'linguistic structures' (e.g. 'referential equivocation') in particular ways (213, 216). 'These possibilities,' he noted, 'give the text the power to *make the law*, beginning with its own' (i.e. to assert its own distinctive literariness) (214). Yet since these represent only a necessary, not a sufficient, condition for the literary to emerge, they are not enough: they 'still remain too general and hold for other texts to which we would hardly ascribe literary value' (213–14).

Here we see the basis for Derrida's anxieties about some of Blanchot's formulations of the 1950s. To exist properly as literature, writing would also need to be *recognised* as such in the ways sceptical anti-scholastics, and indeed Husserlian phenomenologists, would argue were necessary. It would have to 'appear *before the law* of another, more powerful text protected by more powerful guardians', including 'author, publisher, critics, academics, archivists, librarians, lawyers and so on' (214). Indeed, for Derrida, it 'cannot establish law' (i.e. identify itself as literature, as Blanchot sometimes claimed) *unless* 'a more powerful system of laws ("a more powerful guardian") guarantees it, in particular the set of laws and social conventions that legitimates all these things' (214). This looks like a circular argument. To be literature a text must, as a necessary condition, display certain 'Signs of Literature', but this is itself conditional upon these signs already being recognised, in some sense, as literature. The circularity is only an effect of the phrasing, however, which misleadingly traces the history of 'a text'. It would be better to say that Derrida's twofold manoeuvre turns on the idea that writing (think of Joyce's letter), which is literature in the affirmative anti-scholastics' sense, is both enabled and threatened by literature in the sceptics' sense (think of Joyce's envelope).

For Derrida, this doubleness is what makes literature a 'strange institution' as well as an 'extreme experience' which 'puts phenomenology in crisis' (Derrida 1992: 33 and 45–46).

> Perhaps literature has come to occupy, under historical conditions that are not merely linguistic, a position that is always open to a kind of subversive juridicity. This . . . requires that self-identity never be assured, nor reassuring; and it supposes also a power to produce performatively the statements of the law, of the law that literature can be, and not just of the law to which literature submits . . . Therefore, under certain determined conditions, it can exercise the legislative power of linguistic performativity to sidestep existing laws from which, however, it derives protection and receives its conditions of emergence. (Derrida 1992: 216)

Considered in this way, there is no simple choice between sceptical and affirmative anti-scholastic approaches to the question of literature. While there are problems with the way some versions of these positions are formulated, any wholesale rejection of one in favour of the other is not, in the end, possible. Dealing adequately with the challenges of literature would, if we were to follow Derrida and indeed the history of post-war theoretical reflection, require a constant negotiation between the two. It would also involve, as a matter of theoretical necessity, having to embrace irreconcilable inclinations—towards scepticism and affirmation, even critique and engagement; and towards a 'pure' appreciation of the distinctiveness of specific works, which does not ignore their 'impure' situatedness within and dependence on larger social, political and institutional histories.

* * *

This doubleness opens possibilities for literary study because it relates directly to questions associated with another interdisciplinary mode of enquiry, which, like theory, began to emerge in the 1960s. Now generally known in the English-speaking world as 'book history', this field has given new impetus to a number of scholarly traditions—including bibliography, textual criticism, publishing history, library and reception studies—not by fetishising the book as an object, but by focusing on it as the 'product of human agency in complex and highly volatile contexts', with a view to better understanding 'the creation and communication of meaning as the defining characteristic of human societies' (McKenzie, 1999: 4). It has, to that extent, put the radical situatedness of writing, understood in material and institutional terms, at the centre of historical enquiry.

The connections between this field of investigation and the theoretical reflections on literature are worth clarifying and strengthening. They are, however, far from obvious. This is partly because the two enterprises have, in their very different struggles for accreditation in the academy, all too often maintained a resolute distance from one another. The fractiousness of this entrenched standoff was, as we have already seen, reflected in the 1998 prospectus for *Book History*, which invoked the 'after theory' topos in a way Eagleton would rightly have decried. The 'rigorous and empirical approach' associated with this 'new kind of history' was, it claimed, especially attractive given the 'exhaustion of literary theory' (Rose 1998: ix–x). Polarised and polarising forms of self-promotion like this have also dogged theory, which has been championed in terms of a reductive understanding of the 'linguistic turn'—Paul de Man's polemical essay 'The Resistance to Theory' (1982) is a good example—or as a militantly anti-humanist assault on the metaphysics of the unified text encoded in the concept of the author, copyright law and, most obviously, in the materiality of the book itself; as we shall see, the latter played directly into the early euphoria of the digital age, which rallied around similar anti-humanist themes. What these polarisations repress, of course, are the various potential and actual points of connection between these two modes of enquiry, which, if they do not amount to an untroubled common ground, at least put the debate on a more constructive footing.

If it were possible to trace to a single source the confusions that put enterprises like theory and book history at loggerheads, then Derrida's notorious statement '*Il n'y a pas de hors-texte*' has a better claim than most to such a mythic status. This short sentence, which first appeared in *De la grammatologie* (1967), became something of a rallying point during the 'theory wars'. It was exhibit A for theory's prosecutors, for whom it exposed post-structuralism's culpable ahistoricism, and a badge of honour for the defence, for whom it represented a triumphant break with historicism. Predictably in this adversarial situation the words themselves got lost, not least in translation. The heat this statement produced in the English-speaking world was no doubt partly a consequence of Spivak's clumsy 1976 translation (her best bet was '*There is nothing outside of the text*'), which Attridge's 1992 version ('*There is no outside-the-text*') improved only slightly (Derrida 1997: 158; 1992: 102). Both missed the punning force of the original, which set *hors-texte*, a technical book-making term roughly translated as 'plate' (as in 'This book contains five colour plates'), alongside *hors texte*, which Attridge's translation comes closest to capturing.

This play on words (or hyphens), which reflects Derrida's lively bibliographical (and Wakean) imagination—one thinks of his ironised reflections on ©, the structure of *Glas* and his longstanding interest in the technologies of inscription—does not, of course, provide a key to the talismanic sentence's meaning. What it does indicate is that '*Il n'y a pas de hors-texte*' announced neither a triumphant nor a culpable break with history. It inventively underscored Derrida's sustained commitment to putting in question received assumptions about what is 'outside' *and* what is thought to be 'inside' writing (again, recall Joyce's letter and envelope). As the literal rendering suggests ('There are no plates'), the idea that there is a secure division between, say, illustrations and the 'main text' is an illusion fostered by the materiality of the book (e.g. using special high-quality paper for the plates). Since illustrations, like paratexts, frame writing (or *vice versa*), and since writing has a capacity to exceed all frames/envelopes, there can be no assured sense of where the text proper begins or ends. In this way, the sharply focused pun reflected one of Derrida's larger purposes in *De la grammatologie*, which was to declare, too apocalyptically, the 'End of the Book and the Beginning of Writing' (1997: 6). It also echoed his double analysis of the identity of the literary work, in which, as we have already seen, he insisted on the value and challenging instability of the distinction between the affirmative anti-scholastics' emphasis on writing's 'internal' demands and the sceptics' preoccupation with the institutions 'external' to it. Far from rejecting any concern with history, then, '*Il n'y a pas de hors-texte*' reinvented historicism by unsettling traditional *doxa*. It gave 'history' itself a history by figuring it as an *idea* of a context, not a self-evident referent, and by putting the 'problematic of the border and of framing', or letter/envelope, at the centre of enquiry (Derrida 1994: 92).

Understood in this way, Derrida's playful pun illustrates how his thinking connects, rather than separates, theorists and book historians by pointing, in the first instance, to their shared interest in radically rethinking the idea of the book. Both enterprises have, in their largely separate ways, highlighted the book's historical and cultural specificity, not simply in the form of the codex but as an artefact of particular technologies, legal histories, ideologies and institutional practices. Yet whereas theorists have, at least since Blanchot's *The Book to Come* (1959, a key influence on Derrida) and Foucault's 'What is an Author?' (1969), tended to emphasise the ways in which, say, the materiality of print, copyright law, ideas of authorship and paratextual conventions, have *constrained* the 'proliferation of significations', book historians, notably McKenzie and Chartier, have attended to the positive ways in which these historically variable factors of text production have *effected* new and different meanings (Foucault 1988: 209). The relevance of these two perspectives, which once again repeat the double logic of Joyce's letter/envelope, to the theoretical reflections on literature can be demonstrated at the most fundamental level: the ontology of the printed literary text—a basic question, which, as we will see, acquired a new urgency with the advent of the ebook and the cloud.

In their different, but complementary ways, both remind us that the literary text, in its printed form, is a 'multiple instance or type artwork', to use Noël Carroll's succinct formulation (Carroll 1998: 211). Unlike ontologically singular artworks—Carroll's best example is a site-specific sculpture—my copy of *Waiting for the Barbarians*, say, is an instance or token of J. M. Coetzee's fiction, which is the type. This distinction between singular and type artworks, which is different from but, as we shall see, related to Blanchot's conception of literature's singularity, has been a staple of debates about the ontology of art at least since Richard Wollheim's *Art and its Objects*

(1968/80). Yet, as Carroll convincingly argued, in relation to the problem of mass art, it is inadequate, not least because it fails to capture key differences among type artworks. For one thing, it is not 'fine-grained enough,' Carroll notes, 'to distinguish between film performances and theatre performances' (212) in which the routes from the type to the token are tellingly different.

> To get from a film-type [e.g. Tarantino's *Pulp Fiction*] to a token performance [or screening], we require a *template* [standardly the film print or digital copy]; to get from a play-type [e.g. Pinter's *Party Time*] to a token performance, we require an *interpretation* [by directors, actors, etc.]. (Carroll 1998: 212)

It is these differences that make us regard play performances, but not film screenings, as separate artworks, which call for analysis and appreciation in their own right.

This brings us back to my printed copy of *Waiting for the Barbarians*. For Carroll, books follow the same mechanically reproductive logic as films: my copy is simply a token of the printers' or digitisers' template for Coetzee's fiction. Yet, as book historians have consistently argued, editions are, in fact, more like plays. Each act of book production—design, setting, selection of materials, etc.—is itself a creative process, involving interpretative decisions about Joyce's envelope which effect and constrain meaning; moreover, across various editions changes in *mise-en-page*, paratextual framing, cover design, etc. produce different effects irrespective of whether there are significant so-called 'textual variations'. Derrida makes this point in his detailed analysis of the disparate instantiations of Kafka's 'Before the Law', which appears both as a free-standing *récit* and as an interpolated tale in *The Trial* (Derrida 1992: 209–20). Yet if each edition is, in certain respects, more like a play performance than a film screening, this analogy also has its limitations. In the case of the play, theatregoers often have ready access to the play-type—the printed edition of Pinter's script—whereas readers only rarely gain access to the text-type (Coetzee's original typescript), which may or may not have formed the basis of the printers' or digitisers' template. All that comes readily to hand is my token copy of the type, which is, say, the latest Vintage ebook or paperback edition of *Barbarians*. This does not undermine the logic of the type/token distinction as applied to books—that logic is anyway inescapable—but it makes it look less secure and it suggests that, at the level of ontology, the printed and digitised literary work represents a unique case.

Thinking about editions, or any distinct bibliographical documents, as peculiar kinds of play-like performance—i.e. separate artworks in themselves—has a number of implications for the way we understand the scene of reading. Most immediately, it disturbs the conventional assumption that we have unmediated access to an *author's work*—e.g. Coetzee's fiction as type—and encourages a detailed awareness of modes of textual presentation, the envelopes, as forms of interpretation. These are particularly apparent in composite publications such as anthologies, collections, magazines or series—see chapters 10–13—but they are also evident in the case of individual editions. The difference between the original 1980 Secker & Warburg hardback edition of *Waiting for the Barbarians*, which had a purely abstract cover design, and the 1982 Penguin paperback edition, which included a schematic image of a middle-aged white man on his knees washing a pair of broken Black feet, is a case in point. (It is enough to note here that the fiction, which contains no references to blackness or whiteness, represents Coetzee's first attempt to sidestep racialised discourse altogether.) Yet it is not only specific presentational factors, or 'bibliographical codes', to use Jerome McGann's phrase, that make an edition a play-like performance (McGann 1991: 13). The publishers' details—including the date, place of publication and the imprint—which are usually considered to be of merely legal or commercial interest, also contribute to this by marking the edition, including the digital version, as a particular kind of spatio-temporal event. They point, usually only after careful research, to the literary field to which it owes its existence and, in some cases, its continued survival not only as a public document but as literature, in Bourdieu's sceptical anti-scholastic sense.

Indeed, given the shifting hierarchical structure of the field, each edition tends, via the symbolic economy of the signature, also to identify the work as literature in a strongly normative sense. It does so by associating it with the publishers' reputation, project and promotional strategies; by inserting it within a particular series or backlist, which functions as a co-textual (as opposed to a paratextual) frame; and, of course, by locating it in the field at a particular historical juncture (see chapters 10–13). Depending on the categories available at the time, these various factors, which make the field itself function as an interpretive frame/envelope, label the work as, say, 'literary' or 'popular', 'avant garde' or 'mass', 'classic' or 'modern', 'marginal' or 'mainstream', etc., and set it on a particular trajectory through the next series of cultural guardians, including booksellers, reviewers, prize judges, librarians and academics, who then confirm, contest or revise its identity in their own ways. What circulates in the culture, then, is neither an author's work, nor simply the book historian's material document, but a highly institutionalised (i.e. signed and counter-signed) symbolic form. Though Bourdieu tended to restrict his analysis of these larger field effects to a national, specifically French, context, a limitation Pascale Casanova's *La République mondiale des lettres* (1999) attempts to remedy, in the case of English-language publication a more thoroughly globalised approach is required. That *Waiting for the Barbarians*—to stay with my example—appeared in English under three imprints between 1980 and 1982 is not a merely bibliographical fact. The Secker & Warburg, Penguin and Ravan Press editions—the last was the imprint of the most important anti-apartheid publisher in South Africa—all situated it within very different social, political, critical and institutional histories, modifying its identity as a literary work in different national contexts or legally agreed transnational markets accordingly (see chapter 9).

Tied as it is to his version of sceptical anti-scholasticism, Bourdieu's concept of the field does not address the challenges of affirmative anti-scholasticism, nor can it accommodate the kind of double movement on which Derrida insisted. Yet, in my view, it creates the most effective bridge between the concerns of book history and the theoretical reflections on literature detailed in this chapter, making it possible to analyse the changing conditions of literary production, which are not merely linguistic, with a degree of subtlety and historical richness most other forms of sceptical anti-scholasticism do not achieve. By focusing on the diverse and always volatile interests specific to the field and by demonstrating how various cultural guardians or envelope-makers—not simply academic critics, as both Eagleton and Fish tend to imply—exercise performative power over the literary, Bourdieu avoids the vagueness of Fish's 'interpretive communities' and the short-circuiting effects of Eagleton's 'social groups' without losing the sense of political urgency they bring to debates about literature.

Yet do his concept of the field and style of analysis, developed as they were in the final decades of print dominance, have any relevance in the age of Kindle, Google Books and the cloud? Or are they, like the printed book and all the print-era intermediaries, from publishers to booksellers, perhaps even like the concept of authorship itself, anachronistic products of an old and outdated technology?

For some early celebrants of the new digital era, the answer to this last question was yes. Take Kevin Kelly, the founding editor of *Wired*

(1993–), the digital magazine for digital advocacy. Celebrating the coming of 'that Eden of everything', the digitised 'universal library' Google Books presaged in 2004, Kelly was confident that the emergent, supposedly democratic culture of the internet based on 'the universal form of digital bits', and facilitated by the hyperlink and the tag, would 'transform the nature of what we now call the book and the libraries that hold them'—as he acknowledged, the digitising revolution was having as much of an effect on the publishing industry and copyright (Kelly 2006). 'What is the technology telling us?', he asked:

> That copies don't count any more. Copies of isolated books, bound between inert covers, soon won't mean much. Copies of their texts, however, will gain in meaning as they multiply by the millions and are flung around the world, indexed and copied again. What counts are the ways in which these common copies of a creative work can be linked, manipulated, annotated, tagged, highlighted, bookmarked, translated, enlivened by other media and sewn together into the universal library. (Kelly 2006)

The 'universal library,' Kelly added, 'becomes one very, very, very large single text: the world's only book'. This is the digital evangelist's equivalent of 'the End of the Book and the Beginning of Writing' Derrida announced in the 1960s.

Not all members of the tech community shared Kelly's utopian yes to a future seemingly beyond the book and, we could add, beyond Bourdieu's dynamically differentiating concept of the field. For Jaron Lanier, the leading tech developer and dissident, 'the digital flattening of expression into a global mush' Kelly envisaged not only jeopardised the livelihoods of authors, publishers and booksellers (Lanier 2010: 47). It threatened to erase the individuality of books and their authors, and so the prospects of creativity itself. On this analysis, Kelly's single-book utopia, which promises direct access to an undifferentiated 'planetary source of all written material', looks like the obverse of Bourdieu's intricately hierarchical and always dynamic field, the products of which are performance-like in their material and symbolic specificity (Kelly 2006). For Lanier, the prospect of a world beyond such fine-grained particularities was not just dismal in cultural terms. It had political consequences too, ones Bourdieu, given his committed anti-totalitarianism, would have appreciated. 'A continuation of the present trend,' Lanier commented with Kelly's vision in mind, 'will make us like various medieval religious empires, or like North Korea, a society with a single book'—hence his challenge to what he calls 'cybernetic totalism' (Lanier 2010: 45–46).

Yet, to argue for the ongoing relevance of Bourdieu's model for literary and book studies in our multimedia age, we need not trade utopias for dystopias. It is enough simply to point out the continuing co-existence, and ever-deeper entanglements, of print and digital cultures, and to highlight the shaky grounds on which Kelly attempted to distinguish the old world of isolated books from the new utopia of linked texts. As the transmission history of any print-era text shows (see chapters 10–13), republication in any form, digital or print, has always had implications for meaning, as works are 'linked, manipulated, annotated, tagged, highlighted, bookmarked, translated, enlivened by other media and sewn together' in new ways. Most obviously, however, to claim a future for Bourdieu's thinking, we can simply note the centrality of technology and its potentially transformative effects to his analysis. While he expended most energy developing and refining the field as a methodological concept—i.e. as productive *idea* of a context/envelope—he always insisted on the need to consider its embeddedness within larger socio-political and technological histories. Widening the scope of the analysis to include, for instance, the literary field's entanglements with the state or the digital sphere, or, perhaps more pertinently given Lanier's concerns about single-book societies, the state *and* the digital sphere, would represent a natural development of his theoretical rationale and a productive way of investigating multimedia literary cultures today. Here the differential impact of new technologies is especially pertinent. As Simone Murray notes, the Kindle Direct Publishing ebook originals model, to take just one example, which relies on automated algorithmic recommendations, has 'translated very poorly to the literary fiction genre, where eBook originals have largely failed to bypass the book industry's traditional gatekeepers—multinational and independent publishers and literary agents' (Murray, 2021: 206). Any investigation of the literary field today would need to begin not just by understanding these differentially refractive effects but by uncovering why the phrase 'literary fiction', which Murray treats as a given, emerged as a mass-market genre category in the publishing world of the 1990s. This was, in no small measure, a consequence of the dawning of the 'Age of Amazon' in 1994. As McGurl notes, the icon of contemporary mega-retailers began life as an online bookseller that redefined the concept of genre because its business model was 'not so much anti- as omni-literary' (McGurl, 2021: xviii–xix).

Chapter 7

Reclaiming the Future of Book History from an African Perspective

The study of books has a complex genealogy that can be traced back at least to the nineteenth century, especially if we bear in mind the long history of British bibliography. Yet it was only when an international group of historians, literary scholars, bibliographers, sociologists and librarians began to co-ordinate their various activities in the 1960s and 1970s that the 'history of the book' emerged as a distinct scholarly enterprise, and it was only in the following decade that it started to see itself as a discipline in the making. The defining year was 1982, which saw the publication of Robert Darnton's manifesto-essay 'What is the History of Books?' and the appearance of the first volume of the *Histoire de l'édition française*. These two events put the field on the map and set the terms of its development as a discipline over the next two decades, with, as we saw in chapter 5, some regrettable consequences.

Since then, book history has established its credentials as a discipline and had a shaping impact on a wide range of more traditional disciplines within the humanities and social sciences. In the process of acquiring its own professional status, it has encouraged historians to see books themselves not just as indices but as agents of historical change in societies as diverse as France in the 1780s and India in the 1920s; it has fostered a greater awareness among literary scholars of the materiality of the book as a medium, even in its digital forms, and of the institutions in which acts of writing and reading take place; it has led social scientists to analyse the publishing industry as an intricately structured, evolving world of its own, albeit one linked in complex ways to the larger forces at work in social, economic, technological and political history; it has even made inroads into the otherwise rarefied world of philosophy, where it has prompted reflection on the consequences for humanity of the emergence of a new multimedia age in which a paperless, and borderless, future is conceivable if not imminent; and it has led everyone with an interest in cultural history to re-examine the meaning and value of libraries as repositories of the book in all its many forms, and of communications media as a key factor influencing cultural practices of all kinds.

As is the case with any new discipline, the emergence of 'book history studies' was not quite as straightforward as this overview suggests. At one level, this was inevitable. Far from simply seeking a place in what Darnton called 'the canon of scholarly disciplines', a new form of enquiry, if it is worth taking seriously, will always unsettle traditional ways of thinking and challenge previously clear, often vigorously defended disciplinary boundaries (Darnton 1990: 107). This is especially true if its primary object—the book in this case—has long been declared the property of more established disciplines. At another level, however, the unease it sometimes caused was less predictable. To begin with, there were the difficulties of the name itself. 'Book History,' as the founding editors of *Book History* remarked in their inaugural volume, 'is the least unsatisfactory name for this scholarly frontier, which is certainly not limited to books—or to historians' (Rose 1998: ix). Rather, its 'field of play,' they insisted, 'is the entire history of written communication: the creation, dissemination, and uses of script and print in any medium, including books, newspapers, periodicals, manuscripts, and ephemera' (ix). Expansive as it was, this formulation cut two ways. On the one hand, it opened the question of the relations between oral and written forms of communication, which have always remained inextricably entangled with each other. On the other hand, for a claim made in the late 1990s, it oddly left digital modes out of the equation altogether. That the editors concluded their introduction with the 'promise' that their journal would 'change the way we read words on paper' only compounded this last problem (xi). Given these methodological quandaries, it might be better to see the field as involving the study of communications across all linguistic media: oral, manuscript, print and digital.

Yet the term 'book' stuck for reasons that had much to do with the circumstances out of which the discipline emerged in the 1980s and the methodological assumptions against which it was initially defined. For many early champions of the field, its distinctiveness lay primarily in the scrupulous attention it brought to bear on the material history of all media, which more established disciplines all but ignored. As the editors of *Book History* observed, 'historians have always relied on documents to reconstruct the past, and perhaps for that reason they overlooked, until very recently, the history of documents themselves' (ix). Among historians, Elizabeth Eisenstein's *The Printing Press as an Agent of Change* (1979) and Darnton's own *The Business of Enlightenment: A Publishing History of the Encyclopédie* (1979) did much to effect this shift in outlook. Arguing against 'a purely semantic definition of the text' in a seminal essay of 1992, the French book historian Roger Chartier similarly insisted that 'readers, in fact, never confront, abstract idealized texts detached from any materiality' (Chartier 1992: 50). Rather, 'they hold in their hands or perceive objects and forms whose structures and modalities govern their reading or hearing'. Characteristically, in making this claim, Chartier was concerned not just to correct the quantitative methods of the '*Annales* School' of French book history, against which he defined his own more qualitative approach, but what he took to be the neo-Platonic conceptions of text associated with French theory and literary studies. A comparable anti-Platonic drive can be seen in D. F. McKenzie's arguments against traditional forms of bibliography in favour of a 'sociology of texts' (McKenzie 1999). Bringing the documentary medium, which had previously been neglected in favour of its contents, to the fore was, in other words, integral to the new discipline's bid for scholarly recognition. Hence the appeal of the term 'book', the most iconic document in the Euro-American world, which, if used metonymically, could be said to stand for all media.

For all its strategic value, the early emphasis on the materiality of the book in this sense had several unhappy methodological consequences. For one thing, it fostered countless case studies, all of which relentlessly reiterated the basic materialist or new documentalist point, albeit across a wide range of periods and contexts. For another, the focus on transforming 'the way we read words on paper' privileged questions of reception, often at the expense of the other stages in the communicative process. It also privileged ways of thinking about reception which, as we have seen, downplay the generative agency of writing itself. These various dangers are very much on display in the *PMLA*'s otherwise indispensable special issue on 'The History of the Book and the Idea of Literature', which appeared in January 2006. Somewhat perversely, given the anti-Platonic ambitions driving the emergence of book history, this had the effect of turning the book or document into a materialist fetish, which was, from a methodological point of view, almost as abstract as the orthodox literary critic's text. It was as if the book itself, rather than the frames/envelopes it created, or the relations and questions it opened, became the object of study.

Darnton anticipated this particular risk in his founding essay of 1982. As we have seen, his 'communications circuit', a model showing how all the agents involved the creation, dissemination and reception of books relate to each other, was intended precisely to pre-empt narrow specialisation (figure 2. Having sketched the various points on his circuit, which ran in a loop from the author to the reader, via the publisher and bookseller, he added that 'book history concerns each phase of this process and the process as a whole, in all its variations over space and time and in all its relations with other systems, economic, political, and cultural, in the surrounding environment' (Darnton 1990: 111). The other key aspect of Darnton's model was its internationalism. Books, he insisted, 'do not respect limits either linguistic or national': 'they have often been written by authors who belonged to an international republic of letters, composed by printers who did not work in their native tongue, sold by booksellers who operated across national boundaries, and read in one language by readers who spoke another' (135). Reaffirming these two aspects of Darnton's model—its holism and its internationalism—is, I shall argue, essential as we contemplate the future of book history today. To get a clearer sense of the stakes involved, however, I would like first to consider another less well-known context in which an idea for a holistic and international study of the book arose independently of Darnton's.

* * *

In 1980, J. M. Coetzee, then a lecturer in English Literature at the University of Cape Town, offered a course entitled 'The Book in Africa' as a specialist final-year undergraduate option on the university's new African Literature programme. It was a novel undertaking that, as his prospectus made clear, confronted some of the limitations of literary studies at the time.

> We will be exploring some of the determinants of literary production not often dealt with in literary studies: environmental pressures of all kinds on writers, the economics of publishing and distributing literary works, the nature of the readership of literary works, etc. Since much of the information required for this kind of study is not readily available, students are forewarned that the course will entail a certain amount of bibliographical ferreting and a certain amount of practical investigative research. (Coetzee 1980)

Though Coetzee conceived of the course after reading Eisenstein's *The Printing Press as an Agent of Change* (1979), he had not been following the rise of book history as such. His extensive reading list included Richard D. Altick's *The English Common Reader* (1957), Robert Escarpit's *The Book Revolution* (1966), Q. D. Leavis's *Fiction and the Reading Public* (1932), John Sutherland's *Fiction and the Fiction Industry* (1978), as well as a number of Hans Zell's studies on books in Africa, all of which made important, though indirect, contributions to the new field, but he did not cite the work of the more self-consciously pioneering book historians of the 1960s and 1970s, such as Chartier, Darnton, Lucien Febvre, Henri-Jean Martin, McKenzie or, indeed, Eisenstein herself. Instead, he directed his students to the field via a series of questions he had concerning the predicament of African writers in the second half of the twentieth century. His reading list gave special prominence to essays by, among others, Chinua Achebe, Ali Mazrui, Es'kia Mphahlele, Ngugi Wa Thiong'o, Emmanuel Obiechina and Wole Soyinka.

Looked at from the perspective of this generation of African writers, it was impossible, Coetzee suggested, to see the book itself merely as a neutral medium. Given the history of its advent during the era of European colonisation and its role as an agent for change in postcolonial Africa, it had to be seen as a culturally freighted artefact in its own right. Though this downplayed the influence of Islamic scribal culture, which more recent scholarship has shown spread into sub-Saharan Africa in the course of the thirteenth century, it none the less remains the case that the arrival of the book, and eventually the printing press, from Europe after the fifteenth century represented a decisive event for African cultures in which the performing and visual arts, music and varieties of orature constituted the traditionally dominant expressive media (see Jeppie 2008). In Coetzee's view, the consequences of this were not just cultural or political. 'If we accept (following Ong, McLuhan, Goody) that print changes modes of thought,' he remarked in his preparatory notes for the course, 'then printing can be seen as the agent whereby the world is modernized' (Coetzee 1980). Echoing McLuhan's arguments in *Understanding Media: The Extensions of Man* (1964), he added that 'it is the print quality of the artefact, not its content (the medium rather than the message) that is of prime importance'. Yet, to understand this, and so to grasp the full implications of taking the book as an object of study in itself, it was essential to attend not just to the history of its advent in Africa or to 'mundane social factors in the study of the growth of the reading habit, e.g. availability of light, of seating space in trains, etc.'. It was necessary to analyse 'the class structure of so-called emergent African nations' and, above all, the place of the 'intelligentsia' in that structure, since this particular social faction was the 'prime modernizing agent' for whom newspapers, periodicals and books of all kinds were essential media. Coetzee's endorsement of this well-established transformative paradigm, which Robert Fraser rightly challenges in Book History through Postcolonial Eyes (2008), was characteristically cautious, but he was willing to let it define the larger ambitions of his course.

This line of enquiry, which took the publishing industry as its starting point, raised several pressing questions for students of African literature. 'As long as African writers remain bound into a supranational system of publication (in the broadest sense),' Coetzee commented in his notes, 'the old splits in consciousness (which may or may not aid production) will persist: writing for a national audience versus writing for an international audience; writing to foster nationalist values versus writing to foster internationalist values (the values of the international intelligentsia); writing after African models versus writing after metropolitan models; writing by African standards versus writing by metropolitan standards'. Making the book the initial point of departure not only opened key methodological opportunities for Africanists, however. It raised equally compelling questions for literary students in general. As Coetzee remarked, the course presupposed that 'the unit of historical meaning is not who writes what at what time, but that, at a certain time, someone should write X, someone should publish it, someone should bring it to the attention of readers, and someone should read it'. The primary object was 'the complete act of transmission'. For literary students, or scholars for that matter, schooled in one or another tradition of 'close reading', who considered the 'words on the page' to be their chief concern, this entailed a radical shift in orientation. 'From this point of view,' Coetzee continued, 'it is not the publishing industry in isolation that must be examined, and certainly not the activity of writing (or texts in isolation), but the total industry that involves the sponsorship of texts (in part by the creation of a climate, in part by educational processes), the dissemination of texts (publishing, distribution, selling and lending), and the criticism of texts.'

For literary students of the early 1980s, Coetzee's emphasis on the 'total industry', and his effort to displace attention away from the 'activity of writing', was as challengingly novel as it was demanding. In addition to acquiring some expertise in a wide range of disciplines, including literary criticism, sociology, cognitive psychology, media studies, cultural history, politics and economics, he expected his students to have a firm grounding in what would now be called 'book history' and to develop an appreciation of its relevance to African studies and humanistic scholarship generally. Among other things, he encouraged students to investigate 'the location of bookstores in the Cape Peninsula and the types of clientele they serve'; 'the library services in the black residential areas of the Cape'; and the histories and editorial policies of a number of 'South African literary magazines' of the 1960s and 1970s. In addition, he suggested they might consider which 'works by black South African writers' the apartheid censors 'tended to proscribe' and which ones they 'let through'; the 'origin and development of the Heinemann African Writers series'; and, given the emphasis on South and West African contexts, he suggested that students might 'compare and contrast Onitsha market literature with the South African *fotoroman* [photo-novel] in terms of themes and readership'. Given all the ferreting involved, not to mention the fact that the course tested the limits of literary studies at the time, it is perhaps unsurprising that it was not a success. Though the University of Cape Town's embattled African Literature programme continued, Coetzee's 'Book in Africa' option attracted few takers, and it was shelved after the first year.

* * *

Since the turn of the millennium a new generation of scholars has changed the fortunes of the field decisively, establishing book history as a vital part of research and teaching across all areas of African studies.[1] By focusing on the transnational aspects of the trade, which remain as marked today as they did in the colonial era, despite the

---

[1] Besides the titles mentioned in the main text, the key monographs shaping the field in the new millennium include Archie Dick, *The Hidden History of South Africa's Book and Reading Cultures* (Toronto: University of Toronto Press, 2012); Anthea Garman, *Antjie Krog and the Post-Apartheid Public Sphere: Speaking Poetry to Power* (Pietermaritzburg: University of KwaZulu-Natal Press, 2015); Isabel Hofmeyr, *The Portable Bunyan: A Transnational History of* The Pilgrim's Progress (Princeton: Princeton University Press, 2004); David Johnson, *Imagining the Cape Colony: History, Literature and the South African Nation* (Edinburgh: Edinburgh University Press, 2011); Stephanie Newell, *Ghanaian Popular Fiction: 'Thrilling Discoveries in Conjugal Life' and Other Tales* (Oxford: James Currey, 2000), as well as *Literary Culture in Colonial Ghana: How to Play the Game of Life* (Manchester: Manchester University Press, 2002); and Andrew van der Vlies, *South African Textual Cultures: White, black and read all over* (Manchester: Manchester University Press, 2007). While Mcebisi Ndletyana's edited collection *African Intellectuals in 19th and 20th*

relative strength of the local industry in countries such as South Africa, Ghana and Nigeria, they have extended and elaborated the internationalist vision Coetzee shared with Darnton. Caroline Davis's *Creating Postcolonial Literature: African Writers and British Publishers* (2013), which examines Oxford University Press's Three Crowns Series, a key rival to Heinemann's African Writers Series, is exemplary in this regard. Yet, as Isabel Hofmeyr demonstrates in *Gandhi's Printing Press* (2013), not all these networks evolved along established colonial lines. Focusing on the Indian ocean as a trans- or perhaps even supranational space of cultural intersection, she shows that some also formed the basis of complex, highly labile anti-colonial solidarities. As much of this scholarship suggests, however, living up to Darnton's holistic ambitions, or encompassing Coetzee's 'complete act of transmission', has proved more of a challenge. Corinne Sandwith's *A World of Letters* (2014), an engaging study of interventionist literary magazines and newspapers in mid-twentieth-century South Africa, provides a particularly clear instance of the difficulties.

Like many literary scholars influenced by developments within book history, Sandwith gives the forgotten intermediaries of culture, including reviewers, editors, critics and essayists, their rightful place in history as shapers of opinion and as guardians of the public sphere. But unlike many in the first phase of the discipline's emergence, she does not analyse the various periodicals she studies in detail exclusively as material objects or documents. She examines the way they created 'a public space for independent cultural-political debate' and, even more crucially, embodied the priorities of particular reading communities 'that articulated a distinctive set of aesthetic, interpretive and evaluative norms' (Sandwith 2014: 48). The emphasis she places on the norm-creating capacity of these micro-communities of letters is vital, but, unavoidably, the particular weighting she gives them raises questions of method. What place do poets, novelists, dramatists and other less easily identifiable literary practitioners have in this kind of analysis? Or, more pressingly, what

---

century South Africa (Cape Town: HSRC Press, 2008) is invaluable, particularly in relation to the periodical press, *Print, Text and Book Cultures in South Africa* (Johannesburg: Wits University Press, 2012), edited by van der Vlies, and *The Book in Africa: Critical Debates* (London: Palgrave Macmillan, 2015), edited by Caroline Davis and David Johnson, authoritatively map the field and feature important new work by emergent scholars, including Nourdin Bejjit, Ruth Bush, Claire Ducournau, Jack Hogan, Elizabeth le Roux, Lily Saint, Hedley Twidle, Margriet van der Waal and Jarad Zimbler. Equally significant is the special issue on 'Materials of African Literatures', *Cambridge Quarterly*, 49(3), September 2020.

standing might literary writing itself have in any world of letters conceived in these terms? In relegating writers and literary works to the margins, Sandwith was drawing not only on the methods of book history understood in a particular delimited way. On this issue, she owed as much to cultural studies, which, in its more militant versions, rejected the literary altogether in favour of other, seemingly less ideologically burdened, forms of expression, such as film and television. Among the traditional varieties of literariness cultural studies rejected, Sandwith invokes 'the Leavisite ideal of artistic detachment and the privileged place of art' (74). Yet, if we accept that literature has never been reducible to literariness, in one or another of its many generalised definitions (see chapter 6), then I would argue it is not only possible but essential to bring it back into the frame. After all, a properly desacralised literature, which is the only kind worth taking seriously, is a site in which all 'aesthetic, interpretive and evaluative norms' and, indeed, normativity itself are put in question (48).

To illustrate what it might mean to live up to Darnton and Coetzee's holism by keeping literature in this sense in the frame, we can turn briefly to James Currey's recent insider account of the fluctuating fortunes of the Heinemann African Writers Series (AWS) from its inception in 1962 to the late 1980s. Describing the selection of any new title for the series, Currey recalls that, while the 'initial discussion' was always 'literary', the decision to publish had also to reflect 'practical and political realities', most notably relating to the 'economics of the firm and the publishing industry at the time', which, for a series like AWS, had everything to do with changing educational policies and resources, rather than with the vagaries of commercial bookselling (Currey 2008: viii). Billed as a modern literary imprint fashioned 'by Africans for Africa' and modelled on the success of Penguin in the UK, the low-cost paperback series in fact began as a highly successful exercise in rebranding by a colonial educational publisher created by editors in London, Ibadan and Nairobi for, in the first instance, secondary schools and universities in Anglophone Africa (Currey 1993: 4). As Davis has shown, this was equally true of more modest contemporary projects such as Oxford University Press's Three Crowns Series (Davis 2013: 93–192). Unlike the popular, often fictionalised educational pamphlets that were produced locally in Nigeria and sold directly to readers via market stalls in towns like Onitsha, AWS initially flourished as an elite-sponsored, supranational collaboration between a British-based commercial publisher and selected postcolonial African states, or, more accurately, government education departments. Following the wider economic crises of the early 1980s, however, Currey and his colleagues were obliged to shift their attention to the UK and the US, where, coincidentally, the advent of a multicultural approach to education created new opportunities that ensured the ongoing survival of the series just as the African market began to shrink. Taking the 'complete act of transmission' as the 'unit of historical meaning', then, we need to acknowledge not just that Chinua Achebe, say, wrote *Things Fall Apart* in the mid-1950s, but that Heinemann published it as the inaugural AWS volume in 1962, that African educators prescribed it for schools and universities, that a generation of African students consequently studied it, and that, after the economic crises of the 1980s, the book began a new life as part of a very different 'communications circuit' outside Africa. We also need to acknowledge that every decision Currey and his colleagues took as publishers, from the selection of titles to the details of format and presentation, was affected by their understanding of how these disparate and shifting circuits worked as integrated systems.

Currey's account not only reinforces the kind of holistic approach Coetzee and Darnton encouraged. It offers detailed evidence to support their internationalism and the recent transnational turn in African book history. He confirms that, while many Anglograph African writers contributed willingly or testily to a post-colonial project of nation-building, they also depended on a 'supranational system of publication', dating from the colonial era, that was either specifically pan-African or more broadly Commonwealth. Despite the political developments of the 1960s, this legacy was perpetuated in the immediate post-colonial era under the Traditional Markets Agreement, which divided the Anglograph world into two protected trading zones, one British, the other American. When this informal agreement collapsed in the mid-1970s, resulting in a more fluid arrangement of 'open' and 'closed' markets, the mismatch between legally agreed rights territories and politically defined national boundaries became if anything more acute. As always, this has particular significance for works originally written in English. The mismatch is less pronounced when it comes to Africa's numerous smaller languages, many of which continue to be contained within, without necessarily being co-extensive with, national borders.

Just how complex English-language rights agreements became in the 1980s can be seen in the early publishing history of Mtutuzeli Matshoba's short-story collection *Call Me Not a Man*. Initially published in 1979 by Ravan Press as a paperback in apartheid South Africa, where it was immediately banned, the collection appeared simultaneously in a limited hardback edition under a co-publishing arrangement with Rex Collings, a small London publisher who specialised in African books. Two years later Longman produced a new paperback edition as part of its Drumbeat Series, the main rival to AWS, reissuing it as an African Classic in 1987. Though the initial Longman agreement stipulated that Three Continents Press, then one of the principal Africanist publishers in the US, had the first option on the remaining English-language rights, they did not take them up and no US edition was ever produced. Looked at from the perspective of *Call Me Not a Man*, then, the Anglophone world of the 1980s was divided into four distinct territories: South Africa (Ravan); UK (Collings); UK, the Caribbean and Africa north of the Limpopo (Longman); US and Canada (Three Continents). This, of course, covers the book rights for the English-language version only. Ravan also managed to sell translation rights for French, German and Dutch editions; and, given the potential for any twentieth-century book to be translated not just across languages but across media, they sold the drama and film rights for the story 'A Glimpse of Slavery' and rights for a taped edition for the blind.[2] Today this list of subsidiary rights would in all likelihood include digital media as well, which, unconstrained by the limits of physical territory as they are, make national boundaries look even less relevant. Like much literary history, book history is only now finding the resources adequate to the historiographical challenges these technological and legal developments pose.

By focusing on the inner workings of the AWS, Currey also provides a way into understanding the complex interplay between publishers and writers, or, more to the point, the norm-creating capacity of an imprint or series and the literary works it frames, publishes and brings to the attention of readers. This began with the use of the word 'African' in the series title itself. Always eager to prevent the term from being racialised, Heinemann, especially under Currey's direction, intended it to describe the writers' geographical origins, but through the cumulative effect of the day-to-day editorial decisions it quickly acquired a literary significance as well. AWS titles were not just by writers from Africa, they were powerful exemplars of modern African writing, at least in the sense in which the publishers sought to fashion that category. Currey worried that Bessie Head's disturbing study of racism and madness, *A Question of Power* (1974), for example, was not 'really African' but 'more closely related to the mainstream of Anglo-American internal writing' (McDonald 2009:

---

[2] All these rights details are derived from the title file for *Call Me Not a Man* held at the Ravan Press Archives by Macmillan SA in Johannesburg.

111). Though he eventually took it on as something of an experiment for the African market, he turned down J. M. Coetzee's avant-garde debut *Dusklands* (1974), which was arguably even less 'African' in Currey's sense. By contrast, Ayi Kwei Armah's first novel, *The Beautyful Ones Are Not Yet Born* (1969), one of the most successful titles in the series, seemed ideally suited to the AWS project, a point Heinemann underscored through various presentational devices. The blurbs taken from British newspaper reviews drew attention to the novel's topical themes, describing it as 'a story of an upright man resisting the temptations of easy bribes and easy satisfactions', and identifying it generically as 'a clever and uncomfortable moral fable' (Armah 1969: back cover). In addition, the inside pages of a later reissue advertised *The Novels of Ayi Kwei Armah* (1980), a critical study by Robert Fraser, which was also published by Heinemann. As the advertisement noted, Armah emerges from this account not as a moralising Leavisite aesthete but 'as a committed artist attempting to clear the path of cultural reconstruction by means of a dynamic philosophy of history' (Armah 1984: 184). Fraser, as it happens, was also a key editorial advisor for the series. What Heinemann saw itself as doing in the 1960s and 1970s, then, was creating a space, within the territories defined by their rights agreements, for writing that was 'African' in so far as it addressed urgent historical questions in a realistic way and was 'committed' in Sartre's charged sense of that term to the post-colonial project of reconstruction.

To follow this analysis through we would of course need to give a similar account of all the other points in the circuit, since every agent can reframe the book in their own normative terms while enabling its onward transmission. In the case of Armah's novel, for instance, we would need to consider not just which reviewers and critics read it and how they did so, but how African syllabus-designers saw it as fitting with their educational objectives at the time. Prescribing a book is, after all, no less a normative act, subject to institutional conditions, than publishing or reviewing. To complete the circuit, at least in this first African version, we would also need to establish how African students themselves read it. Developing an analysis of this kind is critical for two reasons: first, it makes it possible to track, as Sandwith, Davis and others have shown, the normative effects of production, dissemination and sponsorship—the 'total industry'—on the history of literature; and second, it allows us to return to the 'activity of writing', which, following Darnton and Coetzee, remains in the picture, though no longer as the default starting point. This return is necessary, in part, because we need, as Darnton insisted, to understand 'the nature of a literary career, and how it was pursued', and how writers 'deal with publishers, printers, booksellers, reviewers, and one another' (1982: 125). It is also, as Coetzee argued, because we need to recognise that these contextual factors/envelopes do not simply form the background to any act of writing. Whether serving as a spur or a constraint, they constitute its institutional conditions of possibility and, consequently, become internalised as part of an inner drama of expression. 'As long as African writers remain bound into a supranational system of publication,' Coetzee noted, 'the old splits in consciousness (which may or may not aid production) will persist' (1980).

The strained relations between Armah and Heinemann show just how fraught these potentially creative self-divisions and normative tensions can be. Accepting the manuscript for *The Beautyful Ones* in 1967 was, according to Currey, 'the beginning of by far and away the worst relationship we ever experienced with an author' (2008: 73). Giving his side of the story a few years later, Armah recalled his struggle 'to find an African publisher as opposed to a neo-colonial writers' coffle owned by Europeans but slyly misnamed "African"' (Currey 2008: 75). This acerbic testimony, which is by no means unusual in the history of publishing, confirms the normative power of the publishing process and opens up a series of challenging questions about the role of publishers not just as 'the merchants of culture', to use John B. Thompson's title phrase, but as its sponsors (Thompson 2010). In my view, it also obliges us to go back to the text of *The Beautyful Ones* itself, not to contemplate it in its splendid isolation, or to champion the 'privileged place of art', but to reassess its relationship to the larger project of African writing to which Heinemann and various educational institutions in Africa and elsewhere were committed. The opening paragraph hints at the possibilities.

> The light from the bus moved uncertainly down the road until finally the two vague circles caught some indistinct object on the side of the road where it curved out in front. The bus had come to a stop. Its confused rattle had given place to an endless spastic shudder, as if its pieces were held together by too much rust ever to fall completely apart. (Armah 1984: 1)

The figural language, implied allegory and, perhaps above all, the understated allusion to Achebe's founding AWS title *Things Fall Apart*, itself an allusion to W. B. Yeats's poem 'The Second Coming', invites a reading that goes beyond the protocols of literary realism, opening up the possibility of seeing the novel not just as a supplement to the post-colonial project of cultural reconstruction, as Heinemann presented it, but as a self-consciously disruptive and knowingly literary intervention in a history of writing about Africa. Such a return to the text is needed not because the future of book history depends on its capacity to change how we read, or, indeed, on its historical alliance with literary studies, but because book historians who ignore the challenges some forms of writing pose to normativity itself risk looking like art historians who have abandoned any interest in pictures in order to concentrate on the history of frames, or historians of science who are more eager to study the sociology of laboratories than the meaning of scientific discoveries. In the process, they also risk missing one of the most significant opportunities book history has as an interdisciplinary field for contributing to, and ideally reshaping, the future of literary studies in and beyond Africa.

Chapter 8

Elton John, Libel and the Perils of Close Reading

There are many reasons for studying literature's entanglements with the law. The most engaging, in my view, has to do with the fact that there is no way of telling how to distinguish literature from other kinds of writing either *a priori* or *a posteriori*. Like many artefacts of human endeavour—democracy, say, or Europe—literature does not constitute an object of knowledge as such. As we have already seen in chapter 6, it is not a relatively stable *thing*, which we can learn to identify in the way we learn to distinguish Porsche 911s from other cars or African from Indian elephants. This had become a theoretical orthodoxy by the 1970s and 1980s, though, as noted in chapter 6, the emphasis then tended to be placed on the problems associated with *a priori* definitions (i.e. sceptical anti-scholasticism). The philosopher of art Arthur C. Danto summarised the mainstream view in the following characteristic terms: 'the concept of art [or literature] is not like the concept, say, of cat, where the class of cats do pretty largely resemble one another, and can be recognized as cats more or less by the same criteria' (Danto 1999: 7). Few theorists had much to say about the potentially greater challenges of *a posteriori* definition (i.e. affirmative anti-scholasticism). On this account, literature is not simply an object of theoretical *debate*, perhaps even a quarrel, which, as a matter of principle, can never be resolved. In its most ambitious modes, it is also a self-reflexive, protean cultural *practice*, which often puts established protocols of understanding under extreme pressure, calling for different ways of thinking and new kinds of reader. Whether seen from an *a priori* or an *a posteriori* perspective, these definitional problems create acute difficulties for the law at the level of codification and judicial procedure.

The history of state censorship, which details the repeated failures of the state and its officials to have the last word on literary matters, is essentially an archive of these problems. In the late 1980s, towards the end of the censorship era in apartheid South Africa, J. M. Coetzee put it this way: censors have been 'so ineffectual, century after century,' he said, 'because, in laying down rules that stories may not transgress, and enforcing these rules, they fail to recognise that the offensiveness of stories lies not in their transgressing particular rules but in their faculty for making and changing their own rules' (Coetzee 1988: 3). This is a rare statement of the *a posteriori* quandary. Yet it is not only censors, the traditional enemies of literature, for whom this more radical offensiveness creates difficulties. As a peculiarly disruptive form of public writing, literature is no less of a problem for its defenders, particularly those who turn to the law for help. The challenges they face were well articulated in the late 1970s, during a British government enquiry into the effectiveness of the Obscene Publications Act 1959 the legislation that explicitly incorporated an *exceptio artis*, or literary defence, into the Westminster statute book for the first time. Among other things, it afforded literature protection as a public good and authorised courts to call upon literary experts to testify on its behalf. Here the state is no longer the 'bad' censor but the 'good' guardian of the literary. To put it in the Bourdieuian terms Ralf Grüttemeier and Ted Laros adopt, we could say that the 1959 act constituted an important landmark in the 'institutional autonomy' of literature in England and Wales in so far as it reflected a high degree of 'societal acceptance of the literary field within the field of power' and recognised that 'only literary specialists could evaluate literature' (Grüttemeier 2013: 205 and 210). This is broadly true, though, as my own account of the original Victorian statute of 1857 and its initial implementation shows, the possibility of a literary defence was built into English obscenity law from the start (McDonald 2008). The 1959 act simply made that largely dormant defence more explicit and robust.

The problems associated with the state's well-meaning intervention on behalf of literature were soon clear, however. The product of a concerted campaign in the 1950s, the new defence itself became the focal point of a further protest in the 1960s and 1970s, which eventually prompted the government to establish the commission of enquiry led by the philosopher Bernard Williams. Bearing in mind the temporary banning under the 1959 act of Hubert Selby's controversial novel *Last Exit to Brooklyn* (1966), the commission remarked about the literary defence:

> It is not surprising that [the act] has been criticised as elitist in conception, and as saying in effect that corrupting books are to be permitted so long as they are admired by professors. This criticism is

> largely unjust, but it hits at a basic fault in the Act, its absurd model of the role of expert opinion with regard to artistic or literary merit. The model is not so much elitist, as scholastic: it implies an informed consensus about merit which, for each work, already exists. In the real world, new works have to find their own way, and see whether they elicit appreciation or not. No one may know, for some time, what to think about them. It is not just a matter of the *avant-garde*: works in some despised medium or style may subsequently turn out to have had more meaning than most experts would have originally supposed. (Williams 1979: 110)

The underlying scholasticism of the 1959 act was exacerbated by the fact that it required the experts to establish, *as a matter of evidential proof*, whether a particular work might warrant exemption on the grounds of merit or, indeed, literariness. Given that such questions inevitably involve a long, uncertain process of cultural debate, which, from the theorists' point of view, would be inconclusive in principle, the commission argued that the 'public good' defence was 'misconceived' and recommended lifting all restrictions on the 'printed word' (Williams 1979: 126 and 160). Books with illustrations were another matter. The only workable way of protecting the 'institutional autonomy' of literature was, it concluded, for the courts to play no part in the unavoidably contentious 'Republic of Letters'.

This recommendation, which successive British governments have continued to ignore, has several significant implications. At the most general level, it obliges us to think again about an important further claim Grüttemeier and Laros make, namely, that 'judicial practice can be taken to manifest a kind of crystallisation of ideas on poetics within non-literary elites' (2013: 205). As the Williams commission suggested, and as I argued in *The Literature Police* (2009), my own study of literary censorship under apartheid, this process of 'crystallisation' is inevitably fraught. I am not even sure that the metaphor is appropriate, particularly if it implies that 'ideas on poetics' are not just solidified but somehow clarified in the judicial process. 'Muddying' is a more plausible formulation. Besides, my own inclination is to turn the argument around: given the difficulties literature creates for judicial practice, what we tend to see when 'ideas on poetics' enter the courtroom is a muddying not just of those ideas but of the authority and protocols of the court itself. To demonstrate this, and to show that these concerns are not merely historical, nor, indeed, limited to obscenity trials, I shall focus on an English libel case that addresses the problem of what happens when ideas of the literary are deployed not by literary experts in the context of the law but by 'non-literary elites', in this instance, an Oxford-educated English High Court judge.

Before I turn to the details of the case, it will be worth briefly describing the legal background, especially as my example dates from 2008, that is, five years before the Defamation Act 2013 was passed. This was the first major reform of English libel law since the 1950s. Historically, libel has both an extensive meaning in English law, covering blasphemy, sedition, obscenity and defamation, and a peculiarly precise designation where, in cases of defamation, it is contrasted to slander. Crudely stated, libel is defamatory writing, slander is defamatory speech. This reflects the etymology of the word, which derives from the Latin *libellous*, the diminutive for 'book'. This curious distinction is unknown in most modern jurisdictions. In Scots law, for instance, both libel and slander are treated as 'verbal injury'. Unsurprisingly, the distinction generated problems of its own in the changing media environment of the twentieth century from the advent of radio in the 1920s to the rise of the internet in the 1990s. In response to these developments, 'written' came to be understood, in the words of one English judgement from the 1930s, as 'permanent matter to be seen by the eye' (Deakin 2013: 637).

Yet it was not only the medium of expression that created problems. Perhaps most significantly, unlike slander, libel did not historically require proof of damage from the plaintiff. Once the libel is proved, serious damage is assumed; whereas, in most cases, victims of slander are required to demonstrate actual damage relating to, say, loss of earnings. This idiosyncrasy, which created an opening for trivial or vexatious actions, was readily construed as a bias in favour of plaintiffs, particularly rich or powerful ones who could buy silence by threatening or instituting legal proceedings. The still controversial reforms introduced in 2013 were intended in part to close this loophole, requiring plaintiffs in libel cases to submit evidence of serious harm, as they had been obliged to do in cases of slander. A further key feature of English libel law is its anti-intentionalism. 'Liability for libel does not depend on the intention of the defamer,' one judge noted in the 1920s, 'but on the fact of defamation' (Deakin 2013: 633). Seen from the perspective of literary studies, this kind of anti-intentionalism may look like American New Criticism *avant la lettre*, but, unlike the New Critics of the 1940s, English law did not substitute the vague and debatable intentions of the author/defamer for the apparently more objective 'words on the page', the text of the libel. It shifted the burden onto its reception, which, as we shall see, only created a new set of quandaries with literary and legal consequences.

Unlike obscenity, and to a lesser extent blasphemy and sedition, libel rarely features in the cultural histories of literature and the law in the English-speaking world. Indeed, as Sean Latham comments in *The Scandal of Art* (2009), 'our understanding of the intersection between literature and the law' since the nineteenth century 'has been severely distorted by an almost obsessive focus on the famous obscenity trials of *Ulysses* and *Lady Chatterley's Lover*' (2009: 72). Yet the case history for this period is there. We need only recall Oscar Wilde's libel trials in the 1890s. Wilde's failure to clear his name was largely a consequence of the changes introduced under the Libel Act 1843, which held that in a criminal case the truth of an allegedly libellous claim constituted a legitimate defence, so long as its publication was also in the public interest. Wilde's own aesthetics, and some of the more dramatic moments of the trial, all turned on the question of art's claims to truth. For Latham, the fact that libel has been left out of the story is not surprising. The more famous obscenity trials, he argues, 'have become part of a liberal romance of art's ever-expanding freedom', one of literary history's most cherished grand narratives (2009: 72). By contrast, the various libel cases he discusses, all of which relate to the genre of the roman à clef, oblige us to consider the extent to which 'literary modernism', or, for that matter, Wildean aestheticism, 'failed in what Pierre Bourdieu calls its "conquest of autonomy"' (2009: 73). Noting that his concerns lie as much with the gaps in literary history as with the orthodoxies of literary criticism, Latham opens his study with this playful gesture: 'Be warned: this book commits one of literary criticism's deadliest sins by treating seemingly fictional works from the early twentieth century as if they contained real facts about real people and events' (2009: 3). He then goes on to show how various writers in the early twentieth century, including Joyce, Aldous Huxley, D. H. Lawrence, Wyndham Lewis, Osbert Sitwell and Jean Rhys, experimented with the roman à clef, testing and sometimes falling foul of, English libel law, while at the same time questioning the institutional and aesthetic autonomy of fiction.

It is, however, not only the roman à clef, or, indeed, genres of writing that are generally considered to be literary, that probe the limits of libel law and oblige us to revisit the grand narrative of literature's conquest of freedom. As my own more contemporary example suggests, cases involving apparently mundane forms of writing, which seldom feature in conventional literary histories, also have a bearing on these issues. Here, too, 'ideas on poetics' and 'judicial practice' confront each other with equally unpredictable consequences.

* * *

In late September 2008, Sir Elton John sued the *Guardian* newspaper in the UK for libel. This is not especially remarkable. Elton John had been suing newspapers for over thirty years on a regular basis, often successfully. On this occasion, however, things proved less straightforward, mainly because of the nature of the public comments to which he took exception. The offending text, which first appeared in the *Guardian* on 5 July 2008, is worth citing in full, partly because it is a libel in the original etymological sense. It also has the virtue of being short. The speaker is Sir Elton himself, and the text is a diary entry, covering two days in late June 2008. Sir Elton records his thoughts about attending Nelson Mandela's ninetieth birthday celebrations on 25 June 2008 and about a charity ball he held the following day at his Windsor mansion to raise funds for the Elton John AIDS Foundation.

> What a few days it's been. First I sang Happy Birthday to my dear, dear friend Nelson Mandela—I like to think I'm one of the few people privileged enough to call him Madiba—at a party specially organised to provide white celebrities with a chance to be photographed cuddling him, wearing that patronisingly awestruck smile they all have. It says: 'I love you, you adorable, apartheid-fighting teddy bear.'
> The next night I welcomed the exact same crowd to my place for my annual White Tie & Tiaras ball. Lulu, Kelly Osbourne, Agyness Deyn, Richard Desmond, Liz Hurley, Bill Clinton—I met most of them 10 minutes ago, but we have something very special and magical in common: we're all members of the entertainment industry. You can't manufacture a connection like that.
> Naturally, everyone could afford just to hand over the money if they gave that much of a toss about Aids research—as could the sponsors. But we like to give guests a preposterously lavish evening, because they're the kind of people who wouldn't turn up for anything less. They fork out small fortunes for new dresses and so on, the sponsors blow hundreds of thousands on creating what convention demands we call a 'magical world', and everyone wears immensely smug 'My diamonds are by Chopard' grins in the newspapers and OK. Once we've subtracted all these costs, the leftovers go to my foundation. I call this care-o-nomics (Hyde 2008a: 16).

As I said, Sir Elton did sing at Mandela's ninetieth on 25 June 2008, and his White Tie and Tiara Ball did take place on the 26th, but, as you will have by now guessed, this is not really a diary entry, and the speaker is not really Elton John. Following a well-established journalistic tradition in England, which can be traced back at least to the seventeenth century, it is a spoof involving an act of rhetorical ventriloquism in which Marina Hyde, a *Guardian* staffer, does the smug but also acerbic voice of the celebrity prima donna for satirical purposes by purporting to quote from his diary. The regular column, to which Hyde often contributed, was called 'A Peek at the Diary of'.

This is not how Sir Elton saw it. On his reading Hyde's text was neither a diary entry nor a satirical parody of one. It was a libellous attack on his moral integrity. In a writ issued against the *Guardian* on 7 August 2008, suing the paper for £150,000 damages, he called it a 'gratuitously offensive, nasty and snide' slur, which damaged his reputation as a public-spirited philanthropist and AIDS campaigner by falsely accusing him of being an insincere, uncaring self-promoter (Limbrick 2008). It is important to stress that, given the terms of English libel law and the level of compensation he sought, Sir Elton accused Hyde of knowingly making false claims with malicious intent. In earlier correspondence with the *Guardian*, he also said she had branded him a racist, a charge he subsequently dropped from the formal writ. The *Guardian* accepted none of this and, to get the matter sorted out as quickly and as cheaply as possible, it made an application for a judicial ruling on Hyde's words and their meaning. The hearing eventually took place in early December 2008, with the Hon. Mr Justice Tugendhat presiding. Given the unpredictability of High Court appointment processes, the *Guardian* was lucky to get him. Unlike some of his esteemed colleagues, Tugendhat, then the most senior media judge in England and Wales, had earned a reputation for being an especially robust defender of press freedom. William McCormack, instructed by Carter-Ruck, the UK's leading media law firm, represented Elton John, while Gavin Millar QC and Anthony Hudson, both defamation specialists of Doughty Street Chambers, represented Guardian News & Media Limited.

The hearing turned out to be an oddly academic affair, which has an unexpected bearing on the question of literature's status as an object of knowledge. Not for the first time, and no doubt not for the last, the Royal Courts of Justice in London's Strand became a forum for heated debate not just about the unique intricacies of English libel law, the freedom of expression or, for that matter, the meaning of words, but about how meaning is understood to be made, and what role publishers, readers and ideas of the literary play in the process. Tellingly, though there were several avenues open to the *Guardian*'s lawyers—they could, for instance, have argued that Hyde was justified in making her claims by proving them to be true, following the provisions of the Libel Act 1843; they chose to focus primarily on the defence of fair (now honest) comment in the public interest, which, somewhat surprisingly, turned on the even more subtle question of literariness. In their view, the words to which Sir Elton took exception were not actionable as libellous because they could not be 'understood as statements of fact', or even as allegations of fact (Tugendhat 2008: 27). Rather they were part of a specifically literary mode of writing. In making this argument, which is a particular version of the fair comment defence, they did not appeal to any supposedly inherent idea or unique property of literariness, say, that a literary text is always and only fictional (although, as we shall see, much turned on a particular understanding of irony). They focused on the question of how words might be taken to be literary depending on the context in which they appear. As Justice Tugendhat put it in his summing up, 'it is common ground that the meaning of words, in law as in life, depends on their context', though, as he noted, following the arguments put forward by the defence, the term 'context' (think Joyce's envelope) could be construed in two ways (2008: 20). In the first, the context referred to the larger 'circumstances under which the words were published', which, in this case, included the two key events, Nelson Mandela's birthday and the White Tie and Tiara Ball (20). This has a particular bearing on the truth or falsity of Hyde's claims. The second 'narrower sense', which Tugendhat took to be especially significant from a legal point of view, referred to the material context in which Hyde's words were first published. This has a special pertinence to their literariness (20).

Drawing attention to the details of this narrower context was the burden of Tugendhat's first Joycean lesson in the perils of close reading. By focusing exclusively on some of Hyde's words, he argued, Elton John, like Joyce's 'ornery josser', had made the fatal mistake of failing to give due weight to their precise provenance in the *Weekend* section of the Saturday *Guardian* for 5 July 2008—the legally relevant envelope. Adopting the pose of a careful descriptive bibliographer, Tugendhat explained perhaps a little too pedantically:

> This section is made up of 104 pages (including advertisements), illustrated in full colour, and is itself divided into sections headed Starters, Fashion, Food & Drink, Features and so on. Like the Saturday editions of a number of other English newspapers aimed at an educated readership, *The Guardian* is made up of separate

> or pull out sections, of which Weekend is only one. While different types of speech can appear in any of these sections, the designation of the section assists in understanding the extent to which particular speech is to be understood as factual or not. Weekend is not the news section of the paper. (Tugendhat 2008: 23)

It is worth noting that Tugendhat did not mention the online version of the piece, which displays none of these print-based bibliographical features, making such fine discriminations between factual reportage and other 'types of speech' (strictly writing) much trickier in a digital context, a point to which I shall return (2008: 22).

Having established that the immediate print context was the first legally noteworthy envelope for Hyde's words, Tugendhat then turned to the article itself, and more particularly to its title, which, he argued, functioned as another key framing device, albeit one that was more difficult to read. By presenting the words under the heading 'A Peek at the Diary of Sir Elton John', 'that is, as if they are an extract from a diary written by the Claimant "as seen" by the journalist', the editors, according to Tugendhat, chose not to indicate 'what statement the reader is to expect, as title [sic] to news articles generally do' (2008: 23). By contrast, the headline on page 2 of the main paper, which appeared under the running header 'News', reads: 'Johnson forced to remove his deputy mayor after magistrate claim proves false' (Taylor 2008: 2). The report that follows then gives an account of Boris Johnson's embarrassments over one of his first mayoral appointees who was obliged to resign amid allegations of financial misconduct. In this case, then, the title constitutes a précis of the factual report, helpfully guiding the reader's expectations; whereas 'A Peek at the Diary of' plays all sorts of rhetorical games, setting a trap for unwary readers, especially those like Sir Elton who fixate on the 'letter' and choose to read it too closely.

Yet, as Tugendhat recognised, the argument from bibliographical provenance, though necessary for a literary defence, was not sufficient. After all, despite its location in the *Weekend* section, he noted that Hyde's article contained 'a number of statements of fact attributed to the Claimant [Sir Elton] which are true, and obviously intended to be understood as true' (2008: 27). As everyone in the High Court acknowledged, these included the reference to Mandela's birthday party, to the ball and to the photographs that did appear in the celebrity magazine *OK!*. Tugendhat added that there were also some 'statements of both fact and opinion', citing as an example the spoof Sir Elton's reference to the photographs in *OK!* (fact) and his comments on his fellow celebrities wearing their 'immensely smug' grins (opinion) (2008: 28). For Sir Elton's lawyers, these complexities made it unclear which interpretative protocols applied, especially when it came to what they took to be the most offensive statement in the piece, the penultimate sentence: 'Once we've subtracted all these costs, the leftovers go to my foundation' (Hyde 2008a: 16). In their view, the implications (specifically 'innuendo') of this sentence were clear, unliterary and so libellous: it meant that Sir Elton and the organisers of the ball deducted 'all the costs of providing the lavish evening, including the costs incurred by the guests for new dresses and diamonds, and that it was only the balance that went to the charitable foundation' (Tugendhat 2008: 29).

At this point Tugendhat offered his second lesson in the perils of close reading, shifting the terms of his argument from bibliography to reception theory, from the materiality of the print *Guardian* to what he took to be the interrelated questions of readership and literariness. Having noted that the Saturday *Guardian*, with its various supplements such as *Weekend*, was 'aimed at an educated readership'—the typical *Guardian* reader is popularly regarded as being a left-leaning member of the comfortable middle classes—he focused on what he termed, following legal precedent, the figure of the 'reasonable reader' (2008: 22 and 28). When it came to deciding which interpretative protocols applied to the penultimate sentence, he was in no doubt that this particular reader would understand that 'the words complained of are obviously written by the journalist, who has attributed them to the Claimant as a literary device', and that the 'transparently false attribution is irony', which, he explained, is 'a figure of speech in which the intended meaning is the opposite of what is expressed by the words used' (2008: 24). For this reader, then, the fictionality of the entire piece was obvious. Irony, one of the subtlest, socially coded rhetorical devices, also applied more specifically to the key penultimate sentence, which, Tugendhat noted, is presented not as fact but 'as an allegation that the Claimant is making against himself' (24). Bringing together the two strands of his reading lesson, he suggested that no 'reasonable reader' would understand the sentence in the way Sir Elton had because they would 'expect so serious an allegation to be made without humour, and explicitly, in a part of the newspaper devoted to news' (32). By mistaking a piece of light-hearted, even 'teasing', literary satire for serious reportage, Sir Elton had, he concluded, suffered a sense of humour failure complicated by a bad case of josserish myopia (31). Hyde's article was therefore not actionable under English libel law, and, consequently, Sir Elton's claim for damages had to be struck out.

Tugendhat also ordered him to pay costs, even though the *Guardian* had applied for the hearing.

Not content with this outcome, Sir Elton's lawyers then took their case to the Court of Appeal, only to have it rejected once again. On 26 March 2009, over eight months after Hyde's piece first appeared, they finally conceded defeat and gave up. No doubt the vanity of celebrities—who can also afford the fees—helps to explain their persistence. Yet, since it is unlikely that an established and very successful firm such as Carter-Ruck would put its professional standing on the line without good reason, the tenacity of Elton John's team also says something about the legal niceties of the case.

* * *

This is where the legal story of Sir Elton's lessons in the perils of close reading ended. Yet, for anyone concerned about literature in law, I would argue that it is at this point that the real interest of the case starts. Seen from a literary rather than a legal perspective, the closure Justice Tugendhat brought to the proceedings, which was later confirmed by the Court of Appeal, looks more pragmatic than principled. This is in part because, as I have already suggested, he chose to stabilise the process of meaning-making by privileging the original print version of Hyde's piece, ignoring the complications any mention of the online version might introduce, an issue both legal teams also overlooked. Online publication, whether on the internet or via social media sites like X (formerly known as Twitter), is especially testing for English libel law not just because it raises new questions about the 'written' word, authorship and ownership, which the Defamation Act 2013 has attempted to address, but because it does not necessarily bring with it the extrinsic markers of status and provenance associated with the traditional medium of print, which played such a central part in Tugendhat's determination. As the case history develops, however, the ways in which digital media create new forms of context for 'permanent matter to be seen by the eye' are being taken seriously (Deakin 2013: 637). In one noteworthy case from 2010, for instance, which relates to an allegedly libellous online article, the hyperlinks inserted in some of the words were deemed to constitute a part of the relevant meaning-making context (Deakin 2013: 633). In its online version, Hyde's piece contains no hyperlinks, though it directs the reader to several related categories via a sidebar, including 'music', 'celebrity', 'life and style' and more from 'The Peek at' series, which it also describes as 'a glimpse inside the celebrity mind'. These arguably ensure that the online reader does not mistake the piece for factual reportage, albeit not as clearly as the contextual markers in the print *Weekend* supplement.

Tugendhat's ruling also looks more pragmatic than principled because he cut the interpretive uncertainties short by invoking the legal fiction of the 'reasonable reader'. In so doing he was following sound legal precedents, though, as Markesinis and Deakin point out in their magisterial textbook *Tort Law* (2013), precedents that are a source of much ongoing legal contention. Setting out the key issues, they explain:

> Courts treat the meaning of words as a matter of construction rather than evidence, to be interpreted objectively in their context, with reference to the opinion of right-thinking members of society. (2013: 633)

This is why Tugendhat expressly made no mention of Hyde's intentions in his ruling, and why he focused exclusively on the effects her words might have on what he called the 'reasonable reader', given the precise bibliographical provenance. Yet, as a test, this anti-intentionalist legal convention is, as Markesinis and Deakin observe, 'vague and unsatisfactory', not least because it begs a series of large questions about who the 'reasonable' or 'right-thinking members of society' might actually be (2013: 633). Given the emphasis Tugendhat placed on irony in his ruling, this has a particular bearing on the Elton John case. Did Tugendhat have a particular theory of irony? Based on what he says in his ruling, this is highly unlikely. At best, he was working with a very rudimentary critical lexicon, concerning irony, fiction and satire as literary devices, though, as I have suggested, one that none the less has some theoretical implications. His arguments assumed that irony cannot, for instance, be understood in purely structural terms, since its effects depend on what linguists call its pragmatic context. For Tugendhat, this was defined in part via the legal fiction of the 'reasonable reader', but, as I have already noted, irony is among the most precarious and socially charged rhetorical devices, relying as it does on easily missed (often veiled) markers, subtle inference and implied background knowledge, which only some readers might possess. It is, in fact, often used precisely to separate a narrow circle of those in the know (one version of the 'right-thinking') from a wider audience who cannot pick up the signals. As such, it is a consciously disruptive mode that invites misreading and cannot be understood independently of the complex, never wholly assured social contexts of its use.

As Tugendhat noted at various points, such intricate interpretative issues would be a matter for the jury if the case went to court. This was written into English law with 'Fox's' Libel Act 1792, which made juries the ultimate arbiters of whether a text is libellous. Until that point, judges had decided, and juries were required only to determine if the defendant had published the text. In the absence of a jury, Tugendhat was obliged to invoke the 'reasonable reader', which opened other uncertainties. As the shifting legal terminology during the latter half of the twentieth century shows, deciding who the 'right-thinking' or 'reasonable' might be is far from obvious. In the 1960s these readers were deemed to be 'ordinary' rather than 'logical' men; in the slightly less sexist 1980s, the 'hypothetical reader who is not unduly suspicious, but who can read between the lines'; and, a decade later, the 'substantial and respectable proportion of society' (2013: 633–34). The terminological challenges are relatively minor, however. As Markesinis and Deakin note, the more pressing question is: 'Is the test of defamation what right-thinking persons belonging to the class to which the statement is published think? Or right-thinking persons *generally*?' (2013: 634). The case history since the 1930s shows that the latter view has prevailed in English courts, but, as we have seen, Tugendhat focused on the 'reasonable reader' of the Saturday *Guardian*, rather than reasonable readers in general. As a challenging recent case suggests, this judgement has particularly fraught implications in contemporary inter- or multicultural societies. Echoing the kinds of argument associated with the literary theorist Stanley Fish, who championed the idea of 'interpretative community' as the arbiter of meaning in the 1970s, an English court of appeal in 2000 respected the construction members of the Muslim community might give to certain statements about women and sexuality. As Markesinis and Deakin then comment, this opens the worrying possibility of 'the same statement having certain consequences for one section of the population of one state but not for other citizens of the very same state'. 'In an increasingly pluralistic society,' they add in their rather bland textbook prose, 'the designation of one or more sections as "right-thinking" [or 'reasonable'] results in difficulties' (2013: 635).

For the *Guardian* the outcome of the Elton John case was 'A victory for irony', but, in her own reflections on the episode, Marina Hyde, the journalist at the centre of it all, registered some mordant disquiet: 'We British have a rich tradition of irony and satire but there is very little case law protecting what may well turn out to be one of the few comforts left to us in these darkening times' (Campbell 2008: 1–2; Hyde 2008b: 2). Moreover, she added, 'there is something absurd about a silly little piece of fluff about Elton John's annual White Tie and Tiara ball being used to enshrine such important principles' (2008b: 2). She was none the less pleased that she had helped to defend 'our right to be a tiny bit ironic about a diamond-encrusted celebrity Aids fundraiser' (2). She was also happy to report that, according to the *Guardian*'s 'head of legal', 'we made good law' (2). I am not so sure. Seen against the broader background I have been sketching, Justice Tugendhat's appeal to the 'reasonable reader', coupled with his decision to restrict himself to the print version of Hyde's article, begins to look less like an assured 'victory', and the Royal Courts of Justice, for all their Victorian Gothic magnificence, start to lose some of their comfortingly impressive institutional solidity. They begin to seem less like authoritative bastions of interpretive clarity and more like vulnerable, because always questionable, sites of hermeneutic closure.

From a legal and journalistic point of view, Tugendhat may have determined the saving literariness of Hyde's 'piece of fluff' by accepting the *Guardian*'s defence, thereby bringing the meaning of Hyde's words to a judicially defensible end and making 'good law'. From a literary point of view, it is clear that he could do so only by relying on a restricted conception of their public context, on the legal fiction of the 'reasonable reader', and on a socially laden and inescapably precarious idea of irony as a 'literary device'. Far from manifesting 'a kind of crystallisation of ideas on poetics' in the context of 'judicial practice' as exemplified by a member of a 'non-literary elite', then, this case reflects the challenges courts and other tribunals face when they attempt to treat literature as a clearly identifiable object of knowledge, or to apply secure tests for literariness, exposing the gulf between literary and legal approaches to language, cultural value and meaning. As I have argued, it also suggests that the problem of scholasticism, which Bernard Williams's enquiry identified as one of the main faults of the British Obscene Publications Act 1959, may be more pervasive than we like to think and may, in fact, be impossible to eradicate from the courtroom, given the particular, and ultimately pragmatic, imperatives of the law and the protean qualities of the literary as ever-changing creative practice. Since no one is safe from the perils of reading, whether closely or not, the Elton John case offers little assurance about the future of 'irony and satire' in England and Wales, and every assurance about the ongoing trouble literature will bring when it gets entangled with the law. And so the 'liberal romance' of literature's autonomy or 'art's ever-expanding freedom' remains as alluring and as unworkable as ever.

Chapter 9

The Worldliness of Books

> A finger is needed to point at the moon, but what a calamity it would be if one took the finger for the moon.
>
> Ancient Zen saying

As a matter of principle, I begin with a particular case—not a case study but a specific experience of writing and reading, albeit a partly hypothetical one.

Towards the end of *In the Heart of the Country*, J. M. Coetzee's second foray into literary writing, a young boy called Piet delivers a letter to Magda, the main protagonist and first-person narrator. Addressed to Magda's father, it comes in a 'buff envelope with a cross drawn heavily over it in blue pencil', indicating that it is both official and that it has been sent registered mail (1978, 124). Opening it, Magda finds 'a printed letter in two languages requesting the payment of taxes' (124). Piet does not know who sent it but insists that she acknowledge receipt in 'a little notebook' (124). Rather than sign her name, she writes: '*EK HET NIE GELD NIE*' (124). By this stage in the narrative, Magda is an aged, arthritic 'crone' who uses 'block letters because of the pain in my fingers' (124).

In the Heart of the Country does not attempt to conjure up a precise historical and geographical world—it is not an exercise in realist fiction—but the action evidently takes place sometime in the late nineteenth or early twentieth century on a remote sheep farm in the Karoo, a semi-desert region in South Africa's hinterland. Extrapolating from some of the details in this scene, however, our hypothetical reader might be tempted to be a little more exact about the historical moment. If she takes the two official languages of the letter to be English and Afrikaans, then she may well infer that Magda's father is being chased by tax collectors working on behalf of the Union of South Africa sometime after 1925, the year in which Afrikaans effectively replaced Dutch as the second official language of the unitary state created in 1910. Magda certainly chooses to address the revenue authorities in Afrikaans, as she does not write 'Ik heb geen geld', the Dutch equivalent of 'Ek het nie geld nie'.

As these extrapolations suggest, our reader has some familiarity with South African history as well as some competence in English, Dutch and Afrikaans. Less obviously, she is reading a particular edition of *Country*: the paperback brought out by the leading Johannesburg-based anti-apartheid publisher Ravan Press in 1978. Now a rare book, it is the only 'bilingual' (English-Afrikaans) version ever published. Today all the English-language editions are based on the 'monolingual' version Coetzee prepared for his American and British publishers, Secker & Warburg (London) and Harper & Row (New York), who published separate hardback editions in 1977. After acquiring the paperback rights, Penguin (UK) and Viking (US) reissued the same self-translation in 1982. Despite various changes of ownership, the English-language digital rights have been apportioned in the same way. So, if you buy, say, the 2015 Vintage ebook from Amazon.co.uk on Kindle today, then you will find not only that Magda writes 'I HAVE NO MONEY' (no italics) but that she speaks a rather neutral, unidiomatic English to Piet rather than Afrikaans, more or less the same English in which she composes the diary-like entries that make up the main body of the narrative (2015, 136). In the original, 'bilingual' edition only the dialogue is in Afrikaans.

Magda receives other visitations from the world beyond the farm besides the tax letter. 'I also hear voices,' she notes: 'The voices speak to me out of machines that fly in the sky. They speak to me in Spanish' (1978, 125). Though she has no knowledge of the language, she finds everything they say 'immediately comprehensible' (125). This puzzles her. Perhaps there is some 'continuous miraculous intervention on my behalf in the form of translation'—as if she has acquired a Babel fish from *The Hitchhiker's Guide to the Galaxy* (1979), a set of Pixel Buds from Google or some other translation device from the future (126). She dismisses this possibility, however, preferring to think that the men in their flying machines speak 'a Spanish of pure meanings such as might be dreamed of by the philosophers' (125). She also prefers not to think of the voices as mere delusions on her part. Whatever the explanation, she is clear that, given the state of isolation in which she now finds herself—all the farm workers have abandoned her by this point—the voices keep her 'from becoming a beast' (125). After comparing her fate to a Crusoe-like castaway who, with only his barking dog and squawking parrot for company, ends up 'bounding on all fours, clubbing the indigenous goats with thighbones, eating their flesh raw,' she declares: 'It is not speech that makes man man but the speech of others' (125).

Being rather learned, our reader recognises that what the voices say is really a pastiche of unattributed quotations from the writings of various European thinkers and poets, including Blake, Calvin, Cernuda, Hegel, Lacan, Nietzsche, Pascal, Rousseau, Spinoza and Weil. These are all rendered in English (and in italics), though Magda of course hears them as 'crystal Spanish vocables' (126). '*It is a world of words that creates a world of things*,' one voice says, implicitly citing, as our reader picks up, Lacan's 1966 formulation of the linguistic relativity thesis in *Écrits* (134). Magda rejects this claim with a brusque 'Pah!' (134). Only too aware of language as a potential prison-house, she spends much of the narrative trying vainly to escape the entrapments of her 'father-tongue', Afrikaans, and the racialised feudal order it encodes, by attempting to fashion a new language and, she hopes, a new egalitarian community on the farm (97).

Though Magda believes the voices help preserve her fragile human dignity, they also create a problem for her. If the 'sky-creatures' promise the kind of human reciprocity she craves throughout, a reciprocity she pointedly fails to establish with the farm workers, she needs to find some way of opening a genuine dialogue with them (133). She makes various attempts. To begin with she tries gesturing and calling out, first in English, then in rudimentary Spanish. Then, again recalling the 'classic castaways', she lights 'a pyre', but this too fails—she wonders what might make them think it 'a signal', rather than 'a mere phenomenon' (131). Next, she turns to writing. Recognising that her words will need to be read from the sky, she gathers a pile of stones 'the size of small pumpkins', again like Crusoe making use of 'every odd and end', paints them white and forms them 'into letters twelve feet high' spelling out 'messages to my saviours' in her garbled Esperanto-like Spanish (132). First, already worried that she might be seen as a pitiable 'ugly sister', she writes: 'CINDRLA ES MI', then 'VENE AL TERRA', 'QUEIRO UN AUTR' and 'SON ISOLADO' (132). However, after realising that mere 'importunities' are unlikely to have the desired effect, she switches to poetry, composing a series of 'POEMAS CREPUSCLRS, intending CREPUSCULARIAS but running short of stones', as she did with the word 'CINDERELLA' (132). Finally, accepting that even poetry is unlikely to succeed and 'descending to ideographs', she uses the remaining stones to make 'a sketch of a woman lying on her back, her figure fuller than mine, her legs parted, younger than myself too'. 'How vulgar,' she thinks, 'yet how necessary!' (133). Still there is no response.

For our reader, Magda's various attempts at communication, which run the gamut of human sign-making, are most productively construed as Wittgensteinian language-games on at least two levels. *In* the world of the fiction, the 'POEMAS CREPUSCULARIAS', for instance—the phrase would normally be rendered as 'Poemas Crepusculares' ('Twilight Poems') in Spanish—are for Magda less acts of poetic self-expression than desperate appeals like the 'importunities' and the ideograph. Yet they also constitute one of the many writing-games *of* the fiction itself—in this case the games of unattributed, even indeterminate allusion and pastiche. Perhaps, our reader wonders, the phrase is an oblique reference to Pablo Neruda's first book, *Crepusculario* (1923), which is itself 'a curious pastiche of compositions' imitating 'the refined aesthetic norms of Hispanic Modernism' (de Costa 1979: 19). Or maybe it is an allusion to the generation of Italian poets, the so-called 'Poeti Crepuscolari' of the early 1900s, who rejected the lofty nationalism and oratorical style of their precursors, notably Gabriele D'Annunzio, and sought instead to write about everyday life as simply and directly as possible, striving for something like an Italian of 'pure meanings'.

For anyone 'interested in developing the concept of World Literature,' as the 2016 prospectus for the new *Journal of World Literature* puts it, seeing these various acts of reading/writing or hearing/speaking as language-games in Wittgenstein's sense points to a third possibility as well ('Overview' 2016). In this case, they serve as a cautionary tale. If you believe that literary works, especially works of world literature in translation, speak to you out of the sky in an English of 'pure meanings', then you risk being accused of wishfulness at best, delusions at worst. True, as Magda's oblique reference to the dreams of 'the philosophers' suggests, you might be in illustrious company, but there may be little consolation in that given the doubts Coetzee himself expressed about such dreams in his early essay 'Isaac Newton and the Ideal of a Transparent Scientific Language' (1982). The essay considers Newton's engaging but ultimately unsuccessful struggle as a writer-translator 'to bridge the gap between the nonreferential symbolism of mathematics and a language too protean to be tied down to single, pure meanings', identifying the purist aspiration with 'the no-nonsense "mathematical plainness" that stood for the ideal of Bishop Sprat and the Royal Society of Newton's day' (Coetzee 1992: 193–94). Coetzee could just as easily have traced a longer genealogy from, say, Francis Bacon to the varieties of positivism, including those from early Wittgenstein, that emerged in the early twentieth century. His principal point is clear, however: Newton's failure to fashion a 'metaphor-free language' that might achieve an 'unambiguous one-to-one mapping of reality', escaping the prison-house or at least the imperfections of, in his case, everyday Latin and English, raises the question of whether 'anything significant or new' might ever be said in the 'pure language' the philosophers of his day dreamed of making the foundation of knowledge (1992: 193).

In the Heart of the Country itself puts this aspiration under extreme pressure by insisting at every point on its own status not as a crystalline speaking *voice* but as a fallible artefact of *writing*—most obviously Magda's unreliable narrative is set out as a numbered, sometimes contradictory series of 266 diary-like entries. The vignette of the tax letter underscores this by analogy: literary works, the scene suggests, are more like tax letters than aerial voices, since they come into our hands through the agency of various intermediaries—many Hermes-Piets are involved—as all-too-human documents printed in particular languages and writing systems and enclosed in envelopes of one kind or another. The analogy of course belongs to the age of print and so now looks dated or at least of little obvious relevance in the world of the digital download.

To bring things closer to our own multimedia moment, we can turn again to Coetzee writing in his own person. At one point in *Here and Now* (2013), a series of letters he exchanged with Paul Auster between 2008 and 2011, he considers the effects of the digital revolution via an anecdote about the moment he bought a copy of *War and Peace* for his 'personal library' when he was sixteen (i.e. *c*.1956). This was Aylmer Maude's translation first published by Oxford University Press in 1922–23:

> Aylmer Maude's *War and Peace*, in its original maroon and cream wrapper, has accompanied me through half a century's moves from continent to continent. I have a sentimental relation with it—not with Tolstoy's *War and Peace*, that vast construct of words and ideas, but the object that emerged from the printing house of Richard Clay and Sons in 1952 and was shipped from the warehouse of Oxford University Press somewhere in London to the press's distribution agent in Cape Town and thence to Juta's bookshop and to me. (Coetzee 2013: 180)

By distinguishing two versions of the novel—the translator's and the author's—and highlighting the difference between the work ('that vast construct of words and ideas') and the material object (the 'bulky little book printed on thin India paper'), the anecdote can be read as a short philosophical lesson in the ontologies of writing, perhaps even of world literature, in the age of print—recall also Coetzee's course on the 'Book in Africa' described in chapter 7.

Yet, as the detailed itinerary of the book's journey indicates, Coetzee's own 'sentimental' attachment is not so much to the book itself, qua material artefact, as to the interconnected world, or Darntonian circuit, it reveals, a world of authors, translators, publishers, printers, warehouses, ships, agents, booksellers and readers, linking mid-nineteenth-century Russia to early twentieth-century England, the London and the Cape Town of the 1950s and, ultimately, Coetzee's teenage self to Tolstoy. Given the new technologies of dissemination in the digital age, Coetzee concludes, this 'kind of relationship with an author—extremely tenuous and highly indirect, conducted perhaps through a dozen intermediaries—will be less and less possible in the future' (Coetzee 2013: 180).

Taken together with the vignette of the tax letter, these wistful observations reflect Coetzee's nostalgia for the age of print. They also make him seem like an ally of the book historians who have for the last three decades or more been insisting, as Roger Chartier put it in 1992, that readers 'never confront abstract, idealized texts detached from any materiality' (50). A historian by profession, Chartier intended this primarily as a rebuke to the textualist delusions of 1980s literary critics and theorists. But Coetzee's position is in fact more subtle than this connection suggests. For one thing, he is only too aware of the potential absurdity of nostalgia. 'How does one escape the entirely risible fate of turning into Gramps,' he goes on to ask Auster, 'the old codger who, when he embarks on one of his "Back in my time" discourses, makes the children roll their eyes in silent despair?' (Coetzee 2013: 181). For another, he is far from convinced by the materialist fundamentalism to which many book historians subscribe, since, as he puts it, 'books are not real, not in any important sense': 'The fact that what we call a book can be picked up in one's hands, has a smell and a feel of its own, is an accident of its production with no relevance to what the book conveys' (180). What, we might ask, has happened to the Coetzee who designed a course on 'The Book in Africa' (see chapter 7)? His next claim is even more questionable: 'The very letters on the page are signs, images of sounds, which are images of ideas' (180). What about the Coetzee who had the author-figure Foe insist that 'writing is not doomed to be the shadow of speech' (Coetzee 1986: 142)? Returning to his copy of *War and*

Peace and the web of relations it disclosed—that is, to the focal point of his own comments on the advent of the digital age—he draws a more cautious conclusion, closer to his earlier thoughts: 'Whether such relationships have any value seems to me an open question, as is the question of whether it is better to own a physical copy of a book than to have the power to download an image of its text' (Coetzee 2013: 180–81). These differences are certainly debateable, though, as we have seen at various points (chapters 6 and 8 especially), we ignore the 'envelopes' of writing at our peril.

Let's return to our hypothetical reader with these questions in mind. She was, you will recall, reading the 'bilingual' Ravan edition which came into her hands not only as a specific paperback book with a cover design (part of its unique envelope) by the Scottish-born South African artist Richard Smith but as a piece of intellectual property restricted 'for sale in the Republic of South Africa only' (Coetzee 1978: iv). For some critics of the latest iteration of the world literature project, this last detail is vital. 'World Literature seems to be one more way of not talking about the world,' Joseph R. Slaughter comments, 'especially when it fails to recognize the material inequalities and imbalances that subtend creative production and the monopoly model of copyrighted culture that are the conditions of its own contemporary possibility' (Slaughter 2014: 34). As the telling phrase 'one more way' implies, Slaughter, who writes as a no-nonsense materialist, sees this as an expression of a deeper malaise within traditions of literary study that remain aloof from, if not indifferent to, the inequities of real economic and political power.

Country's early publishing history bears out his concerns. As Peter Randall, Ravan's publisher at the time, later recalled about Coetzee's move to Secker and Harper, 'it was painful to know that as a small publisher we could not compete with international houses to retain authors for whom we had taken the initial risks' (de Villiers 1997: 9). Though Ravan's contract for Coetzee's first fiction, *Dusklands* (1974), 'contained the usual clause about being offered his next work', Randall decided that, given his limited resources and the structural realities of the publishing world at the time, 'we could not stand in the way of possible international recognition and world sales' (9). Yet he did in the end produce his own uniquely 'bilingual' edition after Coetzee himself negotiated a compromise with Secker. Partly out of personal loyalty to Randall and partly out of his commitment to Ravan's anti-apartheid activism, he did the same with *Waiting for the Barbarians* (1980), *Life & Times of Michael K* (1983) and *Foe* (1986)—these were not strictly separate editions, however, as the text they reproduced was identical to Secker's (Wittenberg 2008).

For Slaughter, intellectual property is real in an important sense because it reflects the asymmetries of an international book trade in which small, local publishers (and producers of knowledge more generally) cannot compete with the major metropolitan brokers who dominate Pascale Casanova's 'World Republic of Letters', and because it exposes the unworldly idealisations implicit in many traditions of academic literary criticism. Yet, returning to Coetzee's question of value as it pertains to the tenuous author-reader relations embodied in his copy of *War and Peace*, the seemingly legalistic matters of copyright could be said to have a further significance as well, one that brings us back to the analogy with the tax letter and its limits. Though literary works do not speak to us from the sky, neither can they be said to have addressees in the sense that most letters do. Yet, as intellectual property subject to copyright, they do inhabit particular geographical territories, many of which cross national borders and all of which create specific communities of readers. While the 'bilingual' Ravan edition of *Country* circulated within a national sphere, for example, the Secker and Harper 'monolingual' versions were distributed transnationally not to a 'world' audience but to the particular supranational sections of the global Anglosphere which Secker/Penguin and Harper/Viking divided among themselves. By the late 1970s, following the collapse of the Traditional Markets Agreement of 1947, UK and US publishers agreed on a more flexible map of the world defined in terms of 'open' (non-exclusive) and 'closed' (exclusive) markets. In practice, this generally means the Americans operate exclusively within their own national borders and the Philippines, while the British sell their books across the UK, Europe and the Commonwealth, including countries in Asia and Africa. This is true of the paperback versions of *Country* today, the rights to which are now owned by Penguin in the US and Vintage in the UK—the name changes reflect the rise of a new, conglomerate multinationalism in publishing. Again, following the typical pattern, and reflecting the ongoing entanglement of the digital and print spheres, the exclusive digital/ebook territories match those of the print editions. Looked at in terms of the geographies of copyright, then, any viable concept of world literature has to come to terms not just with the structural transformation and imbalances of the global trade in books, whether print or digital, but with a shifting patchwork of contractually and linguistically defined worlds of literary circulation which the digital age has complicated rather than transformed.

Circulating within a restricted national territory, the 'bilingual' Ravan paperback created a particular relationship between our reader and Coetzee. To give her more of a biography, let's say she was a young lecturer teaching English at Rhodes University in Grahamstown, South Africa in the early 1980s. Replicating the circuit linking Coetzee's teenage self to Tolstoy, we could then trace a line back to her local bookshop, University Publishers and Booksellers, via the South African postal system to Ravan and its printers both of 60 Juta Street, Braamfontein, Johannesburg and finally to Coetzee as a bilingual author (not self-translator) in Cape Town where he was himself a lecturer in English. Yet, we might again ask with Coetzee, does *this* tenuous and indirect relationship have any value? As it happens, the absence of one key intermediary in this case is far from negligible. Unlike the British hardback edition, the Ravan paperback did not pass through the apartheid censorship bureaucracy. To secure its own copyright, Secker shipped a limited consignment of its edition to South Africa in July 1977 which customs officers then embargoed, submitting one copy to the censors for inspection. For the same fate to have befallen the local edition, either an individual member of public or the police would have had to make the submission, but this never happened.

This is not to say that it was wholly untouched by the system. Because the blurb Coetzee produced for the Secker edition referred explicitly to Magda's father being 'trapped with serfs in a web of reciprocal oppression' and to his 'lurch across the colour-bar' in 'a bid for private salvation in the arms of a black concubine', Coetzee suggested Randall use a less provocative quotation from Maev Kennedy's review of the British edition which appeared in the *Irish Times* of 11 June 1977 (Coetzee 1978: inside flap). This had the effect of bringing another globally displaced intermediary into the circuit, adding an additional world-feature to the Ravan edition's unique envelope. Though Kennedy mentioned the father taking 'a black concubine', the section of the short review Randall chose centred on Magda's 'searing loneliness', Coetzee's experimentalism and the story's universality—'putting its finger on several common terrors of mankind' (1978, back cover). Tellingly, in the sentence Randall cut from the opening, Kennedy informed her Irish readership that *Country* stood out 'as an alien', particularly when seen 'against the intense Englishness' of the other more conventional novels she was reviewing, with its 'utterly foreign environment and period producing a character deeply estranged from any Western norm'—a revealing but moot point, given Magda's own sense of the culture in which she is inescapably embedded (Kennedy 1977: 8).

The concerns Coetzee and Randall had about the censors proved unfounded, however, as even the Secker edition with its more provocative blurb was passed, largely because the censors judged it a major literary achievement. As Anna M. Louw, a prominent Afrikaans writer, put it in her censor's report, 'this product of our own *bodem* [literally soil, but also existential or spiritual home] is one of the few works of stature in the world of South African English letters'—though equally moot, the contrast between her reading and Kennedy's could not be more marked (McDonald 2009: 314). The censors' decision nonetheless left our young lecturer in the strange position of reading the local edition which they never scrutinised, rather than the import which they approved.

The censors' surprisingly sympathetic and more or less exclusively literary assessment highlights a key dimension of the circuits of publication that Coetzee's own relational model underplays. Again, revealing the limits of the analogy with the tax letter, these circuits never simply track the mechanics of transmission. They also reflect the operations of what James English, following Pascale Casanova (who in turn follows Pierre Bourdieu), dubs 'the economy of prestige', the focus and product of which is literary value itself (English 2005). Like Slaughter's literal rights economy, this symbolic 'economy' has imbalances of its own—think of Casanova's 'Greenwich meridian of literature'—and, again like Slaughter's, it can be national, trans- or supranational, or all three at once (Casanova 2005: 87). Gesturing towards its potential expansiveness, Coetzee notes in a passing comment to Auster that he bought *War and Peace* as an intellectually ambitious sixteen-year-old in 1950s Cape Town 'because *Time* magazine said it was the greatest novel ever written' (Coetzee 2013: 180). In the case of our reader, the value brokers included Randall in Johannesburg, Kennedy in Dublin, the judges of the South African CNA prize, and—to fill out the details of her predicament further still—her senior colleagues at Rhodes University who had prescribed *Country* as part of a course on African literature she was teaching. Tracing a lineage from *The Epic of Sundiata*, an oral narrative about the founding of the Empire of Mali in the thirteenth century, to Ayi Kwei Armah's novel *The Beautyful Ones Are Not Yet Born* (1969), the course, which drew extensively on the Heinemann African Writers Series for its materials, was designed to encourage students to situate various South African writers, including Es'kia Mphahlele, Nadine Gordimer, Miriam Tlali and Coetzee, in a wider *continental* context. For our junior lecturer, however, this only raised more questions about the actual experience of reading the Ravan edition. On the one hand, given its 'content'—at least its setting, its main languages and its political preoccupations—not to mention the writing-games it plays with the Afrikaans tradition of the realist *plaasroman* ('farm-novel'), it seemed, to her mind, to achieve its primary effects only when seen in 'a national frame' ('Overview' 2016). On the other hand, given its many 'cosmopolitan threads', it was impossible to treat it simply as 'a product of our *bodem*', as the censor put it or, indeed, to consider 1970s South Africa its 'culture of origin' in any straightforward sense ('Overview'; Damrosch 2003: 4). Thinking of the 'POEMAS CREPUSCULARIAS', for instance, which linked it to Chile and Italy in the early part of the last century, our reader was more inclined to understand it in internationalist and transhistorical terms, say as a work engaged with traditions of Hispanic and Italian modernism, though that hardly captured the full range of the many literary, philosophical and other 'networks' it both inhabited and created ('Overview' 2016).

Our reader's experience of the Ravan edition may now be a thing of the past—the world has moved on and that edition has been out of print since the early 1990s—but the questions it asked of her and the culture she inhabited have, if anything, become more pertinent today, given *Country*'s extended afterlife in translation. Since the first French edition appeared in 1981, it has been published in twenty languages (Norwegian, Danish, Finnish, German, Serbian, Hebrew, Italian, Polish, Portuguese, Japanese, Dutch, Slovenian, Greek, Spanish, Swedish, Russian, Albanian, Estonian and Mandarin) and six scripts (Latin, Hebrew, Cyrillic, Greek, Chinese and Japanese), making it, at least on one measure, an exemplary instance of world literature. It is still some way off *Disgrace* (1999), Coetzee's most translated work, however, which has now appeared in forty languages and fourteen scripts. Of the twenty, only Peter Bergsma's 1985 Dutch version (*In het hart van het land*) recasts the 'bilingual' experience of the original, retaining the Afrikaans dialogue and, for instance, having Magda write 'EK HET NIE GELD NIE' (165). Again, following the basic language divisions of the original, Bergsma also preserves Magda's broken Spanish while rewording the aerial voices she hears in Dutch. Yet the Dutch-Afrikaans 'bilingualism' his readers experience is still inevitably different to the English-Afrikaans original. It also produces anomalies of its own. In a few cases, for instance, Coetzee retained some Afrikaans words in his English self-translation, 'baas' being the most telling example (see van der Vlies 2007: 138–42). The word is originally of Dutch origin, and the *OED* gives its primary meaning as 'master, employer of labour'—it also notes that the word has been a naturalised part of the English language since the seventeenth century, albeit mainly in its South African variety (*OED*). Coetzee no doubt kept the Afrikaans form as a distinctive linguistic marker of the farm's equally distinctive feudal code. So, in the original English-Afrikaans version, Magda, commenting on the testy master-serf relations between her father and the farm workers, asks: 'And was it their provocation to reply *Ja baas* to his provocation, casting their eyes down, hiding their smiles, biding their time till he overreached himself?' (Coetzee 1978: 130). Preserving the freighted key term, Coetzee translated the Afrikaans phrase as '*Yes baas*', while Bergsma blended the Afrikaans into the Dutch, inescapably reducing, if not eliminating, the word's foreignising effect as well as the culturally and politically specific resonance (Coetzee 1977: 142). Following Coetzee's lead, all the translations in languages based on the Latinate writing system preserve the Afrikaans term in its original orthography.

For David Damrosch, who makes circulation a key to his own concept of world literature, 'a work only has an *effective* life as world literature whenever, and wherever, it is actively present within a literary system beyond that of its original culture' (2003: 4). As we have already seen, *Country* puts this formulation under pressure in part because its 'original culture' is a matter of debate rather than a given, but also because it exceeds the confines of any 'literary system'. For one thing, it engages with many such systems, not just those in English and Afrikaans; for another, its targets are not only literary: it takes on philosophy, theology and much else besides. To avoid these restrictions, we could say the translations make *Country* an instance of world literature in Damrosch's sense because they give it life in a new *language* and, in some cases, a new *writing system*. And yet, as Coetzee's comments on Maude's *War and Peace* indicate, and as the cautionary tale about Magda's vocalised 'pure meanings' underscores, even this formulation falls short because it fails to address the fact that Coetzee's *Country* becomes present in these other systems as a new work, as, say, Bergsma's *Land*, much as Coetzee's own self-translation entered the global Anglosphere as a new 'monolingual' English edition. Given Gisèle Sapiro's work on the unequal and uneven flows of translation—a concern organisations like PEN International and UNESCO have addressed for many years—it is worth noting that this became the standard source or mediating text for translators; again, Bergsma is the exception (Sapiro 2016 and McDonald 2017). Sometimes this difference is explicitly signalled in the choice of title. While most translators opt, like Bergsma, for a rough equivalent of Coetzee's original (though does the Dutch 'land', or the French 'pays', or the Hebrew הארץ *Haaretz* really have the same resonance as the English 'country'?), some recast it completely as, for example, *I det mørke landet* (Norwegian, *In the dark country*, possibly conjuring up ideas of Africa as 'det mørke kontinent'), *Deserto* (Italian, *Desert/Wasteland/Wilderness*), *Askund* (Albanian, *Nowhere*), 内 陆 深 处 (Mandarin, Nèi lù shēn chù, *Deep Inland*), *En medio de ninguna parte* (Spanish, *In the middle of nowhere*) and 石の女 (Japanese, Ishi no onna, *Stone Woman*), avoiding the specific idiomatic colouring of the original English altogether.

For translators and students of translation, these differences are central and worth detailed scrutiny. But is there anything English readers of Coetzee might gain by keeping these other versions in view, thinking beyond the 'monolingual' self-translation currently in circulation?

At one level, the opportunities a lateral comparison affords are philosophical and linguistic rather than literary. For instance, reading across the translations opens ways of developing Coetzee's critique of the philosophers' ideal language of 'pure meanings', since as a quick comparison shows, actual languages, even those that share the Latinate writing system, do not agree when it comes to the onomatopoeic rendering, let alone the graphic notation, of pure (non-human) vocalisations. Consider the sounds Magda's imagined dog and parrot make: her 'Woof!' and 'Squawk!' (Coetzee 1978, 125) become variously '¡Guau!' and 'Ca-ca-ca-ca' (Spanish, 171), 'Woef!' and 'Lorre!' (Dutch, 166), 'Ouah!' and 'Jaco!' (French, 169), 'Voff!' and 'Kræ!' (Norwegian, 146), 'Vuh!' and 'Vaak!' (Finnish, 159–60), 'Au!' and 'Currupaco' (Portuguese, 163), 'Vuf!' and 'Orkk!' (Danish, 158), 'Wuff!' and 'Quak!' (German, 186), 'abbaia' and 'squittisce' (Italian, 145), 'Hau, hau!' and 'Krra, krra!' (Polish, 177). The Mandarin has 汪！汪！ and 呱！呱！ ('wang, wang' and 'guāguā', 187).

At another level, reading with an eye on these differences casts new light on Coetzee's own forays into a wider multilingualism via Spanish, since this plays out differently across the translations, creating various effects. Translators using the Latinate writing system retain most of the capitalised Spanish words in their original (corrupted) orthography, as does the Hebrew, though when it comes to Magda's self-identification as 'CINDRLA' (1978, 132), the Danish translator opted for 'ASKPOT', a deformed version of 'Askepot' (literally: 'Ashpot', 166), while the Spanish has 'CENICNT', a misspelling of 'la Cenicienta' (181). Inevitably, all Magda's attempts at Spanish lose some of their foreignising effect in the Spanish version, which on one occasion also alters her misspelling, giving 'SON AISOLADO' for 'SON ISOLADO'—the grammatically and orthographically correct rendering of 'I am isolated', if that is what Magda intends, would be 'soy aislado' or 'estoy aislado' (181).

These shifts in language, orthography and even graphic presentation inevitably created a challenge for the Chinese translator. Her solution was to reproduce the originals, adding a Mandarin translation in parenthesis. She also included the following explanatory footnote accompanying the first occurrence in paragraph 251:

> ES MI in Spanish could refer to something like 'it is me,' but it is not a typical Spanish word. In the text that follows, there are more such examples in capitalized letters. We could understand some of them by guessing (if so, I shall put the Chinese equivalents just after these coined words, rather than give them any footnote). However, some of these words are really confusing, and thus beyond us. They sometimes seem to be a mixture of Italian and Catalan, but this is not always the case. What is worse, it is more incomprehensible because Coetzee creates a deliberately fragmented narrative. The translator believes Coetzee himself coins these words and wants to show the reader a 'universal' language, which, as he puts in paragraph 241, 'belong[s] in fact not to a local Spanish but to a Spanish of pure meanings'. Thus the translator has guessed one of its meanings based on their common Latin root. The translator believes Coetzee wants to create a puzzle for his readers. (Chinese: 195)

The 'equivalents' the translator guessed were, however, often rather different in kind. In the case of CINDRLA ES MI, for instance, she decided to mix translation with transliteration, rendering the letters as 我是辛德瑞拉, giving the back translation and the Pinyin version of the name 'I am *xin de ri la*' (198). With POEMAS CREPUSCLRS, however, she chose a more direct, if surprising, translation: 黎明之歌 (*li ming zhi ge*, 'dawn song', 198).

Occasionally, however, the translator's choice of a single word or phrase produces a fundamental difference, again casting new light on Coetzee's own preoccupations. Considering Magda's views on writing in the 'bilingual' and 'monolingual' originals, for example, it is clear that she is not always 'deeply estranged from any Western norm', as Kennedy put it. When she describes herself as 'descending to ideographs' in her final effort to communicate with the 'sky-creatures', she voices a very entrenched Euro-American alphabetic prejudice (1978, 133). Since she produces a glamourised and sexualised self-portrait in stones, she evidently has something like Chinese characters or Egyptian hieroglyphs in mind, rather than, say, Indian-Arabic numerals which are more purely ideographic—they also form a central non-phonetic part of all Latinate writing systems. 'Descending' of course implies that supposedly ideographic writing systems are less advanced than purportedly phonetic ones. The idea that there is a categorical and evolutionary difference is itself part of the standard prejudicial story in which the ideal writing system is envisaged not just as phonetic but as 'one in which each letter would stand for just one individual sound', much as each word has one meaning in the dreams of the philosophers (Harris 1986: 39). Most translators reflect Magda's entrapment within this prejudice by finding an equivalent for 'descending'. Bergsma, for instance, has 'En vervolgens verlaagde ik me tot beeldschrift' ('And then I lowered myself to image-writing', 177); while the Spanish translator gives 'descendiendo ya a los ideogramas' ('descending then to ideographs', 182). For readers of the Italian, German and Norwegian versions, however, this feature of Magda's cultural prison-house is downplayed or excised altogether. While the Italian renders the verb simply as 'passando' ('passing/moving', 154), the German construes the clause as 'Und dann ging ich zu Ideogrammen über' ('And then I switched to ideographs', 198), while the Norwegian has the slightly less neutral 'Jeg tydde til ideogrammer' ('I resorted to ideographs', 155). More unexpectedly, given the history of Euro-American attitudes, the Mandarin is as neutral as the German: 我把字母转化为象形文字 (*wo ba zi mu zhuan wei xiang xing wen zi*, or 'I transform these letters into ideographs', 200).

What relevance might all this have for scholars 'interested in developing the concept of World Literature'? By 'all this' I mean not just the details about *In the Heart of the Country* and its publishing history, but the various actual, hypothetical and finally possible reading experiences it affords, both in its original forms and in its translations.

To address this question I propose, by way of conclusion, to revisit and retranslate the 1907 essay in which Rabindranath Tagore developed his own concept, or rather anti-concept, of বিশ্ব সাহিত্য (which can be Romanised from the Bengali as *Vishva Sahitya* and translated as 'World Literature'). In his anthology *World Literature in Theory*, which includes Swapan Chakravorty's 2001 translation of the essay, Damrosch describes it as a 'path-breaking' statement that 'speaks of the universal values that world literature can embody' (Damrosch 2014: 6). In a similar but charier vein, Pheng Cheah cites it in the epilogue to *What is a World?*, setting it up, like Damrosch, alongside Goethe's pronouncements on *Weltliteratur*, as a parallel non-Euro-American formulation of what he calls 'the older vision of world literature as the expression of universal humanity' (Cheah 2016: 310). Though more attuned to the intricacies of Tagore's writing and to questions of translation, Supriya Chaudhuri falls back on the same formulation in her otherwise astute essay 'Singular Universals', claiming that, for Tagore, literature 'serves to express universal humanity' (Chaudhuri 2016: 81). There is much in Chakravorty's translation that makes such claims understandable, not least his version of Tagore's concluding sentence: 'It is time we pledged that our goal is to view universal humanity in universal literature by freeing ourselves from rustic uncatholicity; that we shall recognise a totality in each particular author's work, and that in this totality we shall perceive the interrelations among all human efforts at expression' (Tagore 2001: 150). Yet to take this as a straightforward articulation of Tagore's *concept* of world literature is not just to treat him as a mysteriously comprehensible voice from the sky, ignoring all the promise and perils of translation, but to miss at least two key elements of his thinking, both of which reflect his partly Buddhist-inspired wariness of conceptualisation as such.

The first concerns Tagore's idea of literature. 'We do not properly understand literature (*sahitya*),' he notes at one pivotal point in his wide-ranging discussion, 'if we reduce it to place-time-pot (*desh-kāl-pātra*)'—*pātra* could also be 'vessel' or 'individual/person', and so single author (Tagore 1961: 771). Chakravorty gives the whole sentence as 'literature is not viewed in its true light if we see it confined to a particular space and time', making it plausible to see the compound *desh-kāl-pātra* as something like 'context' in English (Tagore 2001: 147–8). Yet why limit translation to a search for linguistic correspondences or even rough equivalents—or, conversely, to an affirmation or acceptance of the untranslatable? Is it not sometimes more productive, linguistically, intellectually and culturally, to extend the expressive capacities of the target via the source language, creating a new *English* compound in this case? Considering the very long history of loans and calques, such transformative movements are after all part of the ordinary life of languages—recall the emergence of the Dutch word 'baas' into seventeenth-century English.

As it happens, the creative potential of such movements was also central to Tagore's understanding of translation. Indeed, by marking the particular, Bangla-inflected character of his thinking, the foreignising neologism 'place-time-pot' highlights an important feature of his interlingual practice as a writer, while also reflecting the intercultural ideals he championed as an educationalist. For Tagore, literary creativity is above all an act of resistance directed against all forms of containment and reification, including the conceptual kinds that many varieties of literary criticism and academic scholarship favour either actively or by default. He is, to this extent, a pioneering proponent of the affirmative anti-scholastic position European thinkers like Blanchot began to develop in the 1950s (see chapter 9). So if literature cannot be reduced to 'place-time-pot' (say, the historicist's or bibliographer's curatorial object), neither can it be seen merely as a 'constructed artefact' (say, the formalist's well-wrought urn), because it constitutes 'a world' (*ekti jagat*), the creative potential of which is, 'like the material world', always 'ongoing' and 'incomplete' (Tagore 1961: 772).

Why is this? Because, as Tagore explains in the opening paragraphs of the essay, it is an expression of '*ananda*' ('joy' or 'delight'). This has two important consequences. First, it sets literature apart from the sphere of calculating rationality, which Tagore associates with an arrogant will to power over others, and from the sphere of practical necessity or need, which he also links to power, though this time over the environment—'water, air, and fire' become 'our unpaid servants' (Tagore 2001: 138). Second, and conversely, seeing literature as an expression of *ananda* connects it to a wide range of other seemingly gratuitous or superfluous everyday activities, from the elaborate rituals of a wedding ceremony to the needless theatricality of warfare. These are also manifestations of 'man's excess (*prachurya*), his wealth (*aisharya*), that which overflows all his need' and, for that matter, all forms of rationalistic calculation, whether political, economic or, indeed, literary-critical (Tagore 1961: 769). As Chaudhuri puts it, literature for Tagore is 'a movement of affect which binds human beings together' (2016: 84). It is partly because of this affective overflowing that it cannot be contained within a 'place-time-pot'.

The second key element of his thinking concerns his idea of the world. Here the difficulties have less to do with translation as such than with the many unattributed allusions to the Bangla literary traditions that permeate the essay. When it comes to his understanding of the world, the principal figure is the medieval *bhakti* poet Chandidas, and the main point of reference is the song Jeanne Openshaw translates as follows:

> I have made the world my home
> And my home the world.
> I have made 'others' my own people,
> And my own people 'others.' (Openshaw 2002: vi)

Tagore echoes the second two lines when explaining the 'connection' (Chakravorty has 'bond') *ananda* creates: 'It is when we know the other as our self and our self as other', or, as Chakravorty has it, 'it is nothing but knowing others as our own, and ourselves as others' (1961: 763; 2001: 139). Again, Tagore contrasts this with the connections rationality, particularly political rationality, fashions (it is 'like the bond between the hunter and his prey') and with the alliances required to satisfy basic needs—he mentions 'the English trader' who 'once secured his aims by bowing to the Nawab' but 'eventually ascended to the throne himself' (2001: 138).

Political and economic domination over others drive both these forms of connectedness. Whereas, when it comes to the ties created in a spirit of *ananda*, the self and the other are both undone in a process of reciprocal transformation that involves simultaneously reaching out and embracing the foreign, on the one hand, and turning inward, discovering the foreign within, on the other. Later in the essay, Tagore echoes Chandidas's first two lines: 'the heart is constantly at pains to find the world in our self and our self in the world', which Chakravorty renders as 'the heart's longing to make the world its own and itself the world's' (1961: 767; 2001: 144). Crucially, for Tagore, 'the world' in this context is neither a geographical space nor a determinate set of universal values: it is an aspiration toward an ever greater understanding of and feeling for interconnectedness which, like the creative potential of literature, is always in the making, never complete. For this he took his cue as much from Chandidas as from the itinerant Bāul singers of Bengal whose vagabond, quasi-anarchic humanism shaped his own self-understanding as a poet and his ambitions as an educationalist (McDonald 2017). Hence the name he gave the university he founded in Shantiniketan in 1921: Visva-Bharati, which, as Dutta and Robinson explain, is 'a compound made from the Sanskrit word for universe [or world] and Bharati, a goddess in the *Rig Veda* associated with the Hindu goddess of learning, Saraswati' (literally 'world-learning', Dutta 1995: 220).

With these two key elements of his thinking in mind, we can return to the sentence with which he concludes the essay, retranslating it as follows: 'The time has come to try to free ourselves from narrow parochialism [or village-provincialism] and to aim to see the World-Man (*vishva-manab*) within world literature; to find in the works of particular writers a whole, and in that whole the interrelations among all forms of human expression' (Tagore 1961: 773). Importantly, the 'whole' may, on this formulation, be a consequence of the writer's own creativity (the relations actively produced in each work) or simply an effect of the medium they choose to adopt—the relations already embedded in the novel form, say, or the English language. As importantly, for Tagore this understanding of world literature as an intercultural aspiration has nothing to do with reified values of any kind, whether 'universal' or 'cosmopolitan', or, indeed, with simple oppositions or choices between 'nationalism/provincialism' and 'cosmopolitanism/universalism'. Nor is it viable on this model to see world literature merely as an effect of translation and circulation understood in book historical, economic, geographical or cultural terms. Encountering the world in Tagore's sense via literature in his sense is about the way we experience the ongoing creative potential of each individual work as an intercultural effort on the writer's part in the first instance to re-make the self and the other, the indigenous and the foreign, in an open-ended, superfluous, even gratuitously wasteful spirit of *ananda*. This is why he offered his anti-concept *Vishva Sahitya* as an alternative to what he called in a doubly self-distancing gesture 'Comparative Literature'—he used the English phrase—which left too much securely in place (1961: 771; 2001: 148).

So what might it mean to experience *In the Heart of the Country* as world literature in this sense? To begin with, it would require us to become attuned to the ways in which Coetzee foreignises his own elective cultural heritage, including the genre of the Afrikaans *plaasroman*, what he would later call the 'transplanted European novel', and some dominant philosophies of language in the European tradition (Coetzee 1981: 161). At the same time, we would need to recognise the connections he creates with other cultures and languages, and those in which he is already embedded simply because of the literary media, languages and writing systems in which he chooses to work. Extending this author-centred analysis, we could then track *Country*'s circulation and reception in its original 'bilingual' form within South Africa, and the fate of the self-translated 'monolingual' version across the various copyright territories of the English-reading world. We could also consider the varied impact it had on very differently located readers ranging from, say, the Afrikaans censor who remained committed to seeing it in exclusively national terms to our hypothetical reader who hesitatingly embraced its apparent cosmopolitanism, and to Kennedy, who championed its foreignness for her Irish readership in the late 1970s. Adding the translations would raise other questions, allowing us to gauge the success with which each translator, drawing on the resources of each new language and writing system, re-makes the world Coetzee created, enabling readers of Wen Min's 内陆深处, for instance, to engage with the unique intercultural and interlingual connections her version opens up.

Exactly which figure in this unfolding story we choose to emphasise—the author, the publisher, the translator, the reader—is only one, relatively contingent consideration. What matters is that we acknowledge with Tagore that, when it comes to experiencing *Country* in its various iterations as world literature, the *concept* as such is at best only a means, a way of pointing to the many worlds it both inhabits and creates, each of which reveals something more about the connections that reifying and rationalistic modes of thought obscure, ignore or exclude. The reason? For Tagore, as Chaudhuri notes, 'there is no world literature, only a relation of literature to the world' (2016: 86), or, as I would put it, only the experience of relating to an ever-widening range of intersecting worlds via some forms of literary writing.

Acknowledgements

I would like to thank Amazwi in South Africa and Rema Dilanyan of the Peter Lampack Agency for the details about the translation of Coetzee's works, and David Evans of David Higham Associates for the information about his copyright agreements. I am also grateful to the following for help with translation: Supriya Chaudhuri, Liang Dong, Joshua Getzler, Roger Goodman, Anne Goriely, Ben Goriely-McDonald, Akiko Hashimoto, Tom Kuhn, Tore Rem, Donglai Shi, Giuseppe Stellardi and Bart van Es. Special thanks to Rosinka Chaudhuri for her eye-opening re-translations of Tagore.

Translations of *In the Heart of the Country*

- *Au coeur de ce pays*. Trans. Sophie Mayoux. Paris: Lettres Nouvelles, 1981 (subsequently reissued by other publishers).
- *I det mørke landet*. Trans. Aud Grieff. Oslo: Cappelens, 1985.
- *I landets hjerte*. Trans. Niels Brunse. Copenhagen: Hekla, 1986.
- *Maan sydamessa*. Trans. Kimmo Rentola. Helsinki: Otava, 1986.
- *Im Herzen Landes*. Trans. Wulf Teichmann. Munich: Hanser, 1987 (subsequently reissued by other publishers).
- *U srtsu zemle*. Trans. Ksenia Todorovic. Belgrade: Pismo, 1987.
- בלב הארץ. Trans. Naomi Carmel. Tel Aviv: Ma'ariv, 1989.
- *Deserto*. Trans. Paola Splendore. Rome: Donzelli, 1993.

- *W sercu kraju. Zycie i czasy Michaela K. Foe.* Trans. Magdalena Konikowska. Warsaw: Panstwowy Instytut Wydawniczy, 1996.
- *No coração do país.* Trans. Luiz A. de Araújo. Sao Paulo: Circulo do livro, 1997.
- 石の女. Trans. Yasuko Murata. Tokyo: 3-A Corporation, 1997.
- *In het hart van het land.* Trans. Peter Bergsma. Rotterdam: Aristos, 1999.
- *V srcu dezele.* Trans. Jure Potokar. Ljubljana: Cankarjeva zalozba, 2001.
- *Στην καρδιά της χώρας.* Trans. Athena Dimitriadou. Athens: Scripta, 2002.
- *En medio de ninguna parte.* Trans. Miguel Martinez-Lage. Barcelona: Mondadori, 2003.
- *I hjärete av landet.* Trans. Thomas Preis. Stockholm: Brombergs, 2004.
- *Nel cuore del paese.* Trans. Franca Cavagnoli. Turin: Einaudi, 2004.
- *V serdtse strany.* Trans. E. Z. Fradkina. Moscow: Amfora, 2005.
- *Askund.* Trans. Zymber Elshani. Tirana: Skanderbeg, 2005.
- *No coração desta terra.* Trans. Maria João Delgado. Lisbon: Dom Quixote, 2005.
- *Südamaal.* Trans. Urve Hanko. Tallinn: Eesti Raamat, 2006.
- 内陆深处. Trans. Wen Min. Hangzhou: Zhejiang Literature & Art Publishing House, 2007.

Reading Envelopes: Four Examples

Chapter 10

Republishing Yeats's 'The Lake Isle of Innisfree' in the 1890s

Whether digital or print, books are not neutral media. They have designs on the texts they curate and on their readers. For Yeats's more discerning commentators this much has been clear since the beginning of his publishing career. No doubt with *Poems* (1895) on his mind, T. W. Rolleston remarked as early as 1900:

> Few poets have revised and retouched their work more than Mr. Yeats, and this may perhaps be one cause of the singular unity of the impression which it leaves upon the mind. In the final edition of his poems, where much is altered and much early work struck out altogether, one sees naturally but little sign of the immature and experimental stages which every poet must go through. He appears to have struck the rock, and the water flowed; we do not see it led with pain and toil from distant sources, through miry channels, and by feeble streamlets into its true bed. (Brooke 1900: 492)

While many might now feel less confident about the 'singular unity' of Yeats's early work, few would dispute Rolleston's claims about the artful effects of his books. Indeed, taking up what soon became a dominant theme in Yeats studies, George Bornstein developed Rolleston's early impressions in his 1991 essay 'Remaking Himself: Yeats's Revisions of His Early Canon'. Like Rolleston, he argued that Yeats's impulse to revision involved much more than the stylistic alteration of individual poems. Tracing the process back to *The Wanderings of Oisin* (1889), he showed it also entailed 'a complex and deliberate reworking of the larger divisions into which he organised his work', which amounted to 'a careful construction both of a canon and of an appropriate poetic self' (Bornstein 1991: 340). A book like

Poems (1895) is, he suggested, not simply a calculated selection of revised texts arranged in a particular order, but a portrait of the artist as a young man. Of course, like Rolleston, he argued that the result was not a faithful record of a young poet's tortuous development, but a construct projecting an idealised public self-image. As he put it, the principles of selection at work in the first three volumes—*Wanderings* (1889), *The Countess Kathleen and Various Legends and Lyrics* (1892) and *Poems* (1895)—reveal 'a strategy more aesthetic than autobiographic' (340). As Yeats's contemporaries and modern scholars have both recognised, then, books for him were not mere conduits. They were opportunities for poetic self-fashioning.

Taking his cue from Hugh Kenner's remark of the late 1950s that Yeats 'didn't accumulate poems, he wrote books', Bornstein made a compelling case for a bibliographically informed style of reading which resists the allure of the text's ideality (Kenner 1963: 13). He reminds us that we do not read, say, 'The Lake Isle of Innisfree' *in Poems* (1895). We read it *as* the 'The Lake Isle' of *Poems* (1895). Its specific placement in the book as a whole, and among the contending ensemble of poems for the first time entitled 'The Rose'; its relations to the neo-primitive transcendentalism of the volume's 'Prefatory Poem: To Some I have Talked with by the Fire', and to the more equivocal attitudes adopted in the poems that open and close 'The Rose', respectively, 'To the Rose Upon the Rood of Time' and 'To Ireland in the Coming Times'; and the implications for it of Yeats's explanation in the prose preface that the poems in 'The Rose' represent 'the only pathway whereon he can hope to see with his own eyes the Eternal Rose of Beauty and Peace'—all this specifically bibliographical and paratextual scaffolding (again, think of Joyce's envelope), which stands at what Genette in *Paratexts* (1987) calls the threshold of interpretation, influences, more or less effectively, the reader's reception (Yeats 1895: vi).

More generally, demonstrating that books and not simply texts have implied authors, Bornstein suggested that the reader is also implicitly guided by the image of the 'fictive Yeats constructed by the 1895 *Poems*', a figure who emerges 'as an Irish poet devoted to tradition and rural Ireland, to legendary heroes and to the peasantry, and to esoteric pursuit of ideal Beauty', and who shuns 'contemporary causes, urban life, and the emerging middle classes' (1991: 351). This implied author, he added, bore little resemblance to the 'historical young Yeats', who was, among other things, thoroughly metropolitan, worldly and politically engaged (351). In his conclusion, Bornstein paused to reflect on the wider scholarly and theoretical implications of his analysis.

In remaking his poems Yeats remade himself, as his quatrain on the subject reminds us. In so doing, he offers us today a middle ground between the old fixed, stable author and fixed, stable text on the one hand, and the elimination of the author and substitution of endless textual free-play on the other. For what Yeats finally created was a process rather than a product, in which a successive but finite remaking of texts and selves substitutes for the fixing of them. (1991: 778)

Here Bornstein offers us an inviting vision of a world beyond the cold war between history and theory, bibliography and criticism, a world in which authors are neither worryingly absent nor oppressively present. Far from being a stable guarantor of the text's fixed meaning, Yeats appears now as the protean agent of its rich but finite multivocality.

But can the conflicts and divisions within literary studies be so easily and neatly resolved? And does Bornstein's argument really take us forward into a promised land beyond tired polemics about the 'death of the author'? Attractive as it is, his vision loses some of its conciliatory force when set against his own methodological practice. Most importantly, by focusing on the ways in which what we might for now call Yeats's 'own books' affect meaning, he introduced the radical idea of the decentred author while remaining firmly committed to the traditional preoccupation with authorial control. True, a more complex image of the author emerges from his investigation, which uncovered the strategies the 1890s Yeats adopted 'first to create a self-image' and then to devise 'a foil to the allegedly more politically and socially-involved Yeats of the early twentieth century' (Bornstein 1991: 339). But, in the end, all we have is what Yeats, the less integral but still privileged author, created. The modes of publication, and hence the possible meanings and selves, over which he had less direct influence are inevitably obscured. In short, for Bornstein, the meanings of 'The Lake Isle of Innisfree', to stay with my example, are relatively finite, because Yeats is still firmly in charge. What I would like to ask in this chapter is what happens to the meanings of the poem, and indeed to our understanding of Yeats's position in the literary field of the 1890s, if we take a more comprehensive look at the first decade of 'The Lake Isle's' publishing history in Britain. Bearing in mind that it appeared not only in *The Countess Kathleen* (1892) and in *Poems* (1895 and 1899), but in W. E. Henley's *National Observer* (13 December 1890), *The Book of the Rhymers' Club* (1892), the Religious Tract Society's *Leisure Hour* (August 1896), William and Elizabeth Sharp's anthology *Lyra Celtica* (1896), and Stopford Brooke and Rolleston's *A Treasury of Irish Poetry in the English Tongue* (1900), can we remain as confident in the relative stability of its meanings as Bornstein believes? Indeed, is it not possible that the image Yeats wished to project in his 'own books' was not just that he was a particular kind of author, but that he was one who had some control over his text's reception, a privilege not as easily accorded him in other publishing formats?

* * *

In early November 1890, Yeats sent 'The Lake Isle', along with 'The Old Pensioner', directly to Henley, saying 'I enclose two short poems for Scots Observer if suitable' (Yeats, 1986: 232 and 243). Though this marked the beginning of the poem's complex public life, he had been sitting on the manuscript for almost two years. As he told Katharine Tynan in a letter of 21 December 1888, in which he included an incomplete and laboured early draft, the poem was a by-product of his second work of prose fiction, *John Sherman* (1891), which he had begun earlier that year.

> In my story I make one of the charecters [*sic*] whenever he is in trouble long to go away and live alone on that Island—an old daydream of my own. Thinking over his feelings I made these verses about them— (1986: 120–21)

The early two-stanza draft is, in effect, a lyric version of Sherman's narrative recollection of his childhood fantasy (Part IV, Section IV). Not surprisingly, in relocating these 'feelings' from one genre to another, Yeats changed not only the linguistic register and the literary form in which they were expressed, but the nature of their object. In keeping with the practice of the novel as a whole—all the Irish place names are fictionalised—the actual Innisfree becomes the invented Inniscrewin, and, given this was Yeats's first attempt at a *bildungsroman* in a realist mode, the narrator represents Sherman's longings in a studiedly plain, even colloquial style.

> Often when life and its difficulties had seemed to him like the lessons of some elder boy given to a younger by mistake, it had seemed good to dream of going away to that islet and building a wooden hut there and burning a few years out, rowing to and fro, fishing, or lying on the island slopes by day, and listening at night to the ripple of the water and the quivering of the bushes—full always of unknown creatures—and going out at morning to see the island's edge marked by the feet of birds. (Yeats 1990: 58)

Though a solitary place apart, and despite the hint of 'unknown creatures', the Inniscrewin for which the young Sherman longs is firmly of this world. By contrast, Innisfree, the object of the lyric speaker's desire, is, even in the early draft, a far more magical place. Though more concretely realised—the birds have become linnets, the creatures bees and crickets—it is also now a more mysterious refuge where 'peace will come down dropping slow / Dropping from the veils of the morning'; and where Sherman's prosaically contrasting day and night have evolved into an altogether richer chronology encompassing 'dawn', 'morning', 'noontide', 'evening' and 'midnight', each of which offers its own enigmatic consolations. Moreover, while Sherman simply dreams 'of going away to that islet', the lyric speaker's statement of intent already has the oratorical conviction of the biblical 'I will arise and go'—a piece of stagy allusiveness Yeats would later come to regret. As Yeats insisted in his letter to Tynan, the Innisfree he now had in mind was 'a little rocky Island with a legended past' (Yeats 1986: 120).

The version Henley received in late 1890 was radically improved and expanded. The musically and practically unappealing 'dwelling of wattles—of woven wattles and wood work made' has become a 'small cabin . . . of clay and wattles made'; more plausibly, noon now has a 'purple glow' and 'midnight's all a glimmer', not the other way round; and, most importantly, a third stanza, sketching in the speaker's immediate urban context and the profoundly Romantic source of his longing, has been added. Assuming Henley did not tamper with the manuscript—though Yeats claimed he 're-wrote my poems as he re-wrote the early verse of Kipling', there is no evidence to suggest he did in this case—the version he saw, and which subsequently appeared in the *National Observer* (by then its name had changed) for 13 December 1890, was more or less final (Yeats 1972: 38). In fact, in the course of its long public life, the verbal text of 'The Lake Isle'—the 121 words that constitute the literary critic's traditional object of study—remained for Yeats unusually stable. The version we encounter in the *Observer* is not substantially different from the one we find in *Poems* (1895) or, indeed, in Allt and Alspach's *Variorum Edition* (1957). Yet, if the text had already achieved some measure of closure, its meanings and uses, for Yeats and others, had become an open question.

* * *

By mid-December 1890, Yeats had already consolidated his important early relationship with Henley and, with three poems, three reviews and four articles, established himself as one of the *Observer*'s major literary contributors. Only two months after the appearance of his first article in the issue for 2 March 1889, he was on the weekly's promotional list of 'signing contributors', among such leading literary figures as William Archer, Edmund Gosse, Andrew Lang, Richard Garnett and Robert Louis Stevenson (Advertisement 1889: 731). Yet from the start his association with Henley was incongruous. As he admitted in the first draft of his autobiography, written more than a decade after Henley's death in 1903, the political and even literary gulf that divided them was enormous.

> He despised all of Rossetti but 'The Blessed Damozel', never spoke of Pater and probably disliked him, praised Impressionist painting that still meant nothing to me, was a romantic but not of my school, and founded [the] declamatory school of imperialist journalism. (Yeats 1972: 38)

In the end, however, none of this really seemed to matter. 'I always felt that I suffered no loss of dignity from his opposition to all I hoped for Ireland' and that it 'made no difference that I dissented from his judgement of other men'. The advantages of being one of 'Henley's young men' made the gulf between them manageable, if not irrelevant, besides, as he always signed his contributions to the *Observer*, he could, as he put it, 'go my own road in some measure' (1972: 38, and Yeats 1955a: 159). For one thing, at a time of real financial need, Henley was, as Yeats later recalled, 'my chief employer', paying probably as much as £1-1-0 for a short poem like 'A Cradle Song' and £1 a column for reviews and articles (1972: 37). Moreover, as an established man of letters, Henley used his connections and influence to try, not always successfully, to secure him other paid work, and he introduced him to a large, though for Yeats not always congenial, network of writers, critics and journalists.

Yet these financial and social benefits, significant as they were in themselves, were also only a practical expression of Henley's real importance for the young Yeats. What he offered him, above all, was the kind of assurance about his literary quality and status he sought at that stage in his career. As Yeats put it in a letter to Tynan, 'one of his good points is his sympathy with young writers' (1986: 252). Indeed, given his later thoughts about the meaning of their association, it could be argued that Henley played a major part in the formation of his early literary identity. Speculating about Henley's charismatic 'hold' in the draft autobiography, he felt it 'was perhaps that he was never deceived about his taste, that he wished one well, and could not flatter'; or, again, 'I was drawn to him also, I doubt not, by his aristocratic attitudes, his hatred of the crowd and of that logical realism which is but popular oratory' (Yeats 1972: 38–39). On this view, Henley was a distinguished critic whose judgement he could trust, and a prominent man of letters who bolstered his own high-minded anti-populism. A few years later, just before his own father's death in February 1922, he added a further psychological dimension to this analysis. Recalling his early career, and after referring specifically to his father's 'infirmity of will', he noted 'I had to escape this family drifting, innocent, & helpless, & the need for that drew me to dominating men like Henley & Morris' (1986: 520). Part alternative father figure, then, part purist literary role model, and part established impresario, Henley offered Yeats the cultural legitimisation he sought as a young Irish writer on the make in the English 'Republic of Letters'. In what must remain one of the richer ironies of literary history, Henley, the jingoistic author of 'A Song of England', helped fashion Yeats's 1890s Irish poetic self by reflecting back to him the literary self-image he desired.

The other person involved in this dialectical process of self-creation was, of course, Yeats himself. Indeed, any reading of 'The Lake Isle' in the context/envelope of the *Observer* must begin with the fact that the poem was, for Yeats, part of a conscious self-promotional strategy targeted at Henley. Though his general sense of Henley's position, gleaned no doubt from various sources (his own reading, hearsay, etc.) would have enabled him to pursue this odd 'elective affinity', he also had Henley's unsigned review of *The Wanderings of Oisin and Other Poems* to guide him. The image Yeats saw of himself in the review, which appeared in the *Observer* for 9 March 1889, was extremely flattering—he told Tynan it was a 'splendid article'—but it was also tellingly incomplete (1986: 152). Despite the varied nature of his first major book, Henley emphasised Yeats's Irishness by entitling the review 'A New Irish Poet' and by saying his 'verses have the wilding charm, the wayward grace touched with elfishness, characteristic of true Irish song' (Henley 1889: 446). At the same time, he placed him firmly in an English literary tradition by comparing him favourably to Shelley, Tennyson and Morris, and, more importantly, he made sure that his Irishness would be understood in a particular way. Given his own commitment to the late-Victorian cult of manliness, he was, for instance, eager to report that, for all his admirable interest in the 'rainbow-coloured lands of fantasy', this new Irish poet was not an effeminate Arnoldian Celt: 'There are lines in which the tones of war and hunting and heroic comradeship ring out bravely; the writer can stir the blood as well as beguile and lull with sensuous dreams' (1889: 446–47). But, in case this gave the impression that the *Observer* and its editor were backing a manly but also possibly insurrectionary Irish poet—Arnold's effiminate Celts were, of course, famously 'ineffectual in politics'—he hastened to add that none of the poems had any contemporary political relevance (Arnold 1962: 346). Much to Yeats's delight, he praised, among others, *Wanderings*, 'King Goll', 'The Meditation of the Old Fisherman' and 'The Song of the Last Arcadian', but he kept silent about 'How Ferencz Renyi Kept Silent' and insisted that the Fenians mentioned in *Wanderings* were simply part of the mythic past. In his conclusion, he invited his readers to welcome a poet who 'can speak out with the right heroic accent, and kindle the blood with tales of the (strictly historical) deeds that were done in the brave old days "When the Fenians made foray at the morning with Bran, Sgeolan, Lomair"' (Henley 1889: 447).

With this clear opinion at hand, Yeats understandably ensured that Henley got the first option on only a very select range of poems. In the five years from 1890 to 1894, during which his sixteen *Observer* poems appeared, he also contributed eleven others to a wide range of periodicals, including the Parnellite *United Ireland* (the *Observer*'s Irish *bête noire*), the nationalist *Irish Weekly Independent*, the new populist London literary review *The Bookman* and the Religious Tract Society's illustrated family monthly *Leisure Hour*.[1] Not all of these would have suited Henley's taste. Some, like 'In the Firelight' (*Leisure Hour*, March 1891), were immature, not to say mawkish, but others, like 'Mourn—and Then Onward!' (*United Ireland*, 10 October 1891), the elegy for Parnell, and the nationalist 'Ballad of Earl Paul' (*Irish Weekly Independent*, 8 April 1893), were too overtly political. Just how conscious Yeats's careful selection of poems for Henley was can be seen from one of his remarks to Tynan. 'You should not have sent the poem [most probably 'The Wild Geese:

---

[1] See Allan Wade, *A Bibliography of the Writings of W. B. Yeats* (London: Rupert Hart-Davis, 1951), pp. 291–303. Besides 'The Lake Isle', Yeats's poetic contributions to the *Observer* were 'A Cradle Song', 'Father Gilligan', 'The Old Pensioner', 'A Man who Dreamed of Fairyland', 'A Fairy Song', 'Kathleen' (later 'A Dream of a Blessed Spirit'), 'An Epitaph' (later 'A Dream of Death'), 'Rosa Mundi' (later 'The Rose of the World'), 'The Peace of the Rose' (later 'The Rose of Peace'), 'The White Birds', 'Fergus and the Druid', 'The Rose in my Heart' (later 'Aedh tells of the Rose in his Heart'), 'The Celtic Twilight' (later 'Into the Twilight'), 'The Faery Host' (later 'The Hosting of the Sidhe'), 'Cap and Bell' (later 'The Cap and Bells').

A Lament for the Irish Jacobites'] to the Scots Observer,' he told her in a letter of May 1890, 'it was too political—Irish exiles are out of their range I think' (Yeats 1986: 217). He then immediately went on to say he had just sent Henley 'Father Gilligan', the wry folk ballad which, in the *Scots Observer* version, came with the authenticating paratext: 'A Legend told by the people of Castleisland, Kerry' (Yeats 1890b: 174–75). Clearly, in Yeats's view, disillusioned priests miraculously saved from disgrace and memorialised by the 'people', not revolutionary exiles, represented an acceptable version of Ireland and Irishness for Henley's *Observer*, a version he was quite willing to help promote.

As importantly, however, the intersection between the set of *Observer* poems and the 1895 canon suggests Yeats treated Henley's weekly as a nursery for the poetic self he created in his first collected volume. Of the thirteen poems from the key section 'The Rose' that first appeared in periodicals (eight never did), twelve came from the *Observer*. Indeed, while less than half (five out of eleven) of the poems not published by Henley in the early 1890s made it into any of Yeats's books—'Mourn—and Then Onward!' and 'The Ballad of Earl Paul', for instance, were excluded—versions of all his *Observer* poems, as well as the two he contributed to Henley's next venture, *The New Review*, became and remained part of the canon. When we think about Yeats's protean existence in the early 1890s, then, we should not focus simply on the *contrast* between his 'poetic' and his 'historical' selves, as Bornstein puts it, but on the more complex *interrelationship* between the various poetic selves embodied in the periodicals and the more selective construct that emerges in the books. With the *Observer* Yeats had designs not only on Henley, but on posterity, or, more likely, he came to think of Henley as a gatekeeper to posterity.

The poetic self he revealed to Henley by selecting suitable poems was also closely related to the implied authorial self he projected in his more consciously inflected prose contributions. In the early articles and reviews, which Henley actively encouraged, he presented himself as a distinctly Irish writer who celebrated the peasantry, folklore and rural life of the West of Ireland—Sligo in particular—and who seemingly had more interest in the 'bloodless, dim nation' than in questions of Irish nationhood (Yeats 1889b: 150). As he remarked in *Autobiographies*, 'that I might avoid unacceptable opinions, I wrote nothing but ghost or fairy stories' (1955a: 160). While his first articles show him to have been especially responsive to Henley's initial Scottish and largely Protestant readership, he also assumed he was writing for an educated, urban, sceptical, generally non-Irish audience, those who 'listen to eloquent speaking, go to discussions, read books and write them, settle all the affairs of the universe', a fair estimation of Henley's intended readership (Yeats 1889a: 692). To them he explained:

> It is far easier to be sensible in cities than in many country places I could tell you off [sic]. When one walks on those grey roads at evening by the scented elder-bushes of the white cottages, watching the faint mountains gathering the clouds upon their heads, one all too readily seems to discover, beyond the thin cobweb veil of the senses, those creatures, the goblins, hurrying from the white square stone door to the north, or from the Heart Lake in the south. (1889b: 101)

'To the wise peasant,' he added later, 'the green hills and woods round him are full of never-fading mystery' (1889c: 550).

For Henley and the readers of the *Observer*, then, he defined himself, as much in these early articles as in a poem like 'The Lake Isle', as a champion of the West of Ireland figured as a lost paradise in which a happily primitive Irish culture, transcendental in outlook though still rooted in the natural world, held out against the disenchantments of modernity. Contemporary political realities formed no part of this mythic vision, though, once, he did allow himself, or he was allowed, to reflect that for the Irish peasant Heaven was much like earth, except that 'now and then a landlord or an agent or a gauger will go by begging his bread, to show how God divides the righteous from the unrighteous' (Yeats 1890a: 409). This was in a signed review of Lady Wilde's *Ancient Cures, Charms, and Usages of Ireland* (1890), in which he none the less remained silent about her nationalist sympathies. Keeping up this intricate balance between his own diverse allegiances and Henley's was, of course, in his interests, but it was not always easy, and on some occasions it defeated him. He found it impossible, for instance, to review Ellen O'Leary's collection *Lays of Country, Home and Friends* (1891) for 'so ultra-Tory a paper'; and about an article on the 'Revival of Irish Literature', he told Henley the 'subject was thorney [sic] & I fear I may not in making it suitable for my own purposes have made it suitable for you' (1986: 250 and 521). Henley evidently agreed, as it never appeared in the *Observer*.

The extent to which Yeats fashioned himself for Henley's *Observer* might suggest that the differences in the degree of influence he had over his reception in periodicals as opposed to his 'own books' was negligible. Yet the realities of periodical publication also inevitably complicated matters. This was not only because a strong editor, like Henley, influenced his output by encouraging, commissioning and/or revising particular contributions. Such interventions were, after all, not the prerogative of periodical editors alone. Rather, it had to do with the effect the specific conditions of periodical publication had on his own stratagems—in particular, the scattered and relatively unadorned appearance of the poems, and the juxtaposition of miscellaneous matter. If books are, on Genette's definition, the natural home of the paratext, periodicals are a mode in which, for those who need a single term, the co-text predominates. This is not to say that Yeats could not add certain paratextual elements to the periodical versions of his poems. Like 'Father Gilligan', 'The White Birds', for instance, appeared in the *National Observer*, but not in any of the books, with a brief explanatory note inserted below the title:

(The birds of fairyland are said to be white as snow. The Danaan Islands are the islands of the fairies.) (Yeats 1892: 641)

If the paratext is, as Genette claims, 'always the conveyor of a commentary that is authorial or more or less legitimated by the author ... at the service of a better reception for the text', then this supplementary note, designed to guide readers not familiar with Irish legends and folklore, and set apart typographically, is, strictly speaking, paratextual (Genette 1997: 2). Yet in the periodical context these important occasional notes, like the poems themselves, were set within a vast body of miscellaneous matter, the effects of which were neither as clear nor as manageable.

To analyse these, it would be useful to distinguish between what we could call the authorial and the non-authorial co-text. As we have seen, the meaning of 'The Lake Isle' in the context of the *Observer* is neither fully determined by, nor separable from our understanding of its function as a part of the mutually acceptable version of Ireland and Irishness negotiated between Yeats and Henley in the early 1890s. Here all the contributions—poems, stories, reviews and articles—authored by Yeats and authorised by Henley are relevant. Together they constitute the authorial co-text: 'authorial' because Yeats still had some measure of control over it, and hence over his self-presentation in the *Observer*; 'co-textual' because it is, unlike the paratext, only indirectly and implicitly 'at the service of a better reception' for the poem. The non-authorial co-text, in contrast, is an editorial matter, but it does not follow from this that it has no bearing on the reception of 'The Lake Isle'. In theory, the persons responsible for the contents and/or layout of the periodical—proprietor, editor, designer, printer, illustrator, etc.—may use the opportunity to create a commentary which may affect, but not necessarily enhance, a particular text's reception.

The most obvious example here would be the addition of accompanying illustrations, a point which is, as Warwick Gould has shown, particularly well demonstrated by the one 1890s version of 'The Lake Isle' I shall not be discussing in detail (Gould 1978). The version of the poem which appeared in *The Leisure Hour* for August 1896 was accompanied by a full-page illustration by the poet's father, John Butler Yeats, who told his daughter in a letter of April that year:

> I drew an Irish longhaired chief in chain armour stalking slowly along using his spear as a staff and leaning heavily on it, an Irish wolf hound following him, its tail between its legs, the place a wood of oak trees black with *forest darkness*. (J. B. Yeats 1972: 32)

This was, on the face of it, a perplexing illustration for a poem which has nothing to say about primitive chieftains, wolfhounds or shady oak forests. Yet, as Gould points out, the image does offer the reader an illuminating if lateral-minded commentary. Most generally, it emphasises, as the young Yeats would have appreciated, the legendary associations Innisfree had for both him and his father; and, more specifically, by placing the figure of the chieftain at the centre of things, it revealed both Yeats's shared indebtedness to William Wood-Martin's *History of Sligo, County and Town* (1882–92)—there Wood-Martin described the island's connection to the legend of Free, an ill-fated young warrior, a story Yeats would use in 'The Danaan Quicken Tree' in 1893. In effect, the illustration as non-authorial co-text said more about the poem's intertextual origins and implicit mythopoeic significance than the young Yeats himself had allowed. Then again, the non-authorial co-text may have no planned effect, but this does not preclude the possibility of its still having some unintended influence, fortunate or unfortunate.

This is especially true of certain materials surrounding 'The Lake Isle' in the *National Observer*. For various reasons, some more obvious than others, Yeats, as we have seen, excluded or played down any explicit political references in his contributions to the stridently unionist *Observer*. Yet, for the same reasons, it is difficult to read 'The Lake Isle' in its periodical context without being aware of contemporary political issues. This is the most telling effect of the non-authorial co-text that begins with Frederick Greenwood's article entitled 'Sedition-Sops for Ireland' which appears alongside 'The Lake Isle', extends to the issue for 13 December 1890 which, given the recent rupture in the Irish Parliamentary Party, devoted twelve and a half columns, almost half the issue, to Irish matters, and finally encompasses the entire run in which the West of Ireland, in particular, figures regularly as a desperate rural backwater populated by an inferior 'race'. In fact, given its political outlook and Henley's sympathy towards Yeats's carefully managed project, the *Observer* not unexpectedly offered its readers two competing images of Ireland, even of the West of Ireland: Yeats's celebratory mythopoeic version, and its own politically expedient 'ultra-Tory' version.

In the contemporary Conservative debates about Balfour's new pacificatory Land Purchase Bill, for instance, which the *Observer* supported but which Greenwood, the fervid but always independently minded unionist, criticised in his article, the West of Ireland figured prominently. As the issue for 31 August 1889 noted, it was deemed to be a special region beyond the reach of any land reforms:

> There is a large tract of country in Ireland, comprising West Donegal, the greater part of Mayo and Sligo, Kerry, and a portion of Galway, which no Land Act of the kind hitherto passed can ever really benefit, or even seriously affect. It is no exaggeration to say that, political expediency apart, it would distinctively pay the Government to buy up every tenant within the whole of this area, and provide him with a pension for life conditional upon his consenting to remove from his present habitation. (Unsigned 1889b: 397)

The problem did not simply have to do with the poverty and overcrowding in these areas officially designated 'congested districts', or with the fact that 'the population was not able to draw from the soil a safe and sufficient living', but with the supposed character of the 'Irish peasant' in the region (Unsigned 1890c: 1). While the *Observer* supported Balfour's plan to provide special state relief to the area—though it predictably preferred to encourage 'emigration or migration' and 'the regeneration of the spirit of self-help'—it also endorsed his view that 'the poverty of the West Coast of Ireland is mainly due to the idleness, the ineptitude, the lazy indifference of the people to the wretchedness in which they live' (Unsigned 1890d: 4–5). True, this did not, in its view, really mean they were all that different from the Irish 'national type'. Characterised as it was by its 'subjection to current needs', its 'utter thriftlessness and waywardness of mind' and its political ineptitude—'not the ruling but the ruled'—the 'peasants' of the West simply reinforced the *Observer*'s anti-Irish stereotype (Unsigned 1890b: 485–86). But it was none the less the case that the problems of the West were exacerbated by the fact that the region was one of the key refuges of the 'unadulterated Irish Celt'.

> For, after all, the history of the settlement of this country is the history of the extrusion of the Celt, westwards and northwards, by the Norman, Saxon, and Dane, until he found security in the impregnable highlands of Scotland, Wales, and West and South Ireland. If such facts do not cover some real difference in the fibre and worth of the contending races, they constitute a class of phenomena wholly anomalous and inexplicable. (Unsigned 1889a: 402)

Still, it was unfortunate that the 'mere Irish' did not 'disappear before the colonists, as the Maoris have done in recent times in New Zealand' (1889a: 402). 'It is not wonderful,' another of Henley's observers added, 'if the wearied Saxon have sometimes heaved a sigh over the strange partiality of Nature which dooms the noble savage of other continents but protects that other kind of wild man he grows at home' (Unsigned 1890a: 692).

Reading 'The Lake Isle' of the *Observer* is, then, in part, a matter of understanding its relations to the authorial co-text. While its elevated language and sonorous metre create an atmosphere all its own, its representation of Innisfree as a magical primitivist idyll which answers to the modern, urban speaker's most profound, unconditioned longings is incidentally informed by the mythic image of the West of Ireland Yeats projected in his other contributions. Reading it in this context involves, I have suggested, not only a textual analysis of these contributions and their interrelationships, but a sociological analysis of Yeats's association with Henley and of his career strategies in the early 1890s. What 'The Lake Isle' meant in the *Observer* and what Yeats used it for, the *literary* interests it was meant to serve, at that point in his career cannot easily be distinguished. At the same time our perception of the poem is coloured by the highly politicised accompanying materials over which he, as a contributor, had no control. Just as his mythopoeic celebration of the mysteries of the Sligo landscape is pitted against the *Observer*'s politically expedient insistence on its destitution, so his idealisation of the primitive is set against a racist idea of the uncivilised 'wild man'.

The extent to which we see these discourses as complementary, contradictory or simply contiguous depends mainly on how we read

Henley. We could, for instance, take John Frayne's sceptical view. He felt Henley's support for Yeats was not 'innocent', since he knew his contributions 'would have confirmed in an English reader the prejudice that the Irish were hopeless dreamers and their affairs had best be kept in capable English hands' (Yeats 1970: 24). Though many of Henley's clubland readers might well have responded in this way, and seen Yeats and 'The Lake Isle' as two good reasons for maintaining the Union, the little available evidence, notably Henley's review of *Wanderings*, suggests he was, for all the violence of his often inconsistent opinions, seldom capable of such cynical calculation. It is more likely that Yeats's contributions were, for him, acceptable because they could be seen to have no contemporary political relevance. 'The Lake Isle's' appearance in the *Observer* was, in other words, less a consequence of Henley's political calculations, and more a result of his no less questionable assumptions about the nature of the 'literary'. Yet the case for considering the promiscuous effects of the non-authorial co-text need not rest on speculations about Henley's motives. Whether taken to be complementary, contradictory or merely contiguous, the simultaneous presence of Yeats's consciously inflected 'literary' version of the West of Ireland and the *Observer*'s tendentiously 'political' version reveals just how contested and unstable the boundaries between these two categories were in the 1890s.

* * *

The subsequent publishing history of 'The Lake Isle' in the 1890s reveals a similar interplay between the diversity of Yeats's alliances and the growing complexity of his evolving interests. If 'The Lake Isle's' appearance in the *Observer* showed something of his eagerness to earn the recognition of the established English avant-garde, its re-emergence in *The Book of the Rhymers' Club* (1892) reinforced his ties to what he called 'the very newest literary generation' in London (Yeats 1989: 57). Though, as he admitted, not all the club's members were young—John Todhunter, for one, was in his fifties—most of the major players were, like him, in their twenties. Their first anthology was, then, intended to be a provocative literary statement—Yeats called it a 'manifesto'—designed to seize the cultural high ground by naming and publicising the new self-appointed 1890s avant-garde (1989: 59). Though published by the enterprising young London publisher Elkin Mathews, the anthology was initiated allegedly by Yeats, edited by a committee of Rhymers—Richard Le Gallienne (Mathews's reader), George Greene, Lionel Johnson, Todhunter and

Ernest Dowson—and financed by the twelve participating members themselves (see Nelson 1971: 151–83). Prefaced by a list of the contributors, many of whom were not English, it was, in effect, the book of and by the arrivistes on the English literary scene. The advantages for Yeats of this dual alliance with London's established and emergent avant-garde were clearly evident in the *Observer*'s review of the anthology. Though its title—'Minors'—ensured the newcomers knew their place, the anonymous reviewer, who gave special praise to 'The Lake Isle', singled out Yeats, who was 'ever an artist and a poet', and added 'for the other contributors, let it in fairness be recorded of them that they do their best' (Unsigned 1892: 646).

The next two anthologies in which 'The Lake Isle' appeared had less to do with Yeats's advances in the English literary field, and more to do with his increasingly intricate Irish and Pan-Celtic connections. *Lyra Celtica* (1896) was a Scottish initiative published by the new firm Patrick Geddes and Colleagues of Edinburgh, edited by Elizabeth Sharp, and introduced and annotated by her husband William (alias 'Fiona Macleod'), who was Geddes's literary adviser. Though Geddes himself had a wide range of interests—he was a progressive biologist, sociologist, town-planner, educationalist and a patriotic Scottish nationalist—he shared the Sharps' commitment to the Pan-Celtic cause. As Elizabeth put it, Geddes and her husband were both 'ardent Celts who believed in the necessity of preserving the finer subtle qualities and the spiritual heritage of their race against the encroaching predominance of the materialistic ideas and aims of the day' (Sharp 1910: 248–49). While the firm's biannual five-shilling magazine *The Evergreen: A Northern Seasonal* (1895–96), edited by William Sharp, reflected its full range of interests, the anthology was the flagship of its 'Celtic Library'. Never as comprehensive as its subtitle announced—*An Anthology of Representative Celtic Poetry: Ancient Irish, Alban, Gaelic, Breton, Cymric, and Modern Scottish and Irish Celtic Poetry*—it was, as Sharp admitted in his introduction, 'intentionally given over mainly to modern poetry' and to the myriad sub-divisions within recent Celtic culture, ranging in twelve sections from the 'Scoto-Celtic (Middle Period)' to the 'Irish (Modern and Contemporary)', and from the 'Contemporary Anglo-Celtic Poets' (Welsh, Cornish and Manx) to the largely North American 'Celtic Fringe' (Sharp 1896: xix). It was, in short, a propaganda vehicle for the Celtic literary revival which, as Yeats remarked in a letter to Sharp, 'is certain to be very influential & to help forward a matter I have myself much at heart—the mutual understanding & sympathy of the Scotch Welsh & Irish Celts' (Yeats 1997: 37).

Though published four years before Brooke and Rolleston's *Treasury of Irish Poetry in the English Tongue* (1900), Sharp's collection was, as he made clear in his introduction, in direct competition with it from the start. Recalling the inaugural address entitled 'The Need and Use of Getting Irish Literature into the English Tongue' which Brooke gave to the new London-based Irish Literary Society in March 1893—it was here that Brooke first called for a 'Golden Treasury' of Irish verse—Sharp gently rebuked him for his 'over-emphasis on the word Irish, which he frequently uses instead of Celtic', and then went on to quote and rewrite the conclusion to his lecture:

> When we have got the old [Celtic] legendary tales rendered into fine prose and verse, I believe we shall open out English poetry to a new and exciting world, an immense range of subjects, entirely fresh and full of inspiration. Therefore, as I said, get them out into English, and then we may bring England and [Celtdom] into a union which never can suffer separation. (Sharp 1896: xxxv)[2]

In their revised form, these were, for Sharp, 'inspiring words' (1896: xxxv). Yet the conflict of interests between the anthologists of the Irish and the Pan-Celtic literary revivals remained chiefly his bugbear. When Brooke's *Treasury* eventually appeared in 1900, it was preoccupied with other disputes, internal to the Irish literary tradition itself. Published by the eminent London firm Smith, Elder & Co.; promulgated at the Irish Literary Society's first meeting; edited by its newly elected President, and his son-in-law, the former Rhymer, T. W. Rolleston, who was its first secretary; and dedicated to Sir Charles Gavan Duffy, its first President, and, as the dedication pointed out, the editor of 'the first worthy collection of Irish National poetry', the *Treasury* embodied the Society's position in book form (1900: v). As the carefully worded title declared, and as Brooke reiterated in his introduction, it was not only intended to be an Irish version of F. T. Palgrave's famous *Golden Treasury* (1861), it was also a rejoinder to those in the Gaelic League who took their inspiration from the President of the Irish National Literary Society, Dublin, Douglas Hyde,

---

[2] Sharp was no doubt working from memory or from his own notes, as the published version of Brooke's lecture reads: 'When we have got them [Irish stories] into fine prose and verse, I believe we shall open out to English Poetry a new and exciting world, an immense range of subjects, entirely fresh and full of inspiration. Therefore, as I said, get them out into English, and then we may bring England and Ireland into a union which never can suffer separation' (See Brooke 1893: 56–57 and 62).

and more particularly from an especially uncompromising reading of his 1892 lecture, 'The Necessity for De-Anglicising Ireland'. Not that the anthology and its nationalist editors were against de-Anglicisation. 'Were it possible that Irish literature should be anglicised,' Brooke insisted, 'there would soon be no literature worth the name in Ireland' (1900: xix). Rather, while retaining some sympathy for the league's efforts in the spheres of education and scholarship, he, like Rolleston, believed Gaelicisation was not the only, or the most effective, means of asserting Ireland's cultural independence. On pragmatic and political grounds, he argued that 'if Irish writers do not deviate into an imitation of English literature, but cling close to the spirit of their native land, they do well for their country when they use the English tongue' (1900: viii). His anthology was, therefore, committed to those poets, like Yeats, who affirmed Ireland's national traditions by translating its 'ancient myths, legends, and stories' into a language that was 'rapidly becoming universal' (viii).

* * *

Yeats was at the centre of the various social networks and cultural controversies out of which these three anthologies emerged. So too was 'The Lake Isle'. The only poem of his to appear in all three, it was repeatedly co-opted by the advocates of these various causes and reframed by the books themselves. By placing it in particular bibliographical, textual and paratextual configurations, each anthology had designs on its reception, designs Yeats implicitly supported but which for the most part remained outside his direct control. *The Book of the Rhymers' Club* was the exception. He had a considerable say in both its production and reception. Though it was, in his view, 'the manifesto of the circle', the book itself contained only the vaguest indications of their collective rationale (Yeats 1989: 59). To obtain any sense of this readers had to rely on the conjunction of the title and the two paratextual poems that opened and closed the volume, respectively 'At the Rhymers' Club: The Toast' by Ernest Rhys and 'The Song of the Songsmiths' by George Greene, both of which were italicised and so typographically set apart from the book's fifty-five other poems. Their central point was that 'Rhyme', their metonym for poetry, was not what it used to be—Rhys looked back to Ben Jonson and Robert Herrick, Greene simply to the 'ancient fire' in 'a far, forgotten clime'—and that its fate lay in their 'prentice-hand' (Yeats 1892: 1 and 92–93). Predictably, they found, as Rhys put it, 'the Muse degraded, / And changed, I fear, and faded' (2). Limited as it was, their diagnosis of this decline was no less expected: poetry was impoverished because it had been sold out to various alien interests. Testifying to the club's new purism, Rhys proclaimed: 'We drink defiance / To-night to all but Rhyme, / And most of all to Science' (1). Adopting a characteristically regal figure to reinforce the idea of poetry's sovereign authority, Greene added that their 'task' was to restore 'the queenly rhyme' with 'reverent toil' (93–94). The only specific indication of the way they intended to undertake this was the selection itself, which expressed their Paterian commitment to the short lyric as the highest form in the hierarchy of poetic genres. Though the anthology contained a wide variety of short forms, including sonnets, ballads, odes and villanelles, it clearly declared itself for concise, highly charged modes of poetic expression and against the potentially impure discursiveness of longer, narrative modes. This new poetic austerity was underscored by the book itself. Derived from the innovative designs associated principally with Whistler and Walter Blaikie, its rather uninspired plain yellow cloth cover, simple, unornamented typographical layout, bold use of white space and untrimmed pages, combined with its five-shilling price and well-advertised limited print run, embodied the Rhymers' modernity and purist exclusivity in bibliographical form.

The person who developed these suggestive generalisations into something more substantial was Yeats himself. He had as much to do with the creation of the anthology as with the production of its meanings, since he spent his career writing and rewriting the club's manifesto, producing, in effect, a series of retrospective paratexts, ranging from the essay of April 1892 entitled 'The Rhymers' Club', which formed part of his 'Celt in London' series for the *Boston Pilot*, to his 1936 Introduction to *The Oxford Book of Modern Verse*. These statements varied according to the period and context in which he was writing, and most often said more about Yeats than about the Rhymers, but each also underscored and developed Rhys and Greene's general claims. As Yeats emphasised from the start, the Rhymers were too dissimilar to be a 'school of poets in the French sense' (Yeats 1989: 57). What united them, more than any particular aesthetic—he mentions, by way of contrast, the French Decadents, Symbolists, Parnassians and Naturalists—was their reaction to the alleged bankruptcy of the English poetic establishment. In the 1892 article, he set the frivolous 'search for new forms merely' of 'the Gosse, Lang and Dobson school'—the 1870s avant-garde—against the new seriousness with which the Rhymers wished to look 'once more upon the world' (1989: 57–58). Referring specifically to the

Music Hall preoccupations of John Davidson (though a regular Rhymer, he was not in the first anthology) and Arthur Symons, he added 'the typical young poet of our day is an aesthete with a surfeit, searching sadly for his lost Philistinism' (59).

Only six months later, however, he was emphasising the Rhymers' continuities with the aestheticism of their immediate predecessors, notably their belief that 'poetry is an end in itself' (Yeats 1970: 248). True, this was in an article for *United Ireland*, entitled 'Hopes and Fears for Irish Literature', in which he typically played the English off against the Irish, and vice versa: he set mature, but enervated, English aestheticism against the youthful, but too highly politicised, energies of the artless Irish. Aware as always of his own sensitive position, for this readership he also distanced himself from the English by stressing the 'dependence, as I conceived it, of all great art and literature upon conviction and upon heroic life' (1970: 248). Yet, over the years, the Rhymers' austere commitment to 'all but Rhyme' established itself in Yeats's mind as the key to their collective rationale. In 1912, after mentioning his own reaction to the 'rhetorical poetry of the Irish politicians'—i.e. the Young Irelanders, in particular—he claimed to have found in London 'a group of young lyric writers who were also against rhetoric' (Yeats 1975: 413). He now saw them, as he put it in 1936, reacting not to the formalist aestheticism of Dobson, Lang and Gosse but to the supposed moral, scientific and political 'discursiveness' of the previous generation—Browning, Tennyson and Swinburne (Yeats 1936: ix). For him, the Rhymers were, in short, purist allies whose generational struggles within the English poetic tradition resembled and reinforced his own quarrels with the Irish literary establishment.

In so far as his association with the Rhymers consolidated his position within the English avant-garde, it built on the achievements of his alliance with Henley's *Observer*. This much is reflected in the poems he contributed to their first anthology. Though 'Dedication of "Irish Tales"', with its references to 'Exiles', Ireland's 'Sorrow' and its nostalgia for the time 'when her own people ruled in wave-worn Eri', is more explicitly political than anything he submitted to Henley, his five other contributions—'The Lake Isle', 'A Man who dreamed of Fairyland', 'Father Gilligan', 'A Fairy Song' and 'An Epitaph'—all came from the *Observer* (Yeats 1892: 54–55). Yet, in the anthology, they not only appeared in a new publishing context/envelope—a miscellaneous collection of fifty-seven short poems under one title—they were made to do new work. Supplemented by Rhys and Greene's paratextual poems and Yeats's own commentaries, the anthology invited its readers to attend to them as a manifestation of the Rhymers' collective bid to redefine poeticity for the 1890s. In this context, for instance, the Irishness of the theme and setting of 'The Lake Isle', which had been crucial in the *Observer*, was now less important than its short first-person lyric form, its metre, diction and syntax. In fact, compared to the many humdrum lyrics that made up the supposedly groundbreaking collection, it was one of the few poems that managed to bring the Rhymers' grand, self-promoting theory somewhere in line with their practice.

In giving voice to the atavistic desires of the first-person speaker, it rejected modernity, and implicitly the authority and advances of 'Science', in a modern poetic idiom the novelty of which was seldom evident elsewhere in the volume. While its determined but pliant rising triple rhythm and variable line lengths hold up well against the ploddingly consistent iambic tetrameter of Ernest Radford's wholly conventional 'A Sundial—Flowers of Time', its precise, often inventive diction ('bee-loud', 'purple glow', etc.) acquires new life when read alongside the stagy abstractions of a poem like Richard Le Gallienne's 'What of the Darkness?' which ends:

> O! is the Darkness too a lying glass,
> Or undistracted do ye find Truth there?—
> What of the Darkness? Is it very fair? (1892: 3 and 85)

Even its familiar languorous tone crackles with surprising energy when compared to the staggering banality of George Greene's lines 'Full of world-weariness, and of the sense / Of unachievement, lies the toiler down' (1892: 18). Indeed, in this motley company its own stylistic flaws seem minor. As Yeats himself recalled in his *Autobiographies*, 'a couple of years later I would not have written that first line with its conventional archaism—'Arise and go'—nor the inversion in the last stanza' (presumably, 'pavements grey'). 'I only understood vaguely and occasionally,' he added, 'that I must for my special purpose use nothing but the common syntax.' Yet, despite these afterthoughts, he was still willing to concede that the poem was 'my first lyric with anything in its rhythm of my own music'. Attesting to the affinity between his own aims and the Rhymers' purist literary values, he explained: 'I had begun to loosen rhythm as an escape from rhetoric and from that emotion of the crowd that rhetoric brings' (Yeats 1955a: 153–54). Read in the context of his own oeuvre, then, it could be argued that the poem is an early partial failure of his individual poetic project. In *The Book of the Rhymers'*

Club, however, it is one of the few poems affirming the partial success of their collective assault on the English poetic establishment.

* * *

If the Rhymers' anthology advocated, with Yeats's explicit support, a formalist reading of 'The Lake Isle', *Lyra Celtica* did precisely the reverse with at most his tacit agreement. It privileged a biographical and thematic reading. This was not only because William Sharp, in his notes, used the last stanza of the poem to confirm Yeats's Celtic roots; or because the poems were arranged according to their authors' geographical and historical origins—'Irish (Contemporary)' in Yeats's case. Rather, it was because the anthology rested on the assumption that 'The Lake Isle' was, like all the other poems it contained, in the first instance an expression of its author's racial origins. As Sharp typically pointed out, with some inventive inaccuracy, in his short biographical note at the back of the volume, Yeats had the right Celtic pedigree and upbringing:

> Born (of an Irish father, and of a Cornish [*sic*, Susan Pollexfen's family were, in fact, originally from Devon] mother come of a family settled in Ireland) at Sandymount, Dublin, in 1866 [*sic*]; but early life chiefly spent in Sligo, and on the Connaught seaboard. Of late years, Mr Yeats has passed much of his time in London, but is never absent from Ireland for any long period—
> ". . . for always night and day
>   I hear lake-water lapping with low sounds on the shore;
> While I stand on the roadway, or on the pavements grey,
>   I hear it in the deep heart's core". (Sharp 1896: 398)

For Sharp, these lines were clearly no longer an expression of an anonymous urban speaker's longing for a primitive, rural idyll; they were a testament to the depth of Yeats's racial feeling, genuine or invented.

Yet, never one to fuss over precise details or restrictive definitions, and eager as he was to avoid the charge of being a 'zealous Celticist', Sharp also accepted that 'Celtic' was as much a cultural as a racial category (1896: xxviii). In the absence of 'Celtic blood', one could always detect the 'Celtic strain'; and, more bizarrely, one also had to recognise that one 'may at any moment encounter the Celtic brain in the Anglo-Saxon flesh' (xxv and xxvii). On these grounds he was willing to make a case for the inclusion in the anthology of Milton,

Keats, Byron, Scott, Burns, Shelley, Coleridge, Swinburne, Tennyson and Stevenson. After all, he rhapsodised, 'it is an unfrontiered land, this pleasant country in the geography of the soul which we call Bohemia; and here all parochial and national, and even racial distinctions fall away' (xxviii). But, he added, in a more pragmatic mood:

> To avoid confusion, the Editor has refrained from representing poets whose 'Celtic strain' is more or less obviously disputable; hence the wise ignoring of the claims even of Scott and Burns. Byron was more Celtic in blood than in brain, and is represented really by virtue of this accidental [sic] kinship. (xliii)

With this makeshift Pan-Celticism without borders, it is not surprising that Yeats occupied the position he did in Sharp's book. He was not simply one indisputably Celtic author among the eighty-seven named in the table of contents. Celtic in blood, brain and style, he was 'pre-eminently representative of the Celtic genius of to-day' (xliv).

Sharp's critical opinions were as derivative as the intricately entwined harps, shamrocks and latticework of the anthology's 'Celtic' cover design and ornamentations by Helen Hay. In his introduction, he simply rehashed Arnold, whom he described as 'the most sympathetic and penetrating critic of the Celtic imagination' (like Arnold, he also cited Renan's 'La Poesie de la Race Celtique' [*Essais* 1859] with approval) (xliii and xlviii). Admittedly, his Arnold was only a pro-Celtic cultural revisionist eager, like him, to reclaim a marginalised sensibility for English literature. He makes no mention of Arnold's view that the Celts were not capable of producing 'true art, the *architectonicé* which shapes great works'; nor does he consider the political interests at stake in Arnold's analysis (Arnold 1962: 345). For Sharp the primary value of the 1867 essay lay in its characterisation of the 'Celtic strain' which he proceeded to rehearse in his introduction. He directed his readers' attention to the 'natural magic', 'strange melancholy', 'rare music', 'deep yearning emotion' and 'cosmic note' of all 'authentic documents of Celtic genius', qualities that justified the juxtaposition of poems as diverse as Byron's doleful love lyric 'When we Two Parted' and the Breton poet Louis Tiercelin's death-wish lyric 'By Menec'hi Shore', which struck 'the keynote of the poetry that is common to all the Celtic races' (1896: xxiii, xxvii, xlix, 421). He also re-affirmed Yeats's particular pre-eminence in explicitly Arnoldian terms. 'In almost every poem he has written,' Sharp noted, 'there is that exquisite remoteness, that dream-like music, and that transporting charm which Matthew Arnold held to be one of the primary tests of poetry, and, in particular, of Celtic poetry' (xliv). This was especially true, of course, of those in the anthology. Though Elizabeth Sharp had wanted to include five of Yeats's poems, in the end, Unwin, the copyright holder, allowed her to publish only three: 'The Lake Isle', 'The White Birds' and 'They went forth to the Battle, but they always fell' (afterwards 'The Rose of Battle') (Yeats 1986: 468–69). William, however, managed to get around these restrictions to some extent by including ample quotations from *The Wanderings of Oisin*, 'The Madness of King Goll', 'The Stolen Child' and 'The Rose of the World' in his introduction. All these confirmed Yeats's status as the exemplary Arnoldian Celt. While the title 'They went forth to Battle, etc.', from Ossian, recalled the epigraph to Arnold's essay, Sharp's reading of 'The Lake Isle' gave some weight to his observation that 'the Irish themselves have given us the most poignant, the most hauntingly sad lyric cries in all modern literature', through which one could hear 'the lament of exiles', 'the history of the Celtic race itself' (1896: xlvi and xlix–l).

The extent to which Yeats endorsed this flamboyant and derivative Arnoldian reading of his poems and position is a vexed question. Initially extremely hostile towards Sharp—when they first met in July 1887, he told Tynan he 'hated his red British face of flaccid contentment'—he soon accepted him as a useful pro-Celtic ally (Yeats 1986: 24). Privately, he supported his Pan-Celtic initiatives, praised *Lyra Celtica*, and made inviting references to 'our movement' (Yeats 1997: 149). In public, he lauded 'Fiona Macleod' as 'le nom le plus intimement lié à ce mouvement, à cette rennaissance celtique, comme disent les journaux' (Yeats 1975: 109). Admittedly, this statement appeared in *L'Irlande Libre*, the propaganda magazine for Maud Gonne's Paris-based Association Irlandaise, in April 1898 when he was most probably still in the dark about 'Fiona's' real identity. And, of course, he agreed to let the Sharps select and comment on some of his work. As he noted in a letter to Unwin about Elizabeth's request for poems, 'Celtic poetry is so much my business that I can hardly refuse her leave to include something' (Yeats 1986: 468–69).

Yet, other factors, notably the fracas over the chairmanship of his own lecture on 'The Celtic Movement' to the Irish Literary Society on 4 December 1897, suggest he was also eager to keep his distance in public from Sharp and his naively Arnoldian views. When faced with the prospect of Sharp chairing the lecture, he was, according to Lady Gregory, 'furious . . . & declared it wd bring ridicule on the whole movement' (Pethica 1996: 156). Tactful and accommodating as ever in private correspondence, he was none the less delighted when Gregory managed to strong arm the reluctant Sharp into backing down. In the lecture, which subsequently appeared, with revisions, as the article entitled 'The Celtic Element in Literature' in the June 1898 issue of Unwin's 'International Review' *Cosmopolis*, he was, after all, far less accepting of Arnold's analysis than Sharp had been. In it he felt obliged to 're-state a little' Arnold's (and Renan's) arguments, to 'see where they are helpful and where they are hurtful' (Yeats 1955b: 174). In fact, the lecture/essay performed an intricate rhetorical manoeuvre which retained the terms of Arnold's argument while subverting its central pro-Celtic point. When Arnold saw 'Celtic melancholy', Yeats saw 'primitive melancholy'; or when he

> asks how much of the Celt must one imagine in the ideal man of genius. I prefer to say, how much of the ancient hunters and fishers and of the ecstatic dancers among hills and woods must one imagine in the ideal man of genius? (1955b: 183–84)

In effect, he shifted the focus of the cultural debate by replacing Arnold's politically charged Celticism with his own more neutral brand of neo-primitivism.

This ostensibly apolitical, even anti-political strategy had its political uses, however, in so far as it left him free to answer any nationalist-motivated scepticism about his own Pan-Celtic sympathies. Responding to D. P. Moran's hard-line public attack on his use of the terms 'Celtic note' and 'Celtic Renaissance', and his supposed Arnoldian enthusiasms, he replied, in a letter to Moran's *The Leader*: 'all I have said or written about Mathew Arnold since I was a boy is an essay in "Cosmopolis", in which I have argued that the characteristics he has called Celtic, mark all races just in so far as they preserve the qualities of the early races of the world' (Yeats 1997: 568). Far from being un-Irish, in other words, his affirmation of Ireland's ancient Celtic roots had everything to do with his reaction to the hollow materialism of modern, especially English, 'civilisation'. On this analysis, the 'heart's deep core' in 'The Lake Isle' was the site of the modern speaker's longings for a primitive Ireland which happened to be Celtic, not of his buried racial feelings as a displaced Celt, a reading Yeats encouraged in *Poems* (1895) and even to some extent in the *Observer*, but which Sharp occluded in *Lyra Celtica*.

* * *

Despite Yeats's often uneasy personal relations with its editors—especially Rolleston—*A Treasury of Irish Poetry in the English*

Tongue was in many ways a more promising venue for 'The Lake Isle' than Sharp's *Lyra Celtica*. This time, at least, he supported both the cause the anthology was intended to advance *and* the editors' interpretation of it. Though Brooke had initially planned to make literary merit—what he called a 'relatively high standard of excellence'—the sole principle of editorial selection, Rolleston convinced him to produce a 'history of Irish poetry in English', partly to promote their cause by documenting the diversity of that tradition, partly to differentiate their product from Yeats's own 'brief Anthology', *A Book of Irish Verse* (1895) (Brooke 1900: ix). This did not mean they saw it as a work of disinterested historical scholarship, however. The 'history of Irish poetry in English' was, for them, not a comprehensive record but a triumphant *bildungsroman*. As Brooke put it in his introduction, readers would find 'here a school of poetry in the making, a child growing into a man' (x). In another rhapsodic blend of figures, he shed a light of sorts on what this developmental process entailed.

> The river of Irish poetry in the English language . . . rose a hundred years ago in the far-off hills, and wrought its turbulent way down the channelled gorge it carved for its stream out of its own mountains. Other streams have joined it, bearing with them various waters; and it has only just now issued from the hills, and begun to flow in quieter and lovelier lands, glancing from ripple to pool and from pool to ripple, among woods and meadows, happy, and making its lovers happy. It is the youngest child of the Goddess Poesy. (1900: xxxiv)

Despite the confusing return of the child figure, used now to situate Irish poetry in relation to world (especially English) literature, his general point is clear enough. The story of Irish poetry in English was, for Brooke, not simply one of growing cultural richness and diversity, but one of progressive autonomy. Without ceasing to be 'Irish', the tradition had gradually become more universally 'poetic', i.e. less narrowly 'political', particularly after the decline of the Fenian movement. 'After '67,' Brooke noted, 'patriotic rage seldom recurs as a separate motive for poetry' (xiii). Hence his lofty image of the 'youngest child of the Goddess Poesy': 'it is only quite lately that modern Irish poetry can claim to be a fine art' (ix). The aim of his value-laden *Treasury* was, then, not only to answer the Gaelic League hard-liners by promoting an alternative version of Irishness but to reconstruct the 'history of the development of a special national art' (x).

These aims governed the arrangement of the book and, most importantly, the physical placement of Yeats's nine poems. Located at the end of Book V, they were placed for the reader not simply in the context of a century-old Irish poetic tradition, but as its telos. They marked the highest literary achievement to date of a history that began, according to the anthology, with 'The Wearin' o' the Green', dated 1798 by the editors and described as the 'finest of Irish street-ballads' (1900: 2). The exact significance of this positioning is not immediately obvious. For one thing, we should notice that the twenty-nine authors included in Book V (among others, Todhunter, Johnson, 'Æ' [George Russell], Tynan-Hinkson, Hyde, Rolleston and Brooke) are not arranged alphabetically or in order of seniority. For once, Yeats is at the end of the list not simply because his surname happened to begin with a 'Y'. For another, we need to see that Book V is intellectually, if not physically, the end of the anthology. The concluding section, Book VI, which includes such figures as Edward Dowden, George Savage-Armstrong—two of Yeats's key Irish enemies—and the Rhymer George Greene, is beyond the pale of the editors' official Irish canon, the site of the poetic West Britons. As Brooke commented charitably but firmly, and no doubt with an eye on his Gaelic League critics:

> It is impossible not to admire the subtlety, tenderness, and love of nature of these poets, but their place is apart in an Anthology of Irish poetry. They have not kept, along with their devotion to their art, the spirit of their native land. (xiv)

The arrangement of the six books was, in other words, not simply chronological. They were intended loosely to represent 'on the whole distinct phases' in the 'general movement of Irish poetry during the nineteenth century', from the popular 'ballads and songs' of the late eighteenth century in Book I, to the patriotic and humorous early nineteenth-century poems of Book II, to the 'propaganda' 'Poets of *The Nation*' included in Book III, to Mangan and Ferguson, who are credited with starting 'a new Celtic movement', and so given Book IV to themselves (ix–xiii and 113). While the poets in Book VI represent an unfortunate coda to the triumphal narrative from 'popular' to 'high' Irish culture, from 'political' to 'fine' national poetry, those in Book V formed its latest and most promising chapter, with Yeats as the final paragraph. Though they, like Yeats, had 'studied and honoured the great masters of song, and, as they write in English, the English masters', they had 'yet endeavoured to secure and retain in their poetry not only the national and spiritual elements of the character of the Irish people, but also that appealing emotion which lives like a soul in the natural scenery of Ireland' (xv).

This combination of values—'national', 'spiritual' and 'natural'—explained not only Yeats's particular eminence as the last author in Book V, but the significance of the inclusion of 'The Lake Isle' in the anthology. For both editors, Yeats's status was partly a consequence of his prominent role among the new generation of Irish poets who rejected 'political poetry' and 'consecrated their verse towards the support of a vigorous and vital nationality: first, by the representation in a modern dress of the Irish myths and sagas; and secondly, by the representation of the spiritual elements of the modern world from an Irish standpoint, and in an Irish spirit' (1900: xxix). Yet what made Yeats stand out among his 'fellow-poets' was the fact that his poetry had 'a wider range' (xxxii). While never losing his distinctive Irishness, he 'proved his universality', as Brooke put it, by combining his interest in 'mysticism' and the 'spiritualised representation of the ancient Celtic stories' with 'some work, direct, simple, and humane, on actual life' (xxxii). For a neo-Wordsworthian and Unitarian like Brooke this last aspect of his oeuvre was crucial. For him, 'the better food and pleasanter delights of poetry' could best be found, not in 'a hundred passionate and mystic things', but 'in the daily life of men and women spiritualised by natural passion' (xviii). So, while he ensured the anthology reflected the generic and thematic diversity of Yeats's output, from the occultism of 'The Two Trees' to the legendary appeal of 'The Island of Sleep' (from *Oisin*), and from the confident transcendentalism of 'The Rose of the World' to the defiant realism of 'The Lamentation of the Old Pensioner', he had a special investment in 'The Lake Isle', or, rather, in a particular reading of it.[3] On this issue he had the full support of his son-in-law, who shared his reservations about Yeats's mystical tendencies. In his headnote to Yeats's poems, Rolleston commented 'the mystic in him is sometimes, especially in his later work, found adoring the mere stigmata of mysticism; and then one thinks with dismay that a finer and stronger genius than Blake's may someday lose itself in that dreary waste inhabited by Los and Orc and Enitharmion'. 'But,' he went on, 'these forebodings soon vanish when one hears again the "lake water lapping" on the shores of Innisfree' (497). In the *Treasury*, then, 'The Lake Isle' was presented to readers not only with Yeats's other contributions as the

---

[3] The *Treasury* also included 'The Hosting of the Sidhe', 'Michael Robartes remembers Forgotten Beauty', 'When you are Old' and 'A Dream of a Blessed Spirit'.

clearest evidence of the 'development' of the tradition of Irish poetry in English. It was also offered as a justification of his particular eminence, based on his range, and as a special illustration of the fact that, despite his mystical otherworldliness, he had not forgotten the 'natural scenery of Ireland'. It was, in short, to be read as a gratifyingly 'fine', distinctly Irish, and reassuringly topographical lyric in English.

Yeats was broadly in sympathy with the *Treasury*'s position on several issues. He supported its opposition to hard-line nativists, like Moran, who predictably fuelled a protracted controversy in *The Leader* on its publication in December 1900; he saw Brooke and Rolleston as allies in his disputes with West Britons like Dowden; and he shared their outlook on the intricate relations among politics, poetry and nationalism (see Yeats 1994: 6, 10 and 25). But he also had some misgivings about the way the anthology represented him. As he told George Russell, when Russell was enquiring about which poems of his to include in another anthology, 'Rolleston did not please me over well by giving long extracts from what I think immature verse' (Yeats 1994: 493). In his headnote to Yeats, Rolleston not only drew attention to his selective self-presentation in *Poems* (1895), he included twenty-two lines from *The Island of the Statues* (Act II, Scene 3, ll. 131–34, 160–65, 201, 203–13), the suppressed classical verse drama Yeats had published in *The Dublin University Review* (April–July 1885). This was not the dispassionate scholarly gesture it might seem. Rolleston no doubt took it a little personally that Yeats expunged poems he, as the former editor of the review, had initially deemed worthy of publication. Moreover, there were evidently some implicit tensions between Yeats's and the editors' views on the mystical tendencies in contemporary Irish poetry. In the four headnotes Yeats himself contributed to the *Treasury* on Lionel Johnson, Æ, Nora Hopper and Althea Gyles, he spoke of little else but their various interests in 'a spiritual life'; and, whereas Brooke chastised Æ for ignoring 'universal human life' and 'Nature as she seems to the senses', he called his poems 'the most delicate and subtle that any Irishman of our time has written'. He thought particularly highly of them 'because their writer has not come from any of our seats of literature and scholarship [*vide* Trinity College, Dublin men like Brooke and Rolleston], but from among sectaries and visionaries' (Brooke 1900: 465 and 486–87). These differences of opinion on aesthetic and metaphysical matters may well have made him uneasy about the way the *Treasury* presented 'The Lake Isle'. After all, as he had mentioned to Tynan, as his father's illustration in *The Leisure Hour* had reiterated, and as he also made clear in a note appended to the suppressed poem 'The Danaan Quicken Tree', which appeared in *The Bookman* for May 1893, he saw Innisfree not simply as a scenic spot on the West of Ireland, but as a mystical place with a long history.

> It is said that an enchanted tree grew once on the little lake-island of Innisfree, and that its berries were, according to one legend, poisonous to mortals, and according to another, able to endow them with more than mortal powers. Both legends say that the berries were the food of the *Tuatha de Danaan*, or faeries. (Yeats 1957: 117 and 742)

Attesting, once again, to the inseparability of the meanings of 'The Lake Isle' and its publishing history, and to the important but limited part Yeats, as author, had to play in the overall process, this periodical paratext to another poem becomes, via a footnote, a direct commentary on 'The Lake Isle' itself in Allt and Alspach's *Variorum Edition* (1957).

* * *

One of the axioms of publishing history is that authors have little to do with book production. As Roger Stoddard succinctly reminded us in 1987:

> Whatever they may do, authors do not write books. Books are not written at all. They are manufactured by scribes and other artisans, by mechanics and other engineers, and by printing presses and other machines. (Stoddard 1987: 4)

Yet it is important to bear in mind the differences between the politics of publication and the material processes of book production. While most authors may indeed never participate in the physical production of their books, many may have a considerable say in (and hence responsibility for) the overall design process. This was certainly true for Yeats. Though *Poems* (1895)—to take the most striking early example—was published by T. Fisher Unwin, London, printed by the leading Edinburgh firm T. and A. Constable, with decorative designs by H. Granville Fell, Yeats, as Bornstein has argued, had an extraordinary influence over its total design, and hence over the way it presented him and his poems to the reader (1991: 348). In this context, for instance 'The Lake Isle', which now formed part of the complex, multi-voiced section entitled 'The Rose', represented an especially resolute assertion of his otherwise often ambivalent poetic quest for 'the Eternal Rose of Beauty and Peace'.

Yet, as we have seen, the poem also appeared in many other publishing contexts in the 1890s, where Yeats's powers over its reception as author and book designer were significantly, if not completely, restricted. Entering the gravitational field of the *National Observer*, *The Book of the Rhymers' Club*, *The Leisure Hour*, *Lyra Celtica* or *The Treasury*, and on each occasion subject to the planned and unplanned effects of new paratextual or co-textual commentaries, bibliographical conditions and sociocultural interests, it began a rich public life in which Yeats's own designs were variously embellished, subverted or effaced. Depending on the form in which they happened to come across it, readers of the 1890s could have found a judiciously 'literary' celebration of the West of Ireland uneasily entangled in an otherwise hostile 'political' portrayal of its destitution, a short lyric asserting the new purist imperatives of a young group opposed to the English poetic establishment, a poetic accompaniment to an illustration of an ancient Irish legend, a particularly clear expression of Arnoldian Celticism, or an especially 'fine', but also fortunately topographical, example of the latest achievements in the tradition of Irish poetry in English. Of course, whether these readers actually interpreted the poem in these ways is another question, and one which falls outside the scope of this argument. All we need say now is that these various bibliographical forms created, with or without Yeats's full support, deliberately or incidentally, the material and textual conditions that legitimised such readings. After all, just as the history of meaning should not be confined to the history of the author's intended meanings, so it should not be restricted to the history of reception, since it is generated as much by the producers of bibliographical forms, who have palpable designs on the texts they transmit, as by their consumers, who have minds and interests of their own.

Chapter 11

Rereading Pound's 'In a Station of the Metro'

Where and how were the texts that constitute the literary culture of the period 1880 to 1939 first published?

Questions of this kind are generally considered the preserve of bibliographers and scholarly editors, academic specialists in the material history of text production and transmission. For bibliographers, such questions direct one of their primary aims: to list and describe as comprehensively as possible the total output of a period, a publishing house or, most commonly, a specific author. For scholarly editors, these questions are motivated, not necessarily by an interest in changing publishing venues *per se*, but by an editorial concern with the history of textual variation these changes evince. Since the 1980s, however, questions of publishing provenance have come to interest a larger constituency within and beyond literary studies. This was in part because of developments in literary theory and criticism—the influence of Stephen Greenblatt's 'new historicism', Janice Radway's feminist studies of women readers, and Raymond Williams's 'cultural materialism' are especially pertinent—and in part due to the cross-disciplinary impact of revisionist bibliographers and scholarly editors themselves, most notably D. F. McKenzie and Jerome McGann. It is also a consequence of the new prominence given in the 1980s to the emergent interdisciplinary field of 'book history' (after the French *histoire du livre*) by American and French historians, particularly Robert Darnton, Elizabeth Eisenstein and Roger Chartier. These very different but intersecting initiatives transformed the study of text production and opened new modes of inquiry.

They also contributed, directly or indirectly, to the much vaunted '(re)turn to history' in the 1980s and 1990s, and in so doing they situated the more widespread preoccupation with publishing in a broader intellectual and institutional context. Asking the question 'Where and how were texts first published?'—and, of course, many other 'historical' questions—at that time not only meant, in a positive sense, rethinking the possibilities of bibliographical and editorial inquiry. It also frequently meant, in a negative sense, marshaling evidence against 'theory' (poststructuralism in particular) which allegedly occluded the complex social, political and economic conditions of reading and writing by promoting an empty, ahistorical textualism. For some—Greenblatt, for instance—slaying the dragon of poststructural ahistoricism (Derrida himself called this bogey a 'monstrosity' in 1990) played a significant part in their successful quest for academic credibility (Carroll 1990: 79). For others, the bogey was more like an unwelcome ghost haunting the archives and present less directly in the style and tone of their writing. There were also those who favoured the quiet life and who chose, sometimes conspicuously, to ignore the bogey altogether. This larger context—which is inevitably more complex than my brief account makes out—is worth bearing in mind, not least because all questions, even the seemingly modest, empirical one I am asking, bear witness to the concrete debates and institutional energies that define the time and place in which they are asked. And this is no less true of the answers they yield. What we need to consider, then, is why, at this historical juncture, we should want to ask where and how the novels and poems written at the outset of the twentieth century were first published. What is the value of this question? To whom? And what is at stake?

I would like to approach these large issues by examining a key book to emerge out of these debates: Lawrence Rainey's *Institutions of Modernism: Literary Elites and Public Culture* (Yale 1998). In the first part of this chapter, I evaluate what Rainey says about the possibilities for publishing history as a special mode of *cultural analysis*; in the second, I briefly consider his resistance to *reading* before proposing an alternative perspective on the question of the relevance of publishing history to literary studies, focusing mainly on the first appearance of Ezra Pound's 'In a Station of the Metro'.

* * *

Institutions of Modernism was one of the most ambitious, stylish and richly researched studies of modernism and publishing to have emerged out of the reconsideration of text production as a field of study in the 1980s. Focusing mainly on the years 1912 to 1924—conventionally identified as the zenith of 'high modernism'—it is arranged as a series of closely observed microhistories detailing the 'institutional profile of modernism in the social spaces and staging venues where it operated' (Rainey 1998: 5) To this extent it is not only about publishing. The first case study, for instance, contrasts F. T. Marinetti's loud championing of Futurism to large audiences in London's Coliseum theatre with Ezra Pound's lectures on medieval poetry to a select elite at the London home of Lord and Lady Glenconner. Yet the four remaining chapters—on the first appearance of *Ulysses* and *The Waste Land*, on the composition of Pound's Malatesta Cantos, and on H. D. and coterie culture—are centrally concerned with the role that publishing, especially in the form of the 'little review' and the limited deluxe edition, played in modernism's apparent 'withdrawal from the public sphere' (1998: 75). Hence Rainey's principal, and much reiterated, claim that modernist writers, 'by restricting supply, could exploit the limited demand for modernist literature, turning each book into an objet d'art that acquired potential investment value for collectors' (1998: 154). This cultural generalisation is contentious, as we shall see, but, stated thus baldly, it fails to capture the significance of *Institutions of Modernism* as a contribution to publishing history at the level of methodology.

According to Rainey's grandish narrative, modernism was poised in a precarious state of uncertainty between a mid-Victorian confidence in an expanding literary marketplace (he opens with Dickens's 1853 paean to 'the people' who have 'set Literature free' from patronage) and post-modernism's knowing embrace of culture as a commodity— he refers at one point to Andy Warhol and the *'tristes tropiques* of late capitalism' (1998: 1, 41). The exclusive modes of modernist publication are, then, of interest, he claims, as a particularly clear manifestation of, and means of understanding, this equivocal episode in the history of Anglo-American culture. More importantly, for Rainey the rigours of his methodology—all that archival digging—make possible new ways of challenging the mythologies of modernism invented by the writers themselves (and their publishers) and too often uncritically rehearsed by subsequent commentators.

The most well-known of these are the heroic authorial self-constructions encoded in the stock oppositions between 'high' and 'low', the 'intellectuals' and the 'masses', or 'literary purists' and 'commercial profiteers'. Taking issue with Terry Eagleton's account in 'Capitalism, Modernism, and Postmodernism' (1985), for instance, Rainey argues:

> Modernism is commonly considered a 'strategy whereby the work of art resists commodification, holds out by the skin of its teeth' against

the loss of aesthetic autonomy. But it may be that just the opposite would be a more accurate account: that modernism, among other things, is a strategy whereby the work of art invites and solicits its commodification, but does so in a way that it becomes a commodity of a special sort ... integrated into a different economic circuit of patronage, collecting, speculation, and investment. (1998: 3)

Though Rainey often takes a little too much delight in the easy disenchantments this line of argument affords—the anti-commercial is *really* commercial after all—it does enable him to make a strong case for seeing publishing history as a sophisticated mode of cultural analysis and critique, an appealingly ambitious prospect.

Difficulties begin to arise, however, when we consider his account of the background to the crisis of cultural value, which gives a larger significance to the local details he amasses so assiduously. In his view, three events 'epitomized' the 'growing complexity of cultural exchange and circulation in modern society' which put pay to any 'rigorous opposition between "high" and "low"': the *Daily Mail*'s (1896) record-breaking sales of a million copies a day in 1902; the construction, in 1904, of the Coliseum theatre, a new, upmarket version of the traditional music hall; and the first recorded appearance of the word 'middlebrow', in 1906 (1998: 2–3). These are sound observations. The *Daily Mail* did, like the Coliseum, provide a forum for Marinetti's Futurist assault on the 'high/low' divide. Later, as Rainey shows, the Sunday *Observer*, another of Alfred Harmsworth's popular papers, boomed the deluxe first edition of *Ulysses*, boosting its sales (1998: 57–58). These details reveal lines of diffusion more intricate and interconnected than any envisaged by critics, such as Andreas Huyssen and John Carey, who define modernism in terms of its hostility to 'mass culture'. Rightly resisting the rigid dichotomy between 'high' and 'low' that such definitions presuppose, Rainey argues that modernism's 'ambiguous achievement' was 'to probe the interstices dividing that variegated field and to forge within it a *strange* and *unprecedented* space for cultural production' (1998: 3, my italics). But just how odd or unique was this space? And just how definitive of modernism was it?

Part of the problem is that Rainey's emphasis on the four years from 1902 to 1906 gives the impression that the modernists were responding directly to a new set of conditions peculiar to the beginning of the twentieth century. The causality implied—the modernists' space was unique *because* the cultural conditions were unprecedented—seems less clear, however, if we take the longer history of cultural transformation in the late nineteenth century into consideration.

In one of its most popular versions, this is a relatively simple story of the rapid and radical incursion of the market economy into every aspect of late Victorian literary culture. An enlarged reading public, created in part by the broad expansion of educational opportunities after 1870, attracted a new generation of modernising publishers—George Newnes was the first, followed by Harmsworth and C. Arthur Pearson—who turned the gentlemanly world of Victorian publishing into a large-scale culture industry. Taking advantage of new printing technologies—Hoe rotary presses, linotype machines, etc.—and energetically adopting new promotional strategies (prize competitions, advertising stunts), they created a highly commercialised 'mass culture' for a new socially diverse population of suburban consumers. Newnes pioneered its major forms first with *Tit-Bits* (1881), a penny weekly, and then with *The Strand Magazine* (1891), a sixpenny monthly. These changes in the magazine culture were echoed, in the book market, by the rise of the 'bestseller' made possible, in part, by the death of the three-volume novel in the mid-1890s. At the same time, the Society of Authors, founded by Walter Besant in 1884, and the emergence of literary agents signaled a new era of literary professionalisation. By the late 1880s, then, literary publishing in the dominant sector of the market was big business, and the gulf between 'high' and 'low', the purists and the profiteers, was plain and unbridgeable.

Or so it seemed, particularly to the established literary intelligentsia—George Gissing's *New Grub Street* (1891) is the clearest single expression of their polarised view. In fact, things were not so straightforward. This was partly because the new mass-market publishers were not profiteers out to exploit the 'low', as their detractors claimed. They were sometimes socially responsible entrepreneurs who, in effect, created the new cultural space later called the 'middlebrow'. (While quietly abandoning the piety of most mid-Victorian family periodicals, Newnes, for instance, was as averse to the 'unwholesome' elements of the established popular press as he was to the latest risqué literary experiments.) The story of the advent of 'mass culture' was also complicated by the fact that many other editors and publishers at the time took Matthew Arnold at his word. Though their motivations were always complex—some had political objectives, some were hoping to make money—they saw themselves as Arnold's 'true apostles of equality', with a 'passion for diffusing, for making prevail, for carrying from one end of society to the other, the best knowledge, the best ideas of their time' (Arnold 1867: 79).

Some, like Archibald Grove, the founding editor of the *New Review* (1889), were not particularly successful—Grove wanted to democratise the mid-Victorian review by pricing his at sixpence rather than two shillings and sixpence, but, despite some real achievements, this proved unsustainable. Others, most notably W. T. Stead and T. P. O'Connor, prospered. In 1890, Stead, the controversial former editor of the *Pall Mall Gazette*, launched the *Review of Reviews*, a popular digest of all the 'high cultural' periodicals, priced at sixpence. And in 1902, T. P. O'Connor, another pioneering 'New Journalist' of the 1880s, started the equally successful *T. P.'s Weekly*, a penny *Tit-Bits*-style miscellany intended 'to bring to many thousands a love of letters'. Each weekly issue included 'Cameos from the Classics', extracts from, among others, Plutarch, Byron, Shelley, Wordsworth, Browning and Carlyle. The book publishers' equivalent to this was the cheap 'classic' reprint series, another important late Victorian initiative. This can be traced back at least to Cassell's 'Library of English Literature' (1875), but it was given new life and popularity by the next generation of publishers, notably Grant Richards ('World's Classics'), Newnes ('Pocket Classics') and J. M. Dent ('Everyman' and 'Temple Classics').

Seen from the perspective of publishing history, then, the cultural dynamics of the period were neither quite as simple, nor as ominous, as *New Grub Street* made out. The late Victorian period did not see the abyss between 'high' and 'low' yawn ever wider, nor was it a time when a new, autonomous 'mass culture' threatened to obliterate the literary elite. It was, as younger writers like Arnold Bennett and H. G. Wells recognised—the former most notably in *Fame and Fiction* (1901), the latter in *Anticipations* (1901)—the moment when instability became the most conspicuous feature of all cultural hierarchies, and new cultural spaces began to open up. What was, for some, an apocalyptic crisis of value was, for others, a new opportunity for cultural mobility and innovation. This longer history makes Rainey's emphasis on the special complexity of the Edwardian period arguable. It also weakens his claims about the uniqueness of the Georgian modernists' position. Culturally speaking—that is, in terms of their attitudes, career strategies and publishing practices—the modernists were not responding to a wholly new set of conditions. They were the inheritors of a late Victorian legacy which included both a highly volatile cultural climate and a range of possible reactions to it.

Rainey is right to remind us, especially in respect of Joyce, Pound and H. D., that 'much of the literature that we now designate "modernist" was produced under the aegis of a revived patronage that flourished on a remarkable scale' (1998: 73). This was one effect of the late Victorian inheritance, representing one response, on the part of writers and publishers, to the complexities of cultural value. How unprecedented it was is another matter, however. Though it is true that few individual writers in the 1890s received the kind of lavish direct patronage Joyce or H. D. enjoyed, many of the boldest late Victorian cultural projects, and so, indirectly, their contributors, were privately financed. The most outspoken and important forum for the literary elite, W. E. Henley's *Scots* (later *National*) *Observer* (1888–94), was funded by a group of wealthy Scottish Tories; an elite circle of subscribers connected to Lady Randolf Spencer Churchill supported the stylish *Anglo-Saxon Review* (1899–1901); and John Lane, the most innovative publisher of the 1890s, was able to create the prestige of the Bodley Head, which published *The Yellow Book* (1894–97), *The Anglo-Saxon Review* and, later, *Blast* (1914), only by actively nurturing a network of private investors.

True, these publications were still intended for a general readership, not just for a coterie of collectors, but their existence had little to do with the market economy, and they often traded on the idea of collectability. It could be argued, for instance, that John Lane pioneered the equivocal cultural position which Rainey identifies as peculiarly modernist. With *The Yellow Book* and his controversial 'Keynotes Series' in particular—both are still too often wrongly considered the emblems of aesthetic autonomy in the 1890s—he turned 'high art' into a successful marketing strategy. Capitalising on the prestige of the 'limited edition', the 'beautiful book' and the appeal of the risqué, he commodified and popularised 1890s aestheticism in a way that both manifested and fell foul of the contemporary instability of value. Pointing to one of the key problems, one group of high-minded critics remarked in response to a promotional announcement for the new *Yellow Book*: 'we should like to know ... what the promoters take to be the best sense of the word "popular", and how they imagine that anything concerned with art or letters can be at once popular ... and distinguished' (Unsigned, 1894: 588–89). Rainey's culturally ambiguous space, which entailed neither 'a straightforward resistance nor an outright capitulation to commodification', was, in other words, not news to late Victorian writers, publishers and readers (1998: 3).

What about Rainey's other central claim? If the modernist modes of publication were not as 'strange and unprecedented' as he urges, did they still in some way define modernism? There is no doubt that Georgian modernism was shaped by a series of small magazines and publishing houses—the *Dial*, John Middleton Murry's *Rhythm* and

The Blue Review, Ford Madox Ford's *English Review*, Wyndham Lewis's *Blast*, the *Little Review*, *The New Freewoman* (later *The Egoist*), Shakespeare & Co., The Hogarth Press—all of which existed outside or on the margins of the market economy. They made the modernist movement viable by providing (temporary) refuge from censorship; by creating a space relatively free from the various constraints of large-scale commercial publishing; and by becoming centres of association, cultural solidarity and self-promotion. Yet does it follow from this that 'literary modernism constitutes . . . a retreat into a divided world of patronage, investment, and collecting' and away from 'public culture' (Rainey 1998: 75)? Part of the difficulty here is conceptual since it is not clear how Rainey's phrase 'public culture' is related to Jürgen Habermas's influential concept of the 'public sphere', from which it derives. For Rainey, the *act of publication* in, say, the form of a limited deluxe edition targeted at collectors, seems sufficient to epitomise modernism's 'tactical retreat' from 'public culture' (1998: 5). Yet this either makes too much of publishing, or too little of the concept of the public sphere. If the modernists did rely on the cultural economy of the coterie to get their work in print—and it is not the case that they all did—their books were also news that stayed news, even, as the case of *Ulysses* and the Sunday *Observer* illustrates, for mass-market newspapers. Through reviews, interviews, advertisements, high-profile court cases and more, their public presence in the 1920s and 1930s was marked, even if their books were not being bought or read by most readers.

The other problem with Rainey's claim about the modernists' definitive retreat is historical. Here the value of his methodological contribution—making publishing history a platform for archivally rich cultural critique—is qualified by his tendency to oversell his detailed case studies. His unparalleled narratives of the first appearance of *Ulysses* or *The Waste Land* tell us an enormous amount about Joyce, Eliot and their 'agent', Pound; about the ironies and complexities of publishing; and about the intricate, contradictory relationship between the literary elites of the 1920s and 'public culture'. It is far from clear how much they tell us about 'modernism', however, despite Rainey's assertions. The fact that the deluxe first edition of *Ulysses* (1922) published by Shakespeare & Co. was less a book than an investment opportunity is, for him, 'the final and consummate paradox of modernism' (1998: 56). On this logic, we could argue that the serialisation of Conrad's *Nostromo* in *T. P.'s Weekly* in 1904, or *Chance* in the *New York Herald* in 1912, is evidence of modernism's consummate populism.

More importantly, such generalisations sit uneasily with Rainey's narrow, focused approach, since his case studies inevitably obscure the modernists' many other publishing strategies and markets. For one thing, though some of their publishers—Elkin Mathews, John Lane, The Hogarth Press, Faber—were small and exclusive, they were not limited to the coterie. Conversely, others were larger-scale commercial publishers who, on occasion, took cautious risks, as Methuen did with Lawrence's *The Rainbow* (1915). For another, the diversity of contemporary English-language publishing markets—Britain, America, the colonies, Europe—and the complexities of the trade meant that their works seldom remained fixed in one place or mode for long. By 1929, for instance, Bernhard Tauchnitz, the Leipzig publisher who sold inexpensive paper-covered English-language books in Europe, had May Sinclair, Conrad, Woolf and Lawrence as well as Conan Doyle, Edgar Wallace, Wells and Bennett on his list. And if we include the illegal trade, the field becomes even larger, as Lawrence discovered to his cost when a host of pirated editions of the 'privately printed' *Lady Chatterley's Lover* (1928) rapidly entered circulation. The pirating of the Florence edition, which was as exclusive as the first edition of *Ulysses*, forced him to bring out the cheap Paris edition in 1929.

Institutions of Modernism convincingly demonstrates that publishing history—still a marginal area in literary studies—can be used to rethink and rewrite cultural history. At the same time, its doubtful generalisations and historical gaps indicate how much work is left to be done. Given the diversity of modernist spaces, the multiplicity of publishing strategies and the chanciness of the whole business, it is clear that the many cultural meanings of publishing in the period have yet to be fully deciphered.

* * *

Where does all this leave us as readers? Or, to put it more bluntly, does publishing history have anything to do with meaning? Rainey's position on this is bracingly uncompromising. One of his favourite devices is the witty, self-justifying punchline designed to put close readers in their place. 'Reconsidering the publication history of *The Waste Land* might prompt us,' he notes, 'to question the dominant methodology of modern literary studies' (1998: 106). The fact that the editors of the *Dial* never actually read the poem before publishing it—they accepted Pound's opinion on it—leads him to wonder if 'the best reading of a work may, on some occasions, be one that does not read it at all' (1998: 106). In his introduction, he formulates this resistance to reading more programmatically: 'I reject the idea that history or theory are acceptable only if they take on the role of humble handmaiden to the aesthetic artifact. Further, juxtaposing the analysis of specific works with discussion of institutional networks would encourage, however inadvertently, a vulgar materialism that I also disclaim' (1998: 6–7). Intended to justify his own work as a cultural historian—especially to sceptical literary theorists and critics—this is an admirably robust defense of publishing history as a mode of cultural analysis in its own right. Yet it also betrays an anxiety about reading—and hence criticism and 'theory'—evident in the tone and style of the book as a whole and especially apparent in the final chapter on H. D. (In an unusually moralistic moment, Rainey dismisses her writing—and recent feminist reappraisals of it—largely because she was a coterie poet.) Though he was never one to shy away from the questions raised by 'theory'—his first book engaged with post-structuralism directly—his resolute rejection of reading says something about the polarised institutional context out of which his book emerged. Reading is for critics and theorists (who, it is assumed, dominate the field); the study of publishing provenance is for bibliographers, scholarly editors and cultural historians (assumed to be the dominated). Does this hierarchical division of labour hold up? To address this question, let us turn to the early public life of Pound's 'In a Station of the Metro', not simply as cultural historians, but as readers interested in the history and shifting modalities of meaning.

I have chosen this example in part because the lyric has traditionally been considered the form most amenable to rigorous close reading.

In a Station of the Metro

THE apparition of these faces in the crowd ;
Petals on a wet, black bough.

For those trained in one or another tradition of detailed exegesis, this highly compressed, free-verse lyric would rightly demand careful critical scrutiny. Such readers might want to begin, for example, by asking about its peculiar, minimalist rhetoric and grammar (it contains no verbs, no logical connectives, no explicit lyric 'I', no rhyme, no fixed meter, etc.). They would, in other words, approach the poem as a complex verbal icon, privileging its linguistic codes and anomalies. This classical reading protocol, which bibliographers and scholarly editors questioned to little avail throughout the twentieth century, came under concerted attack in the 1980s and 1990s from French book historians like Chartier and revisionist Anglo-American textual scholars like McKenzie and McGann. They insisted on seeing the text, not as an abstract linguistic form, but as a mediated material artefact, a redescription which, they urged, entailed a significant shift in our understanding of the scene of reading. If this scene were defined for close readers by their critical engagement with what we could call the transcendent 'text-type' (the free-floating, idealised verbal text—see chapter 9) *written* by the author, it was structured more immediately for materialist readers by their physical encounter with an immanent 'text-token' (a particular material document) *produced* by various cultural mediators (editors, publishers, printers, etc.) for specific markets. For them, in other words, you are looking not so much at Pound's 'Metro' but at my facsimile reproduction of a version abstracted from *Lustra* (1916), his seventh volume of poems.

Seen in the context of the theoretical debates of the 1980s, this determinedly anti-Platonic view of reading moved in two opposite directions. On the one hand, by insisting on the role of cultural mediators, it seemed to endorse the critique of author-centred criticism formulated most persuasively by the poststructuralists; but, on the other, by privileging the self-contained document, it seemed to reject the new concept of 'text' as the borderless space of writing that justified the 'death of the author' in the first place. ('The idea of the book,' Derrida wrote in *Of Grammatology*, 'is profoundly alien to the sense of writing' [1976: 18].) This ambiguity, exacerbated by the contentious climate of debate, soon hardened into a polemical opposition as ahistorical textualists determinedly held out against historical documentalists, and vice versa. Predictably, few were willing to recognise any common ground. Yet what the textualists (who were not so ahistorical after all) and the documentalists (who were not all antiquarians) shared—albeit against the background of their radically different intellectual traditions—was a new interest in the problematics of dissemination and its implications for classical ideas of close reading.

For the poststructuralists, this was a broad conceptual issue central to their general theory of meaning: texts have meaning, they argued, only in a context, but since contexts are infinitely variable, meanings are never final. It followed that any attempt to police meaning, to contain it once and for all, was seen as a form of interpretative coercion. 'Poststructuralism,' as Derrida wrote in 1990, 'dislocates the borders, the framing of texts, everything which should preserve their immanence and make possible an internal reading' (Carroll 1990: 92).

On the face of it, the documentalists were committed to the opposite view, given their investment in the preservation and analysis of the immanent 'text-token'. Yet, as many recognised, immanence did not entail stability, since, even in material terms, there is no end to the process of dissemination. As we have already seen with Yeats's 'Lake Isle', proliferation, not fixity, is the norm, as texts are successively put to new uses in new forms. This is not, it should be stressed, simply a reassertion of the scholarly editor's traditional insistence on *textual variation*. It is a matter of recognising the variability of material *envelopes* and the unpredictability of *readings*. Produced and reproduced by new cultural mediators, in new contexts, and for new readers, the successive versions represent unique episodes in the constitution of meaning. This complements, rather than contradicts, the post-structuralists' primary insight. If the Derridian reader is a permanent nomad who refuses to accept the finality of any border, the documentalist's ideal reader is a stateless cartographer mapping the frontiers as they change. The point, then, is not to celebrate the document at the expense of writing—in Derrida's sense of the term—but to study its attempts to contain the disruptive energies of dissemination, and, in so doing, to make publishing history the foundation of a larger history of reading.

Even at the most elementary level—typographical format—the publication history of 'In a Station of the Metro' illustrates these investigative opportunities. Of course, in a relatively banal sense the poem has been in a constant state of typographical flux, through all its numerous printings and reprintings, from one publisher's house style to another, or as fashions changed. More compelling, however, is the fact that when it first appeared in *Poetry*, Harriet Monroe's Chicago monthly, in April 1913, and then again in Dora Marsden's *The New Freewoman* in London four months later (15 August), it was printed, at Pound's insistence, in this arresting format:

IN A STATION OF THE METRO.

The apparition   of these faces   in the crowd   :
Petals   on a wet, black   bough   .

In a letter to Monroe on 30 March 1913, Pound noted 'In the "Metro" hokku, I was careful, I think, to indicate spaces between the rhythmic units, and I want them observed' (Pound 1951: 53). The trouble is no other version printed in his lifetime followed these strictures. This created a problem for subsequent editors and anthologists. Most quietly opted for the 1916 text as it appeared, in the form I cited first (note the changed punctuation as well), in *Lustra*, no doubt on the traditional grounds that this was the author's 'final version'. Peter Jones took this route in his still popular 1972 Penguin anthology *Imagist Poetry* and this is generally how you will find it on the internet today—see, for instance poetryfoundation.org, which, beguilingly, includes a facsimile of the cover for *Poetry*, April 1913, but not an image of the poem in its original form. By the 1990s, however, those who kept up with developments in textual theory found ways of being more transparent about the problems. The editors of *The Norton Anthology of Poetry* (fourth edition), for instance, who 'introduced notes' to 'challenge and problematize the idea of textual "authority"', used the *Lustra* format but alerted their large, mainly undergraduate readership to the alternatives by dating it '1913, 1916' (Ferguson et al. 1996: lvii). By contrast, Thom Gunn, in his slim Faber volume *Ezra Pound: Poems selected by Thom Gunn* (2000)—part of a new series of contemporary poets editing canonical poets—explicitly opted for the more radical *Poetry* version.

In each of these books, then, we encounter a different 'Metro', the mediated product not only of particular editors' decisions, but of changes in textual theory which reflect our historical moment more than any other. Knowing this does not only raise questions of textual authority, however. It also problematises the scene of reading by fragmenting it and, more interestingly, by obliging us to consider the effects peculiar to the 1913 format. These seem clear, if Pound's letter to Monroe is anything to go by. In the absence of a fixed meter, the spaces were meant to indicate the poem's underlying phrasal rhythm (three unequal units per line). The visual cues advertise, more aggressively than the later versions, the aural aspect of Pound's new poetics by emphatically challenging readers to abandon received assumptions about poetic rhythm and foregrounding his desire to 'compose in sequence of the musical phrase, not in sequence of a metronome' (West 1913: 87). Yet this can only be part of the story, since we still need to account for the spaces before the terminal punctuation marks of each line, which have nothing to do with phrasal patterning. On the contrary, their effect seems exclusively visual. This was true of many other effects beginning to preoccupy Pound around 1913. About another poem ('The Garret') he remarked, in the same letter to Monroe, 'I was careful . . . as to line ends and breaking *and capitals*' (Pound 1951: 53, his italics). Here, again, it is the physical appearance of the printed poem, as much as its musicality, that mattered. The visual dimension, of course, became a vital part of Pound's later poetics, particularly after he read Ernest Fenollosa (1853–1908) in late 1913 and discovered (or fantasised his own version of) the rich potentialities of the Chinese ideogram. Yet what are we to make of it at this early stage in his career? Was it simply a self-conscious expression of prosodic experimentalism about which he later had second thoughts?

There is little doubt that the primary effect of the 1913 format is to draw attention to Pound's rejection of a fixed meter in favour of a loose, musical cadence. Yet the fact that it used visual cues to do so, coupled with the seemingly gratuitous spacing before the punctuation marks, opens another possibility as well. As Vincent Sherry has argued, Pound's resistance to Symbolism—conventionally seen to be the driving force behind Imagism—was not conducted only at the level of poetic language (Pound's denotative directness versus, say, early Yeats's connotative suggestiveness) or epistemology (knowing the concrete directly via the 'image', not the transcendent indirectly via the 'symbol'). It also centered on his changing attitudes to the competing poetics of orality and print, the auditory versus the visual effect. Partly because of his reading Remy de Gourmont (1858–1915)—he probably first did so in 1911—he began to move away from his early Provençal-influenced preoccupation with acoustic effects and to give increasing priority to what Sherry calls 'visual values' (Sherry 1993: 52). This happened gradually in the course of 1912 to 1914, and by 1915, with what he took to be Fenollosa's backing, his association of Symbolism with a debased vagueness, bred in part of its reliance on musical evocation for its effects, was firmly entrenched. As his thinking began to change, he started to emphasise not only clear perception but, increasingly, the visible modalities of the poems themselves. This makes the 1913 'Metro' something of a paradox. It used visual cues both to underwrite its innovative musicality and to give new importance to the medium of writing and print. Unlike the 1916 version, then, its unusual format manifests Pound's uncertain position in 1913 as a young poet—he was twenty-eight—determined to redefine his relationship to the oral traditions of the past while creating new forms appropriate to a culture dominated by print, a *vers libre* experimenter on his way to discovering a new poetry for the eye.

When we encounter 'Metro' in *Poetry* or *The New Freewoman*, we cannot, of course, consider its format in isolation from the frames/envelopes created by the periodicals themselves, which had other, often unexpected, effects. Unlike those produced by the format, these are inevitably erased in the process of dissemination—again, think about encountering 'Metro' as a free-standing poem on, say, poetryfoundation.org. It could even be argued that a canonical text, like 'Metro', is by definition one which is capable of countless reframings and remixings in the various documentary envelopes, whether print or digital, that constitute the cultural memory. The challenge is to delineate these changing material contexts and analyse their readerly effects.

In *The New Freewoman*—to keep to one particularly testing example—'Metro' appeared as part of a unique series of six poems grouped together under the heading 'The Contemporania of Ezra Pound'. The significance of this general title is highlighted in 'Salutation the Second', one of two explicitly metapoetic poems in the series. In it Pound reviews the first five years of his career as a published poet and looks to the future. 'My books,' he claims, were 'praised' in part because 'I was twenty years behind the times' (Pound 1913: 88). Now, however, he insists he has entered a new phase.

> Here they stand without quaint devices,
> Here they are with nothing archaic about them.

(Illustrating the shifting effects of context, the deictic 'here' acquires a different force in each material document—in this case, it is *this* issue of *The New Freewoman*.) 'Contemporania' referred, then, not simply to Pound's latest work, but to his own new engagement with modernity and its idioms. In 'Salutation the Second' he drew attention to this change of direction, and, more importantly, attempted to influence his readers' response to it by preempting criticism. He included direct references to the hostile 'reporters', 'professors', 'practical people' and 'pretty ladies' whose conventional ideas of poetry—'the Picturesque', the 'vertigo of emotions', etc.—he gleefully anticipated affronting with their 'little naked and impudent songs'. These were interestingly varied but generalised targets. He also singled out *The Spectator* and its editor John St Loe Strachey—the influential, conservative British weekly had published critical reviews of his early work. Challenging these guardians of the London literary scene, his new poems were intended to 'rejuvenate things' by dealing with sexuality ('the dance of the phallus'), exploiting the license of free verse ('with two light feet, if it please you!') and reinventing poetic language, even at the risk of writing what might appear 'nonsense' to the likes of Strachey. 'Metro', strategically placed as the last poem in the series, appeared immediately below this manifesto statement, presented as an exemplary instance of the risky new idiom. In this immediate context, then, its meaning is strongly determined by Pound's heroic story of his own poetic development, which he sees in ethical as much as literary terms. The oddly formatted poem, in effect, becomes a testament not only to his new experimentalism but to his own purist integrity. As he characteristically put it in 'Tenzone', the opening poem of the series, 'I beg you, my friendly critics, / Do not set about to procure me an audience. // I mate with my free kind upon the crags' (Pound 1913: 87).

The general title and metapoetic surrounding poems were not the only explicit framing devices in *The New Freewoman*, however. Rebecca West (1892–1983) introduced the series with a headnote entitled 'Imagisme'. The main point of her piece was to explain that 'the following are poems written by Mr Ezra Pound since he became an *imagiste*' (West 1913: 87). For the most part, she simply used extracts from F. S. Flint's essay 'Imagisme' and Pound's 'A Few Don'ts by an Imagiste', both of which had appeared in *Poetry* for March 1913 (i.e. a month before Pound's other, larger series of 'Contemporania' appeared in Monroe's monthly). In borrowing from these pieces West started a critical trend, since they subsequently became canonical paratexts in the history of the Imagists, used and reused by critics and editors to comment on the group's poetics and on individual poems like 'Metro'. Yet West also had some, now forgotten, thoughts of her own which had a special resonance in *The New Freewoman*. Under economic pressure, she claimed, recent English poetry had become elitist and self-indulgent: 'because the public will not pay for poetry it has become the occupation of learned persons, given to soft living among veiled things and unaccustomed to being sacked for talking too much'.

> That is why from the beautiful stark bride of Blake it has become the idle hussy hung with ornament kept by Lord Tennyson, handed on to Stephen Phillips [1854–1915, a celebrated turn-of-the-century poet and playwright] and now supported at Devonshire Street by the Georgian School [Edward Marsh's popular anthology, *Georgian Poetry, 1911–1912*, was first published in December 1912] (West 1913: 86).

Rather surprisingly—given Rainey's thesis and Pound's social attitudes and connections—she saw the Imagists as an answer to this decadent coterie culture and its overelaborated forms. Unlike their indulgent drawing-room precursors and contemporaries, they were, according to West's Socialist rhetoric, 'a little band who desire the poet to be as disciplined and efficient at his job as the stevedore' (West 1913: 86). In a more high-minded if politically contrary gesture, she also associated them with 'Taylor and Gilbreth', who wanted 'to introduce scientific management into industry'—Frederick Taylor published *The Principles of Scientific Management* in 1911, and Frank Gilbreth's *Primer of Scientific Management* appeared in 1912.

With this colourful rhetoric West invited her readers to consider Pound's poems in a very particular light: as examples of a new literary movement produced by specific local conditions, as a reaction against decadent *English* poetic traditions, and as a manifestation of other extra-literary modern tendencies. Underlying her analysis was a grand narrative of national decline and regeneration which took Pound's new Imagist poems out of the relatively limited sphere of his personal narrative (as reflected in 'Salutation the Second') and put them in a larger literary and sociopolitical context. With a stevedore's practical good sense—her outlook is noticeably egalitarian—the Imagists were, in her view, intent on bringing the same efficient, rational practices to poetry that Taylor and Gilbreth were applying in industry. As many articles—on topics ranging from masturbation to prostitution, taxation to women's rights—testified, this was very much in keeping with some dominant strains of thought in *The New Freewoman* itself. One article, in the same issue as Pound's 'Contemporania', appealed, for instance, to the latest anthropological research into cultural taboo to explain the 'primeval' resistance to the enfranchisement of women. It argued that the House of Commons was a 'primitive Men's House', with all the associated rites and rituals, organised to 'defend' men from 'the natural sovereignty of the female sex' (F.R.A.I. 1913: 85–86). On West's reading, then, the literary values reflected most clearly in the innovative form and sparse language of 'Metro' embodied the new anti-elitist, scientific spirit of modernity, and echoed *The New Freewoman*'s emancipatory call for a radical transformation of a decadent social and political order.

Despite Pound's editorial influence—he became the journal's literary editor in June 1913—and though he, like T. S. Eliot, was not averse to justifying his poetics in scientific terms, it is unlikely that he would have endorsed West's framing of his poems unreservedly. This is a price many authors pay for periodical publication, which is the product of numerous, sometimes unlikely, collaborations. For Pound it was almost inevitable given the personal and intellectual tensions within *The New Freewoman* in 1913. He never had a high opinion of Dora Marsden (1882–1960) and was at odds with her from the start. Though he and his allies managed to shift its orientation away from feminism to a programmatic individualism as early as December 1913, when they had it renamed *The Egoist*, he was still frustrated by his inability to veto Marsden's editorial decisions some months later. In a letter to Amy Lowell of 18 March 1914, he remarked: 'I'm responsible for what I get into the paper but I am at present nearly, oh we might as well say quite powerless to keep anything out' (Pound 1951: 72). Marsden had very strong editorial views of her own. She had started the *Freewoman*—as it was called until June 1913—in 1911 with the aim of taking the feminist debate beyond the narrow question of the vote. (A committed suffragette since 1908—she was imprisoned in 1909—she left the Women's Social and Political Union in 1910 after becoming disenchanted with the Pankhursts' leadership.) As her ideas evolved, however, the journal also became a forum for her radical individualism—*The New Freewoman* was subtitled 'An Individualist Review'. She, in fact, became England's most fervent advocate of Max Stirner, the obscure early nineteenth-century German philosopher, whose controversial book *Der Einzige und sein Eigentum* (1844, translated as *The Ego and His Own*) remains one of the most uncompromising articulations of philosophical egoism before Ayn Rand. This resolute individualism created tensions with established members of her stable like West. A dedicated socialist and suffragette in her early twenties— she was ten years younger than Marsden—West had been writing for the *Freewoman* from the start, and so her rhetoric, which commented directly on Imagism and 'Contemporania', said more about the journal's past, as a campaigning feminist paper, than its future, as a celebrated modernist 'little review'.

In *The New Freewoman*, then, 'Metro'—and Imagism itself—is explicitly inscribed into a series of multi-authored paratexts and co-texts which bear witness to the diverse currents of opinion shaping the journal at that historical moment. Its possibilities do not end there, however. If we look beyond the poem's explicit framing devices at the readerly effects of the entire journal itself—considered as an implicit or co-textual frame/envelope—other, more challenging, questions arise. Reading the issue for 15 August 1913, it is not difficult to detect the conspicuous correspondences between, for instance, the extracts West cites from Pound's 'A Few Don'ts' and Marsden's editorial, entitled 'Thinking and Thought'. His own maxim—'Go in fear of abstractions'—and his insistence on 'presentation' resonate with her rousing conclusion: 'When men acquire the ability to make and co-ordinate accurate descriptions, that is, when they learn to think, the empire of mere words, "thoughts", will be broken, the sacred pedestals shattered, and the seats of authority cast down' (Marsden 1913: 83). Earlier in the same editorial she had called for the 'purging of language', arguing that the 'vitally true things are all personally revealed' in 'experienced emotion' (Marsden 1913: 82). This again recalls Pound's definition of the 'Image', also cited by West, as 'that which presents an intellectual and emotional complex in an instant of time', and his claim that it is 'better to present one Image in a life-time than to produce voluminous works' (West 1913: 86). As Marsden's conclusion indicates, however, her editorials, unlike Pound's poetic statements, are explicitly political. Her nominalist critique of abstract language was motivated by her radical libertarian politics. Indeed, language and authority, particularly in their elitist male forms, were among the main targets of her fierce editorials for both *The New Freewoman* and *The Egoist*. In 'Thinking and Thought' she attacked the 'cultured', especially the 'pseudo-logicians', who 'prefer to retain inaccurate thinking which breeds thoughts, to accurate thinking which reveals facts'. Sharpening her focus, she set herself against 'the mountain of culture which in the world of the West they have been assiduously piling up since the time of the gentle father of lies and deceits, Plato' (Marsden 1913: 82).

The co-textual links between Pound and Marsden inevitably raise the question of Imagism's own politics. For Michael Levenson and Robert von Hallberg, the resonances are not coincidental. They reveal, in their view, a lost frame of reference for understanding the historical complexity of Pound's political affiliations. Rightly challenging Donald Davie's unsubstantiated claim, first made in the 1950s, that there is a direct line between Pound's Imagist poetics and his later fascism, they have pointed to the historical connections with *The New Freewoman*'s emancipatory, individualist politics. For Levenson, these correspondences, coupled with Pound's intellectual debts to other philosophical egoists like Allen Upward, reveal that 'modernism was individualist before it was anti-individualist, anti-traditional before it was traditional, inclined to anarchism before it was inclined to authoritarianism' (Levenson 1984: 79). This is a useful corrective, not least because it reattaches modernism—and Imagism in particular—to the concrete debates of the time that mixed politics and poetics in uncertain measures.

Yet, seen in the context of *The New Freewoman*, Levenson's revisionist political reading looks too emphatic. For one thing, in its pages Pound insisted on Imagism's traditionalism. Through F. S. Flint— Pound had Flint interview him for the *Poetry* piece—he insisted that, unlike the Futurists, the Imagists were 'not a revolutionary school;

their only endeavour was to write in accordance with the best tradition' (West 1913: 85). In another instance of modernism's cultural mobility, he made the same point, with a more national inflection, in an article, entitled 'Imagisme and England', in *T. P.'s Weekly* for 20 February 1915. For another, if the links between Pound's poetic statements and Marsden's editorials shed light on his prewar politics, they also tell us something about his inability, despite his best efforts, to control the contexts in which his poetry and his poetics might be understood. The extent to which he wished to do so is evident in a characteristic letter, again to Amy Lowell, dated 1 August 1914. He was responding critically to her suggestion that she might bring out another anthology like his own *Des Imagists* (1914), but in a more collaborative way.

> The present machinery [for promoting Imagism] was largely or wholly of my making. I ordered 'the public' (i.e. a few hundred people and a few reviewers) to take note of certain poems . . . I should like the name 'Imagisme' to retain some sort of meaning. It stands, or I should like it to stand, for hard light, clear edges. I cannot trust a democratized committee to maintain that standard. Some will be splay-footed and some sentimental. (Pound 1951: 78)

In *The New Freewoman*, this authoritarian desire to contain the meaning of Imagism was compromised. It was, after all, Marsden and West, not Pound, who in their different ways invoked the larger sociopolitical context. He restricted his own designs on the reader to the ethical and literary domains. Responding to the rigid historicism implicit in Levenson and von Hallberg's accounts, Sherry rightly maintains that 'an understanding of this moment in cultural history is properly grounded when we see the radical Image standing poised—against the continental background impinging on Marsden—between opposite possibilities; between a turn left and a slide to the right' (Sherry 1993: 46). Rereading 'Metro' in *The New Freewoman* suggests we can take this further, since, even in this one material context, the meanings of the 'radical Image'—which are not just political—shift unpredictably within a wide variety of implicit and explicit frames.

This is unsurprising, since, contrary to some of Rainey's claims, publication, even in a 'little review', marks the moment when a text becomes subject to the various, unstable forces that shape the public sphere. Even in the confines of one document, as we have seen with 'Metro' in *The New Freewoman*, texts are caught within an intricate tangle of sometimes competing, sometimes converging interests. If we extend the analysis across a collection of documents, the picture becomes even more complex. Between 1913 and 1916 alone, 'Metro' appeared in a remarkable range of other settings, which once again reveals the extraordinary cultural mobility of modernist writing. It forms part of Pound's short literary autobiography 'How I began' for *T. P.'s Weekly* (6 June 1913)—this was his contribution to the paper's long-running series designed to appeal to the literary aspirations of its large, frequently lower-middle-class readership. It then resurfaced in his article 'Vorticism' published in the eminent *Fortnightly Review* for 1 September 1914 before also appearing in the *Catholic Anthology* (1915), Pound's self-consciously anti-movement (i.e. anti-Lowell and anti-Georgian) anthology, published by Elkin Mathews; in *Lustra* (1916), his seventh volume, published by Mathews in two editions, one unexpurgated and 'privately printed' in September, the other censored version issued for general sale in October; and in *Gaudier-Brzeska* (1916), Pound's experimental biography of the sculptor, published by John Lane.

Each of these material contexts created new, sometimes unique, readerly effects in a process that is, of course, ongoing. Studying these effects, based on the documentary evidence, is one task for publishing history, but it is only a beginning. A more comprehensive approach to the history of meaning also needs to examine the more elusive evidence detailing how readers themselves—reviewers, critics and so-called 'ordinary' readers—interpreted 'Metro' by framing it in their own ways without necessarily acknowledging the designs of its material context. Asking where and how texts were first published is, then, a way into a much larger series of questions which challenge our understanding of how texts relate to their many, shifting contexts. It is also, as we have seen in the case of Levenson and von Hallberg, an analytical tool for critiquing later readings. Approached in this way, publishing history makes possible a nuanced study of the dynamics of meaning which refuses to accept the assurances of traditional historicism, or to define itself against reading, criticism and 'theory'.

Chapter 12

Calder's Beckett

The year 2009 marked the twentieth anniversary of Samuel Beckett's death. It also defined an epochal moment in the ongoing history of his *œuvre's* cultural survival. For the first time, Faber and Faber, who had been publishing the plays for over fifty years, began to issue new editions of the fictions as well, starting with *Murphy* and *Watt*. For Beckett's readers and critics this was a welcome development, since, as Faber rightly declared, their new editions offered 'for the first time a corrected text based on the scholarly appraisal of the manuscripts and textual history' (Beckett 2009: back cover). After decades of slippage and contamination, which the Grove Century edition of 2006 only went some way towards addressing, the Faber paperback editions promised to set the textual record straight in a clear, readable and affordable way.

For publishing historians this development had a different but no less telling significance, since it signalled the end of Beckett's long relationship with John Calder, one of the most important independent British publishers to emerge in the post-war era. Calder was the principal publisher of Beckett's fiction, poetry and criticism in the British sphere of the Anglophone publishing world between 1958, when he brought out an edition of *Malone Dies*, and 2007, when he was obliged, under pressure from the Beckett Estate, to sell his Beckett rights to Faber, who had been making efforts to acquire them since the early 1990s. In 2007, after fifty-eight years in the trade, Calder, aged eighty, also decided to withdraw from active publishing, without exactly retiring—he died in 2018. While his Beckett list went to Faber, he sold the rest of his remaining titles, around 1,000, to Oneworld Classics, a joint venture launched by Oneworld Publications and Alma Books. They started to reissue some of the more successful Calder titles under this new label in 2008, beginning with Alain Robbe-Grillet's *Jealousy* (1960),

Raymond Queneau's *Exercises in Style* (1979) and Alexander Trocchi's *Young Adam* (1983). Given the structural changes in British literary publishing in the last decades of the twentieth century, when huge multimedia conglomerates like Bertelsmann AG absorbed many leading firms and the market became increasingly centralised at all levels, it is significant that the Calder list, though divided, remains in the small, always precarious but still active, independent sector of the British book trade. While Faber, which was founded in 1929, is one of the most established independents, Oneworld and Alma are relative newcomers, the former founded in 1987, the latter in 2005.

What significance Beckett's relocation from Calder to Faber has for literary historians is less evident, since, as Calder himself noted, the role of publishers as 'purveyors of culture' is 'often underestimated in literary history' (Calder 1999: 12). Among these forgotten intermediaries he also included booksellers, literary agents, librarians, teachers and 'the proselytizing admirer'. Since the new millennium, a new generation of literary scholars, inspired partly by developments in book history and cultural studies, began to address this deficiency. As we have seen in chapter 11, Lawrence Rainey's *Institutions of Modernism: Literary Elites and Public Culture* (1998) did much to shape this new line of enquiry, with sometimes questionable results. In particular, his tendency to take a little too much delight in the easy disenchantments his analysis affords—the anti-commercial is *really* commercial after all—set the tone for a predictable line in materialist debunking, evident, in the case of Beckett studies, in Stephen John Dilks's essay 'Portraits of Beckett as a Famous Writer' (2006), a prelude to his full-length and no less desacralising study *Samuel Beckett in the Literary Marketplace* (2011).

Dilks felt driven to adopt the rhetoric of disenchantment primarily in response to Calder's 'effusive celebration' of Beckett as a 'saint'—in his obituary Calder compared him specifically to St Francis of Assisi—a hyperbolically unworldly image which, Dilks argues, James Knowlson's biography *Damned to Fame: The Life of Samuel Beckett* (1996) only reinforced (Dilks 2006: 161). In contrast to these 'proselytizing admirers', Dilks sets himself up as a Rainey-esque man-of-the-world who calls a paradox a paradox: 'the campaign to brand and sell Beckett took as its central proposition that the author was above commercialism and marketing' (163). This is Beckett, or rather 'Beckett', as a commodified postmodern anti-commodity, more Innocent smoothie than Coca-Cola. Just what role Beckett, as opposed to admirers like Calder, played in all this is not clear from Dilks's analysis. It is, he claims, 'evident that Beckett withdrew from any explicit involvement in the marketing of his texts', but he also insists a few sentences later that 'Beckett was more effective than any other twentieth-century writer in the strategic control and dissemination of a personal aesthetic and an authorial persona' (163). The latter claim could plausibly be made of a self-canoniser like W. B. Yeats, as we saw in chapter 10. Making Beckett fit the bill looks like a non-starter, particularly when cast in Dilks's oddly ambivalent but rationalistic terms.

Once again, given the lack of interest literary historians and critics have shown in the inner workings of the book trade, his analysis of the Beckett brand constitutes a useful corrective. Yet, as the tensions in his argument suggest and the implications of his critical rhetoric reveal, it begs too many questions to be convincing. To understand the complex 'elective affinity' that developed between Beckett and Calder, we need a more nuanced mode of analysis, one which avoids the twin traps of admiring hagiography and sceptical anti-hagiography, while also shifting the focus away from the biographical details of the Beckett-Calder friendship. This personal dimension should never be forgotten, of course. In the months before his death Beckett wrote a tribute to Calder expressing in typically allusive but also 'failing words' his 'unfailing affection, appreciation of his efforts on behalf of my work, admiration of his resistance to the slings and arrows' (Calder 1999: 1). Tellingly, when Calder and Marion Boyars went their separate ways in 1975, after an eleven-year publishing partnership as the firm Calder & Boyars, Beckett stayed with Calder. Yet, any analysis that remains at this level, or sees author-publisher relations in overly individualistic terms, risks obscuring the more important institutional dimension of Calder's role as a guardian of the literary in post-war Britain and of Beckett's place in that always over-determined project. Here the language of marketing, branding and selling becomes less helpful, not just because of its implied rationalism—everyone's motives are assumed to be transparent and knowable—but because of its potential cynicism: it is as if there is no substance to Beckett's many refusals or Calder's passionate advocacy and sense of public vocation. Fashioning a different critical language more attuned to the specificities of literary history as well as the circumstances and energies of those who shape it would, in my view, make it possible to speak about Calder's role as a purveyor of Beckett without reducing him, or Beckett for that matter, to a caricature self-promoter whose only interest lies in maximising his visibility in the market.

* * *

Like 'the many-headed monster, whose heads are chopped off by Hercules only to have them grow back again,' Calder wrote in his autobiography, literature 'rises time and again through, and in spite of, opposition, disapproval, censorship, fundamentalist ideology and the incomprehension of the plain reader' (Calder 1999: 11). Though the shape-shifting Proteus is perhaps a more likely figure for the kind of writing Calder championed, his invocation of the Hydra says a lot about his own self-understanding as a publisher, since he, too, fought countless battles, resiliently returning to the fray after every setback. As the blurb on the back of *Pursuit* (2001), his 'Uncensored Memoirs', puts it, he was 'damned by a censorious press, by politicians, by other publishers and by organs of the state, for publishing books on sensitive issues, often against the grain, and for such authors as Henry Miller, William Burroughs, Alexander Trocchi and Hubert Selby, as well as for bringing to public notice the abuses of the army and the security forces in colonial countries'. One of the most significant titles in the latter category was *Gangrene* (1959), which exposed British and French atrocities during the anti-colonial struggle in Africa. Fearing the consequences, especially for British interests in Kenya, the Labour Home Secretary at the time officially requested, via the 'D Notice' system, that Calder withhold publication in the interests of national security. But, as Calder later remarked, he 'successfully ignored' this call for self-censorship 'without prosecution and had reason to be proud of *Gangrene's* influence in righting a wrong and changing the course of history' (2001: 149).

As a literary publisher Calder ought, on the face of it, to have had no such difficulties with the British state. For one thing, he made his publishing debut in 1949, six years after the Council for the Encouragement of Music and Arts was established. One of the great achievements of the post-war welfare state, the Arts Council, as it came to be known, provided vital support to Calder from the late 1960s to the mid-1980s, first in the form of subsidies and then annual grants. For another, Calder first rose to prominence after the *Lady Chatterley* trial, the most famous test case for the 1959 Obscene Publications Act, which was, in part, intended to safeguard adventurous literary publishers like him from prosecution. Following a concerted campaign in the 1950s by liberal politicians, notably Roy Jenkins, the Society of Authors, and established literary publishers, including Secker & Warburg and Heinemann, the new act was expressly designed, as the preamble put it, 'to protect literature'. As Calder soon discovered, however, the consequences of the British state's new commitment to literature and the arts as a 'public good' were far from straightforward.[1]

Anxieties about censorship in the mid-1950s played a role in Calder's acquisition of the rights to Beckett's fiction. When Faber took the plays in 1955, after *Waiting for Godot*'s success in the theatre, they decided against the fictions, which were, in their view, too risky, even though the only trouble Beckett had with the British state was as a dramatist. Before the Lord Chamberlain's office was abolished in 1968, he was obliged to amend both *Godot* and *Endgame* for the British stage. This was very much against Beckett's wishes. Like Joyce, his role model in this respect, he was, and always remained, a passionate opponent of censorship. Some months before *More Pricks than Kicks* (Chatto & Windus 1934) was banned by the new Irish Censorship of Publications Board—*Watt* (Olympia 1953) and *Molloy* (Olympia 1955) subsequently suffered the same fate—he wrote 'Censorship and the Saorstat', a satirical attack on Ireland's 'constitutional belch', and throughout his career he supported numerous anti-censorship initiatives (Beckett 1983: 87). For Calder, publishing Beckett created various difficulties, as we shall see, but it did not bring him into conflict with the British state. The two titles that turned *him* into a fervent anti-censorship campaigner and critic of the apparently reassuring 1959 act were *Cain's Book* (1963), an existentialist account of a Glaswegian heroin addict in New York, by the young Scottish writer Alexander Trocchi, and *Last Exit to Brooklyn* (1966), the cult classic about New York's dispossessed in the 1950s, by the American Hubert Selby Jr. The other controversial Calder title of this period, Henry Miller's *Tropic of Cancer* (1934), which he reissued in 1963, was effectively given official approval after he sought the opinion of the Director of Public Prosecutions in advance of publication. Revealing his willingness to use the threat of censorship for publicity purposes, Calder carefully kept the director's decision to himself, thereby propelling *Cancer* onto the bestseller lists and helping the firm benefit financially from the brouhaha generated by the anticipation of a ban.

As the decisions against *Cain's Book* and *Last Exit* demonstrated, the literary safeguards written into the 1959 act were not as secure

---

[1] Obscene Publications Act 1959 (c. 66), http://www.statutelaw.gov.uk/content.aspx?activeTextDocId=1128038 [accessed 17 May 2023].

as the *Lady Chatterley* trial made out. Indeed, the Trocchi decision, against which Calder appealed unsuccessfully in 1964, not only showed that magistrates were free to disregard the evidence of literary experts, whose testimony was first allowed to be heard under the terms of the new act, but that the legal meaning of obscenity was not confined to 'sexual matters', as Lord Parker, the appeal court judge, put it. It encompassed any depiction of 'the favourable effects of drug-taking' as well, since, as Parker continued, this too could 'deprave and corrupt' those 'into whose hands the book' might fall.[2] Though Calder's appeal against the Selby ban in 1968 succeeded, largely on procedural grounds, it had more significant legal and cultural consequences. To raise funds to fight the case, he founded the Defence for Literature and the Arts Society (DLAS), to which Beckett contributed financially. The DLAS, which still lives on as the Campaign against Censorship, had a significant impact on British cultural life during the Mary Whitehouse era in the 1970s. After the appeal was heard, Calder played an influential role in encouraging the Arts Council of England to set up a Working Party on obscenity. Its report, published in 1969, centred on the legal problems the *Last Exit* appeal had exposed and called for the 1959 act to be abolished.

Calder's involvement in these various initiatives says much about the circumstances in which he operated, the alliances he formed and, above all, the idea of the literary to which he was committed as a member of the white, male-dominated liberal elite in the Britain of the 1960s and 1970s. Other notable members of this influential faction, all key Calder supporters, included Lord Goodman, chair of the Arts Council from 1965 to 1972, Eric White and Charles Osborne, who served on the Council's Literature Committee, and John Mortimer, the writer and barrister who acted for the defence in the *Last Exit* appeal. Calder's ties to this elite circle are worth emphasising, given his tendency to represent himself as an anti-establishment outsider. Describing the readership to which he appealed in the 1960s, he remarked in his memoirs that this was 'the period when a new generation of state-educated intellectuals had arrived on the scene and were open to new ideas and serious culture: many were making that culture' (Calder 2001: 102). Indeed, as a publisher he saw himself as creating space for writers, like Trocchi and Alan Burns, who 'came from the newly-educated upward-thrusting working-class or lower middle', unlike the writers of the self-avowedly anti-modernist 'Movement', notably Philip Larkin and Kingsley Amis, who were

---

[2] John Calder (Publications) Ltd. V. Powell (1964) [1965], 1 Q. B., 515.

'very Oxbridge and middle-class' (277). Calder's stable, 'my group' as he called them, was always more sympathetic to the modernist tradition, though, as he admitted, they never really constituted 'a new school', mainly because they lacked effective leadership (277). Seen in this context Calder's own position was more subtle than he sometimes made out. 'Born into the most conservative of establishment families', as the blurb on the back of *Pursuit* has it, he was always more an insider determined to open a closed world than an outsider trying to break in. In this respect, too, he was very much at one with the kind of thinking that characterised the Arts Council of the 1960s and 1970s.

Despite its Keynesian origins and its commitment to state patronage, the council under Goodman adopted a determinedly liberal, anti-statist position when it came to censorship, which Calder actively supported. Firmly rejecting the idea, which it traced back to 'the days of the Puritans', that a court of law is '*custos morum* of the people', the council's Working Party on obscenity argued that it is 'a somewhat astonishing doctrine these days to say that in the last resort the way we can behave, the things we can read, look at, hear and presumably enjoy, are subject to Big Brother, wigged and gowned on the judicial bench' (Girodias 1971: 241). This kind of thinking had, of course, been at the heart of the campaign to reform the laws on obscenity in the 1950s, but, as the report insisted, the 1959 act (amended in 1964) was at best a confused compromise, which effectively prescribed 'an inept and disabling cure in order to forestall an imagined malady' (246). Among other things, since a book could be judged to be both obscene and worth protecting for the 'public good', the act imposed absurd demands on jurors, who were required to ask 'whether an ounce of depravity-spreading is more or less potent than an ounce of artistic merit' (234). Moreover, by granting 'so-called experts' the right to testify, it made a nonsense of the 'imponderable' question of merit. 'Most unfamiliar art, written, aural or visual,' the Working Party noted, 'has been broadly condemned by its contemporaries' (233). For these reasons, and on the broader liberal grounds, it concluded that the act could only be scrapped, not reformed (see also chapter 8).

This *avant-gardist* idea of an 'unfamiliar art' that tends to affront the 'plain reader' or offend contemporary sensibilities was central to the liberal elite's thinking about the nature and function of the literary. In his defence statement during the *Last Exit* appeal, John Mortimer specifically contrasted a free literature's revelatory power to the 'polite concealment of disturbing truth', while the Working

Party drew attention to the frailty of the legalistic distinction between actionable works that might 'deprave and corrupt' and those that merely 'shock and disgust'.[3] In an attempt to distinguish historically variable standards of acceptability from the unchanging causal logic implied by the phrase 'deprave and corrupt', the judge in the original *Last Exit* case expressly directed the jury to think in terms of the mechanistic Victorian formula that survived in the 1959 act, since, as the he put it, 'the charge is *not* that the tendency of the book is to shock and disgust' (Girodias 1971: 240). *Last Exit* depicts a brutal underworld of gangs, junkies, prostitutes, transvestites and, as Baron Cyril Salmon, then lord justice of appeal, put it, 'homosexuality' and 'other sexual perversions'.[4] Yet, as the Working Party pointed out, Salmon had finally to 'admit that all we could, in practice, expect from a jury was their opinion of "what is acceptable . . . *in the age in which we live*"', that is, what might 'shock and disgust' contemporaries. 'In the last analysis,' the report concluded, 'Obscenity Laws are really about conformity and *mores*', and, therefore, they were both anti-liberal and inimical to avant-garde art (Girodias 1971: 240). In reply to criticisms of the Working Party report, Calder underscored this conclusion, arguing that 'the suppression of unorthodox views of life and society can never be in the public interest; that enforced ignorance of the darker sides of human nature in contrast to its nobilities and glories can only militate against the advancement of goodness and the maturing of human beings' (Calder et al. 1973: 15). On this analysis, which it is worth stressing met the moralistic proponents of censorship on their own terms, the ultimate justification for the disturbing power of 'unfamiliar art' was itself moral, rather than, say, cognitive or aesthetic.

For all his modernist affinities Calder's idea of culture was, as this suggests, informed by an essentially Victorian, indeed, specifically Arnoldian set of ideals. This, too, chimed well with the Arts Council's own sense of mission in the 1960s and 1970s, which was similarly Arnoldian. As Stevenson comments, its founding ambitions, captured in maxims like 'the best for the most' and the 'enjoyment of the "high" arts by a wider public', were 'probably realized most successfully in the late 1960s and the early 1970s' under Goodman's chairmanship (Stevenson 2004: 33). Unlike Arnold's cultural 'apostles of equality', who were supposed to be déclassé social 'aliens',

---

[3] Regina v. Calder & Boyars Ltd., (1968) [1969], 1 Q. B., p. 159; and Girodias 1971, 240.
[4] Regina v. Calder, 172.

this later democratising mission assumed that defining the 'best' remained the prerogative of the metropolitan liberal elite, a point Calder emphasised during a fractious public exchange about Arts Council policy in 1981 (Arnold 1993: 79 and 110). Responding to the suggestion that writers might apply individually for grants, without having to go through a 'sponsor of reputation', Calder fully endorsed Charles Osborne's claim that 'his function is to help literature, i.e. literature that has the status of art' (Calder 1981: 12). 'As an occasional sponsor,' Calder noted, 'I have tried to recommend only writers whose work was on a high literary level.' In his view, writers could not be left to make these judgments themselves, since most 'see themselves as new James Joyces and cannot be persuaded of their lesser status, or do not understand the difference between the really creative writer and the run of the mill'. 'There is no way,' he added, 'that the arts can be made democratic or egalitarian without a corresponding drop in quality and sophistication.' Having said this, he insisted, again in an Arnoldian fashion, that 'the place for democracy is in *access* to the arts' (12). After noting that Calder had misunderstood the central issue—the council was proposing to replace the relatively generous grant system with a more limited set of bursaries for 'established writers'—the writer Eva Figes, who was among those Calder had sponsored, angrily denounced the 'whole tone' of his intervention, which 'reveals the degree of private patronage masquerading as state patronage as perceived by John Calder' (Figes 1981: 8). She could also have pointed out that, after all the council's Working Party had said about 'so-called experts' in its obscenity report, Osborne's confidence in Calder's expertise as a cultural arbiter was, to say the least, moot.

A modernist with an Arnoldian sense of public vocation, a liberal committed to state patronage, an anti-moralist who defended the avant-garde on moral grounds, a democrat who believed passionately in the guardianship of the elite, Calder was driven by a range of contradictory energies. While this made him a sometimes-questionable purveyor of Beckett, as we shall see, it also reflected his situatedness as an influential member of the metropolitan liberal elite of the 1960s and 1970s. If this was a golden age of British liberalism—consider its impact not just on the Arts Council, but on divorce law, capital punishment and gay rights—it was also Calder's moment. Though he never succeeded in having the 1959 Obscene Publications Act abolished, his numerous interventions helped to stop prosecutions against literary works by the end of the 1970s. At the same time, his publishing activities, though always hampered by his casual attitude to the business side of things, flourished partly through the generosity of the Arts Council.

Having started out in 1969 providing subsidies for individual projects, notably *Gambit*, the theatre magazine and Calder's *New Writers* series, the council in 1980 began to give substantial annual grants to the Calder Educational Trust, which it encouraged Calder to establish. In 1982 the amount granted annually rose to a peak of £35,000, at which it stayed for three years. In 1986, following a change in priorities, it fell to £10,000 before finally being stopped altogether. In his memoirs Calder blamed his declining fortunes as a council beneficiary on Thatcherism and, above all, on Sir William Rees-Mogg, the Tory journalist, who, when he was appointed chair of the council in 1982, promptly fired Charles Osborne as Literature Director. Calder also blamed the novelist, critic and journalist Marghanita Laski, who went on to chair the Literature Committee, for damaging 'the previously liberal policy of the Arts Council' (Calder 2001: 503). Contrary to what he claims in his memoirs, however, Laski was not appointed by Rees-Mogg. She began her tenure on the committee in 1980 under Melvyn Bragg and took over as chair in 1981. Though factually inaccurate and overly personalised—it is clear that numerous factors, including general policy shifts and cuts, were at work—Calder's version of events reflects his conviction that Thatcher's advent marked the rise of a new philistinism. During one of many increasingly vain appeals for continued state support, he sensed that the Literature Committee of the mid-1980s, 'then consisting largely of popular thriller writers and children's book writers would not have much sympathy with the kind of serious literature in which I specialized' (504).

* * *

According to the journalist Colin Murphy, Calder has a lot to answer for as the principal British publisher of Beckett's fictions because he compounded the problem of producing inaccurate editions by failing to market them adequately. 'While the plays were popularised,' Murphy commented in 2009, 'the prose has languished in relative obscurity' (Murphy 2009: 58). With the advent of the new Faber editions, he felt this further problem would now also be remedied. This analysis is unjust, but it points to an intractable difficulty facing all undercapitalised independents like Calder. When it comes to marketing, they cannot compete with the conglomerates. It is largely for this reason that so many have been obliged to sell up to their larger rivals.

For Calder, this key handicap had to be set against the virtues of being small, which were, in his view, both cultural and commercial. The 'James Joyces and Virginia Woolfs of the future,' he remarked in 1961, 'are hardly likely to be encouraged by the large publishing corporations, which have to sell an edition in a limited time in order to justify the publication to its shareholders, interested principally in quick growth and dividends'. With lower overheads and a strong editorial emphasis, he was, as a 'small specialized publisher', not only able to give 'time, attention and know-how' to his authors, but to 'take calculated risks of a type inconsistent with the efficient management of larger corporations' and to work for the long term (Calder 1961: 9). Despite his never-ending financial troubles, which the Arts Council support did little to allay, he remained committed to this view throughout his career. His resistance to expansion in fact contributed to the breakup with Marion Boyars in the mid-1970s.

What Calder lacked in financial resources he made up for in energy and inventiveness when it came to bringing Beckett to the attention of booksellers in the first instance and then readers. He not only kept his titles in print, he also used an extraordinarily wide variety of book formats to ensure that they reached as large and diverse a readership as possible. In the 1950s and, indeed, well into the 1970s, British literary publishing was still firmly divided into major hardback publishers like Secker & Warburg, who guaranteed reviews and library sales, and paperback publishers like Penguin, who targeted readers directly through bookshops and the media. Calder was among the first to go against this trend by publishing in both formats, beginning with Calderbooks in 1959 and then with his Jupiter Books series, which, unlike the standard mass-market paperback, was thread-sewn and produced on high-quality paper. While he initially published *Malone Dies* (1958) as a traditional hardback with Brian Sewell's modernist cover featuring a photograph of a human skull, he reissued it as a paperback ten years later, before finally settling on the dual-format edition, with what became the trademark Calder design: the Mondrian-style, two-colour cover (a white background for the author's name, a saturated red, green or orange for the title), which incorporated a photographic portrait of the author, mostly by John Minihan. From 1975 Calder adopted this design for most of his Beckett titles, including *Murphy* and *Watt*, which started out as the inaugural Jupiter Book in 1963. This presentational strategy, which combined photography to emphasise Beckett's singularity and a modernist aesthetic to place his work culturally and historically, became a distinctive feature of Calder's Beckett.

Calder continued to experiment with alternative formats, including deluxe editions for the collectors' market—copies of his last Beckett title, a limited edition of *Stirrings Still* (1988), sold for £1,000 each—or other novelty editions, like the twelve-volume boxed set of 'Beckett Shorts' he produced in 1999. Yet he also negotiated agreements with more mainstream paperback publishers to ensure that Beckett could benefit from their backing and distribution as well. In 1962, for instance, without consulting Beckett, he allowed Penguin to bring out their own paperback edition of *Malone Dies*. As he explained to Jérôme Lindon, 'we do not intend to sell any other Becketts to Penguin, but as the Penguins are able to get into all the little villages, it may help to make a Beckett public and sell all the other works'.[5] Penguin subsequently reissued their edition as a 'Modern Classic' in 1968, a year before Beckett won the Nobel. On the same principle, Calder agreed terms with Picador for *Murphy* (1973), *More Pricks than Kicks* (1974), *The Beckett Trilogy* (1975), *Company* (1982) and *Watt* (1988), with the New English Library for his own *Beckett Reader* (1967) and with Penguin again for *The Expelled and other Novellas* (1980, reissued as *First Love and Other Novellas* in 2000). The latter was based on Calder's *Four Novellas* (1977), which he published only in hardback. These arrangements probably did little to promote his own more expensive titles. Seen against the background of Beckett's early publishing career in the 1930s, however, when firms like Chatto & Windus and Routledge produced very short runs of his books that rapidly went out of print, there can be little doubt that they transformed Beckett's cultural visibility by ensuring that he had a mass-market presence from the early 1960s, not just in Britain but across the Anglophone world.

Yet when it came to promoting Beckett, Calder was not just a publisher: he was a 'proselytizing admirer' and 'popular educator' as well (Calder 2001: 269). Drawing on the experience he gained organising literary conferences at the Edinburgh Festival in the early 1960s, the first of which made headlines when a woman in the audience stripped, he launched his Beckett appreciation initiative in 1964 at the Criterion Theatre in London, where *Godot* had its first success a decade earlier. Setting the pattern for the future, this inaugural event combined a series of readings from Beckett's work by leading actors—Patrick Magee and Jack MacGowran in this case—with supplementary comments by Calder and an academic conference

---

[5] Calder to Lindon, 9 November 1962, Calder and Boyars Archive, Series V, Box IV, Folder 1. Courtesy, The Lilly Library, Indiana University, Bloomington, Indiana.

chaired by the drama critic Martin Esslin. Calder had initially hoped the actors would perform extracts from the plays and fictions, but to comply with the Lord's Day Observance Act (1932), which made fee-charging public performances illegal on Sundays, he had to settle for more restrained readings instead. He continued to develop this project, which he later called the 'Theatre of Literature', well into the 1980s, staging various events at festivals, bookshops and universities to promote all the writers on his list, Beckett above all. In his memoirs, he drew a 'sharp contrast' between his desire 'to popularise the arts and to push up public taste' in this way and 'what governments and the media were to do later', once again reflecting his frustrated Arnoldian ambitions and growing sense of cultural dislocation after Thatcher's rise to power (Calder 2001: 269). Beckett, for his part, was characteristically wary of the whole business—he wanted to know which actors Calder was using and he worried about the extracts he chose—and, unlike Robbe-Grillet and Alan Burns, he refused to participate in any of the events.

For Beckett, this detachment was principled, since, as he always recognised and as Calder's popularising campaign demonstrated, literary works are public documents with public as well as private meanings. The meanings Calder made for British readers can be traced through several sources, including the blurbs he wrote for the books, though his thinking is most clearly articulated in the introduction to the *Beckett Reader*, which he produced in 1967. With its various extracts from the fictions, poems and plays and its surrounding commentary, the *Reader* was a 'Theatre of Literature' in book form, especially in its cheaper paperback format. As Calder remarked in the introduction, his intention was to make Beckett, whose 'fans are found principally among intellectuals', more 'accessible to the average reader' (Calder 1967: 7). Yet, as his analysis revealed, he also used the occasion to reply to reviewers in the British broadsheet press who were generally hostile to the modernist tradition and who routinely labelled Beckett a gloomy pessimist. One of the most consistent proponents of this prevalent view was the *Observer*'s Philip Toynbee. In a typical review-essay of 1966, he lumped Beckett together with Burroughs, dubbing them both 'terrorists of modern literature' and bemoaning their tendency 'to paint only in the extreme colours of chaos and despair'. Reflecting his own Arnoldian inheritance—in this case Arnold's neo-classicism—Toynbee contrasted them to Goethe, 'the olympian, many-sided, panoramic master', who faced the 'spiritual upheavals' of his time in a mood that was 'classical, stately, festive and dignified' (Toynbee 1966: 24). Calder emphatically rejected this reading of Beckett, which, as he noted, was often based on an ill-founded biographical account of his 'supposedly unhappy childhood and Catholic past' (Calder 1967: 9). He acknowledged that Beckett 'will take any situation to its ultimate depth', but 'then, reiterating after all the impossibility of believing anything, even that hope is impossible, he finds that when his eyes are accustomed to the darkness, there is a glimmer of light, a hope, however slight, that something might survive after all'. Citing the endings of *Godot*, *Molloy* and *The Unnameable*, especially 'I can't go on, I'll go on' in the last, he insisted that 'Beckett never leaves his reader without some hope at the very end' (15–16).

Following the logic of his defence of the avant-garde against the moralistic advocates of censorship, Calder once again begged several questions by meeting his opponents on their own terms. Implicitly picking up on Toynbee's larger anti-modernist argument, while also appealing to what he took to be the desires of the 'average' British reader, he went on to claim that Beckett was just as interested in observing 'the human condition' and making 'man greater than he is' as Shakespeare, Sophocles or Goethe (Calder 1967: 11). He specifically compared Molloy to Macbeth, Oedipus and Werther. As he explained, however, Beckett had also achieved a 'double breakthrough', the first sociological, the second psychological, which gave new life to this tradition. In contrast to the great writers of the past who focused on the privileged classes, he chose 'as his heroes the most improbable, the most incapable, the most disgusting and the most handicapped examples of humanity'. At the same time, 'he has made it possible to sweep away . . . all the lumber of tiresome convention that has strangled the novel and the drama in our time, and return to something simpler and more elemental', namely, 'the inner truth of our thoughts, our fears and our passions'. Far from being some sort of literary 'terrorist', Beckett had, according to Calder, effectively restored the high moral seriousness of the Western tradition. By focusing attention on the 'inner truth' of a marginalised figure like Molloy he increased 'our compassion and understanding for those who would normally be below his readers' notice'. Importantly for Calder's popularising campaign, this essentially moral project also had political 'significance in an age when faraway colonial wars are reducing whole populations, and an atomic war could reduce us to the conditions of one of his heroes, or worse!' (Calder 1967: 11–12).

For Christopher Ricks, this defence of Beckett as a politically engaged psychological realist and avant-garde moralist was the ultimate betrayal. In a scornful review of Calder's equally populist festschrift *Beckett at 60*, which he published in the same year as his *Reader*, Ricks argued that there was something 'preposterous about the institutionalising of Beckett, the comfortable assimilation, the pretence that his work isn't really obscure, isn't ever boring, isn't on the face of it cold and hard'. 'John Calder,' he concluded, 'achieves the bizarre and demeaning feat of selling Beckett as a good read' (Ricks 1968: 148). It is difficult not to agree. Yet to see Calder simply as a publisher eager to market his product, as Ricks's language implies, is to miss the complexities of his popular advocacy and to underestimate the forces that shaped it. To assess Calder's Beckett, we need to focus not just on the evident disjunction between the writing and the way Calder curated it, or, indeed, on his various initiatives as a publisher, but on the battles he fought as a guardian of the literary in post-war Britain. By championing Beckett as a modernist sage with a profoundly humane and even ennobling moral vision that would appeal to the 'average reader', Calder undoubtedly made him serve his own purposes, but these were not merely commercial. More icon than brand, his Beckett emerged partly out of the conflicts he had with the British state, partly out of his struggle against British reviewers whose cultural assumptions were even more at odds with the writing than Calder's own, and partly out of the Arnoldian mission to which he dedicated himself as a member of the British liberal elite of the 1960s and 1970s. For Calder, Beckett stood for, even exemplified the 'unfamiliar art' and 'serious literature' he set out to promote as a 'public good'. That he deformed the writing in the process was as much an expression of his cultural ambition as it was a testament to his understanding of the realities of publishing Beckett for a British readership.

* * *

Calder's indebtedness to the Arnoldian tradition of cultural critique is also reflected in his passionate opposition to British insularity. His unfavourable comments about 'The Movement', the group against whom he defined his own stable, focused as much on their privileged class background as on the fact that they were, in his view, 'a very English and inward-looking group, disliking especially Europe and America' (Calder 2001: 277). In his memoirs he was no less severe about Scottish parochialism. Here, too, Beckett played an iconic part, this time as the inventive heir of 1920s cosmopolitan modernism. By developing strong, if often fraught, links with Barney Rosset of Grove Press, Maurice Girodias of Olympia and Jérôme Lindon of Editions Minuit, Calder formed part of a transnational axis of metropolitan

(New York-Paris-London) publishers who created space for Beckett, not as an Irish writer, say, but as a leading figure in a new, post-war cosmopolitan avant-garde. Indeed, it could be argued that Calder was among the most committed champions of a cosmopolitan Beckett, specifically in contrast to Lindon, who made his name publishing the French avant-garde of the 1950s. If Lindon linked Beckett primarily to the French *nouveau roman*, Calder placed him among a wider circle of writers, which looked back to the French Surrealists and German Expressionists, and sideways to a diverse range of contemporaries, including Ionesco, Pirandello and Duras, Miller, Selby and Burroughs, Trocchi, Burns and Bond. In his *Reader* he drew parallels (and important differences) between Beckett and Joyce, who 'developed the same cosmopolitan tastes and outlook'; identified Proust, Kafka and Joyce as 'the greatest of his twentieth-century predecessors'; and called Beckett the 'surest voice' in the 'real revolution in writing that has replaced Rattigan with Pinter, Malraux with Robbe-Grillet, Hemingway with Burroughs' (Calder 1967: 8 and 12).

While Calder presented Beckett as a cosmopolitan for British readers, Beckett also highlighted Calder's own cosmopolitanism. This is particularly evident in the use he made of Beckett in the Signature Series, which he launched in 1969 with *Darker Ends*, a volume of poems by the young English writer Robert Nye. As Calder noted in his memoirs, the series included 'experimental work' by 'Kenneth Gangemi (American), Nicholas Rawson (English and recommended to us by Beckett), Reinhard Lettau (German), Mark Insingel (Flemish), Ted Joans (Black American jazz poet), Peter Bischsel (Swiss), Yuli Daniel (Israeli), Robert Creeley (American), Chris Searle (English) and Eugenio Montale (Italian, later to win the Nobel Prize)'. 'Through this collection of lesser-known names, at least to the British reading public,' he then added, 'we threaded shorter works by Beckett, Sartre, Higgins, Trocchi (his poems) and Artaud' (Calder 2001: 376). Beckett's *Lessness* (1970) appeared as Signature 9 in the series, and *Texts for Nothing* (1974) as Signature 21. Calder also included the short text *Still* in the commemorative *Signature Anthology* (1975), which he produced to celebrate his twenty-five years in publishing. By making Beckett a key figure in the series, Calder used his prestige to bring younger, lesser-known writers from various countries to the attention of British readers, while also confirming and extending his own self-understanding as a publisher at the forefront of a new cosmopolitan culture. In the process, as he later recalled, he also unwittingly created a rich trove of collectibles: 'What I was doing of course, although it did not occur to me at the time, was producing books for the future rare book and first edition market' (Calder 2001: 376).

Seen in cultural rather than commercial terms, the Signature Series was perhaps even more paradoxical. At one level, it stands as a record of a particular cultural moment in which a disparate group of writers and works all came together under the auspices of Calder's cosmopolitanism. Like any publishers' series, it created a co-textual frame/envelope, inviting readers to think about *Lessness*, say, in relation to Christian Enzenberger's *Smut* (1972) or George Bataille's *Literature and Evil* (1973). At another level, since the series was, as its title suggested, intended to celebrate singularity, it put any such linkages in question and all cultural unities in doubt, whether defined in narrowly parochial (even national) or capaciously cosmopolitan terms. As Calder explained on the back cover of the anthology, 'the series was established to publish work by writers of the highest quality that is specifically idiosyncratic in form, length, or subject matter'. Referring to the signature device, he added that each volume 'represents a personal idea not to be expressed or arranged into conventional forms' (Beckett 1975: back cover). All the twenty-one volumes Calder published—Marion Boyars later continued the series under her own imprint—had a facsimile of the author's signature on the cover, a device he repeated on the front of the *Anthology*, which reproduced the signatures of all ten contributors: Beckett, Davie, Nye, Figes, Ionesco, Gangemi, Higgins, Rawson, Ann Quinn and Jan Quackenbush. Yet, simply by highlighting their *shared* 'idiosyncrasy' and arranging them as a new cosmopolitan avant-garde, Calder was inevitably betraying the radical singularity of their writing, once again leaving himself open to Ricks's charge of 'comfortable assimilation'. In this case, however, the problem was less interpretive than structural, and since it is an inescapable part of the publishing process, it was also not peculiar to Calder. As Beach astutely observed of the Signature Series, it 'epitomises that unavoidable and irrevocable process by which, little by little, Beckett's work—singular, unique, new, at its origin—loses its singularity as it is circulated in the public sphere, and as it is read alongside, and so through, the work of other writers' (Beach 2004: 95).

Yet this was a relatively high-minded problem, since for Calder the cosmopolitanism he championed was ultimately doomed for cruder reasons. Recalling the financial difficulties he faced in the 1980s, he once again focused on Thatcher, this time as the enemy of cosmopolitanism, though he also recognised the threat the giant publishing conglomerates posed to his activities. 'Thatcherism was taking its toll in a xenophobic dumbing down of international culture,' he commented, 'while review space was going to the big advertisers, so it was much harder to create awareness of what we were publishing' (Calder 2001: 542). These pressures were undoubtedly reshaping the cultural landscape in Britain, and presaging the end of the Calder era, though other factors were also beginning to make Calder's version of cosmopolitanism look as dated as his liberalism.

In the mid-1980s, for instance, the Arts Council, following broader political developments, for the first time recognised that 'British people of Afro-Caribbean and Asian origin' had 'developed a powerful voice which, if it is heard and acknowledged, will have a profound and enriching influence upon the artistic life of our multi-cultural society.'[6] This new official openness to Britain's diversity was premised on a broader understanding of cosmopolitanism, which extended beyond the northern, metropolitan co-ordinates that defined Calder's version. 'The influences of non-western art forms,' the Council observed in its annual report for 1986, 'have begun to be recognised and they in turn have been influenced by the indigenous cultures of the Caribbean and Europe.' This new thinking lay behind the development of the council's *Glory of the Garden* project in 1986 and its decision to commit 'a minimum of 4%' of its expenditure 'to the development of Afro-Caribbean and Asian arts by the end of two years'. This was, of course, also the year in which it cut Calder's annual grant by £25,000, before finally stopping it altogether. Not surprisingly, as an ardent defender of liberal individualism, Calder decried these new developments, commenting in 1999 that 'democracy has become a sham in every country where there are too many conflicting interests or ethnic minorities in collision' (Calder 1999: 15–16). Reflecting the restrictive assumptions underlying his idea of the cosmopolitan, which centred on Western eclecticism, he added in a similarly testy spirit that 'Beethoven and Shakespeare have no place in African culture, nor do most modern equivalents, but Peter Brook and John Cage would not be so alien there' (16–17). If this said a lot about the limits of Calder's cosmopolitanism, it also revealed his ignorance about the long, often fraught but also creative history of cultural exchange between Africa and Europe.

As I have argued, it is impossible to see Calder's complex relationship to Beckett, which was at once personal and institutional, in merely

---

[6] Arts Council, *41st Annual Report and Accounts 1985/6* (London: Arts Council, 1986), 9. See also Asha Rogers, *State Sponsored Literature: Britain and Cultural Diversity after 1945*, Oxford: Oxford University Press, 2020.

commercial or crudely ideological terms. If Calder was, for Beckett, a tireless if sometimes questionable sponsor who helped to bring his work to the attention of a new generation of British readers and others across the Anglophone world, Beckett was, for Calder, an icon of the liberal, avant-garde, cosmopolitan culture to which he committed himself out of a sense of 'public duty'. As the depth of feeling on both sides reveals, this 'elective affinity' brought obvious benefits to both parties. It also had a transformative impact on British culture of the post-war era. For literary historians, the challenge, as I have suggested and tried to demonstrate, is to develop a mode of analysis with which to understand the forces at work in this relationship and a language with which to appreciate its historical specificity and importance. For literary critics, I would argue the task is to build on this analysis by looking in greater detail at its interpretive consequences, not least to create space for a new, post-Calder Beckett to emerge.

One way of doing this might be to consider how Beckett's writings were absorbed, questioned and transformed by a new generation of writers not just in Europe and America, but in Africa, where, according to Calder, he supposedly had 'no place', a claim at least one major writer's oeuvre calls into question. Towards the end of J. M. Coetzee's fictionalised memoir *Youth* (2002), the young narrator, John, comes across 'a chunky little book with a violet cover: *Watt*, by Samuel Beckett, published by Olympia Press'. It is the early 1960s and he is in London, having fled apartheid South Africa. The book is a puzzling but revelatory discovery, partly because John only knows of Beckett as a dramatist, partly because he associates Olympia Press with pornography. 'It is hardly likely that Samuel Beckett, author of *Waiting for Godot* and *Endgame*, writes pornography,' he thinks. Then, posing the question all readers attuned to the effects publishers have on the writings we encounter, he asks: 'What kind of book, then, is *Watt*?' (Coetzee 2002: 155). As Calder's Beckett passes into history and we try to fashion a new, ideally less iconic Beckett for the twenty-first century, it is difficult to think of a more productive point from which to start, and no doubt fail, again, but perhaps fail better.

Chapter 13

Once upon a Time in a Bookshop: *The Satanic Verses* Revisited

In August 2006, to prepare for a talk I was going to give the following month, I visited a local branch of Waterstones in Oxford, England to buy a book. As the title I wanted was classified under 'Fiction', which in the lexicon of booksellers at the time meant not so much the opposite of 'non-fiction' as the antithesis of 'genre fiction'—not 'Sci-fi', say, or 'Crime' fiction—the book was in a prime position on the ground-floor, immediately behind the latest arrivals and the three-for-two bargains. Given the marketing ingenuity that chains put into designing their retail space, I knew this position signalled the continuing commercial success of 'Fiction' in the booksellers' special sense. I found this reassuring, especially since the old chestnut about the death of literature was then going through one of its perennial revivals. As an object the book was familiar enough, though, as a reasonably diligent follower of book trade practices, I knew by its size, shape and feel that it was not quite the mere paper (pre-digital) thing it appeared to be—remember, this is 2006, the year before Kindle arrived on the scene. Measuring 130 mm by 190 mm, it wore its B-format paperback status as a badge of honour. (As it happens, this is the size Amazon chose for the first Kindle.) These print-era markers indicated that it was published under a prestigious literary imprint and intended to be sold mainly in specialist bookshops, like Waterstones, not in supermarkets. In the unstable but still hierarchical literary marketplace of the early 2000s, B-format paperbacks upheld the distinction between books as culturally esteemed symbolic goods and books as disposable mass-market commodities, a fragile, paper-based order Kindle was about to disrupt.

The bibliographical details on the inside pages confirmed what the format suggested. The book was published by Vintage, then the specialist literary paperback imprint of the Random House Group in the UK, the multinational subsidiary of Random House Inc. in the US, which was in turn the trade publishing division of the German global media conglomerate Bertelsmann AG (it is now part of the Penguin Random House group). Vintage prided itself on the portability and literary quality of its books, which, as the publicity tag on the cover pointedly emphasised, allow you to 'Take your imagination with you'. The elevated cultural status of my B-format Vintage Book was underscored by the laudatory endorsements on the cover from established authors—Nadine Gordimer and Angela Carter—and the Anglo-American broadsheet and literary press. Gordimer called it 'a staggering achievement, brilliantly enjoyable', while the *New York Review of Books* compared it to 'Swift's *Gulliver's Travels*, Voltaire's *Candide* and Sterne's *Tristram Shandy*' (Rushdie 2006: covers). What all these material, institutional and textual markers/envelopes indicated is that by all contemporary measures this was a work of serious literature, belonging to a canonical European tradition dating back to the great Enlightenment fictions of the eighteenth century.

All these minor, seemingly extrinsic, details had a special hold over me because the book in question was the latest paperback edition of Salman Rushdie's *The Satanic Verses* (1988). It was striking enough that the late twentieth century's most iconically controversial novel was readily available in paperback under a mainstream literary imprint, as it had been since 1998. As the book's dedication indicated, this was not always the case. Unlike the first hardback edition, which was published in the UK by Viking in 1988 and which bore a more personal inscription to Rushdie's then wife ('For Marianne'), this edition was dedicated 'to the individuals and organisations who have supported this publication' (Rushdie 1988: v). In 1992, 'this publication' referred to the first paperback edition, which was brought out, amid further controversy, by an anonymous company called 'The Consortium' that had been especially constituted in the US State of Delaware for that purpose. This was after Viking-Penguin, who were still the focus of a campaign of intimidation, ceded the rights back to Rushdie at his request. And 'the individuals and organisations' referred not just to the 'International Committee for the Defence of Salman Rushdie and his Publishers', initiated in 1989 by Article 19, the London-based free expression advocacy group, but to the writers, journalists and politicians who began actively calling for the publication of the paperback after the first anniversary of the *fatwa* in February 1990. By 2006, the dedication had a different, perhaps less urgent, meaning, though the fact that it remained suggested that Rushdie still wished to record the novel's tragic early publishing history and to acknowledge the ongoing support of publishers, like Vintage, who risked keeping the book in print.

So the fact that *The Satanic Verses* was by then widely available as a Vintage paperback was not merely of bibliographical interest. Yet what made my visit to Waterstones an especially sobering, even vertiginous experience was the realisation that my simple act of taking the book off the shelves was made possible not just by the publishers and booksellers who openly supported the novel's publication, but by the more powerful guardians, in this case the British state and European human rights structures, that protected them. This is not just because both bodies uphold certain ideals without which modern European ideas of literature would not exist, notably the autonomy of the public sphere, the rights to intellectual property, to free expression and, in the British case, the special cultural status of books (the UK, unlike most other European states, exempts books from VAT). It is, more particularly, because both bodies dismissed appeals by offended Muslims who attempted to bring a case against Rushdie and his then publishers Viking-Penguin under English and European law. Since these specific decisions had a part to play in my actions in Waterstones, I shall briefly describe some of the salient issues they raised. This will also set up the next part of my discussion, focusing on the history of *The Satanic Verses* in the world beyond Europe, particularly in apartheid and post-apartheid South Africa.

* * *

Early in 1990, two separate, though apparently concerted, cases were brought before the English High Court. The two applicants, who had previously failed to bring criminal prosecutions against Rushdie and his publishers in the Magistrate courts a year before, applied for a judicial review, partly to test the law, partly to have the earlier decisions overruled. The first case, which was brought by Abdul Choudhury, who was acting on behalf of the Muslim Action Front, attempted primarily to argue that English blasphemy laws covered all three major religions: Islam, Christianity and Judaism. The second case, which was brought by Sayid Siadatan, an Iranian living in Britain, invoked the Public Order Act of 1986, focusing on the question of whether the distribution of *The Satanic Verses* would provoke unlawful violence. In both cases the High Court refused the application for review and upheld the Magistrates' earlier rulings.

In the first, the court argued that, since the offence of blasphemy was, under English common law dating from the seventeenth century, inseparable from sedition, it was exclusively and unequivocally linked to the Christian faith. For the courts this meant that a crime against God had to be treated as a crime against the state and, more specifically, the established Anglican Church. As *The Satanic Verses* did not constitute such a crime, it could not be deemed blasphemous under the law. The second case, which, the court admitted, was based on more secure grounds, failed largely because of a technicality. As the Magistrate had noted, the applicant had not produced evidence to show that immediate violence would follow if distribution continued. Significantly, in summing up the High Court's ruling, the leading judge in the first case, who recognised the novel's literary value and the offence it had caused, noted that the courts' powers were limited, since, in this case, there was no uncertainty about the law. Even if the court felt that the laws of blasphemy might be considered 'anomalous or even unjust', or, as one key legal precedent eloquently put it, 'shackled by the chains of history', it could not reach any other determination.[1] Any major review was, he insisted, the prerogative of Parliament alone. It is worth recalling that the Law Commission recommended that the offence of blasphemy be abolished in 1985 and that Tony Benn, the opposition Labour MP, presented a bill, which was not carried, to the House of Commons endorsing the commission's view four years later at the height of the 'Rushdie Affair'—the common law offences of blasphemy in England and Wales were eventually abolished in 2008, with Scotland following in 2021.

Having failed to make any headway at the national level—his application for leave to appeal to the House of Lords was refused in July 1990—Choudury exercised his rights as a British citizen by taking the case to the European Court in September. Developing his other key but ultimately unsuccessful arguments in the High Court hearing, which centred on Britain's obligations under the European Convention of Human Rights (1950), he entered two formal complaints: the first, which fell under Article 9 of the convention, was that 'the United Kingdom has not given the Moslem religion protection against abuse or scurrilous attacks, and that without that protection there will inevitably be a limited enjoyment of the right to freedom of religion provided for by that Article'; the second, which

---

[1] R v Chief Metropolitan Stipendiary Magistrate, ex parte Choudhury [1991] 1 All ER 306; R v Horseferry Road Metropolitan Stipendiary Magistrate, ex parte Siadatan [1991] 1 All ER 324.

fell under Article 14, was that the protection afforded exclusively to the Christian religion under English blasphemy law was discriminatory. The Commissioners, who were at the time responsible for deciding which cases could legitimately go before the court, agreed with the English High Court, and deemed both complaints inadmissible on related grounds. They noted that

> the applicant sought to have criminal proceedings brought against the author and the publisher of the book 'Satanic Verses' in order to vindicate his claim that the book amounted to a scurrilous attack on, inter alia, his religion. He does not claim, and it is clearly not the case, that any State authority, or any body of which the United Kingdom Government may be responsible under the Convention, directly interfered in the applicant's freedom to manifest his religion or belief.[2]

Seeking redress via the convention, which applied to states only, was inappropriate, the Commissioners claimed, because its provisions could not be extended horizontally to guarantee a right, on the part of an individual or group, to bring a criminal case against an author or publisher for offending their religious 'sensitivities'. This claim followed uncontentiously from Article 27 of the convention. By contrast, the Commissioners' claim that the convention applied to states if and only if they 'directly interfered' in a citizen's freedoms was a standard but disputed interpretation.

This summary account of a complex and closely argued series of decisions, which, in turn, opens up the vast, tangled politico-legal histories that have shaped distinctively English and European modernities at least since the seventeenth century, might go some way towards justifying my sense of vertigo on an otherwise ordinary afternoon in Waterstones. It does not, however, explain why my feelings were fixated on the simple act of taking a copy of *The Satanic Verses* off the shelves. What made this an issue for me was the realisation that, at that point in 2006, I could not do the same thing in one of Cape Town's branches of Exclusive Books, South Africa's equivalent to Waterstones.

* * *

Had I been talking about the contrast between South African and British bookshops around seventeen years earlier, say, in 1989, this

---

[2] Choudhury v UK, no. 17439/90, 5 March 1991.

would not have been so striking. After all, in late October 1988, apartheid South Africa, following India, Pakistan and various countries across the Middle East, banned *The Satanic Verses* in its first hardback edition. This was two months before the book burnings in Bradford in the UK and the demonstrations in Hyde Park, and three months before the *fatwa* was proclaimed. As we shall see, this decision, which tested anti-apartheid solidarities and divided South Africa's minority Muslim community, was not as predictable as it seemed at the time. It was, however, not inconsistent with the apartheid government's disregard for basic freedoms. The same cannot, of course, be said for South Africa's young democracy in 2006, which was underpinned by one of the most progressive constitutions in the world. Given the terms of the European Convention, it is worth noting that the South African Bill of Rights, which places as much emphasis on traditional freedoms as it does on more recent ideas of human dignity, is unconditionally binding on all organs of the state and conditionally binding on all 'natural or juristic' persons—so it allows for some horizontal extension beyond state bodies to individuals and groups.

Why, then, could I not take a copy of *The Satanic Verses* off the shelves at Exclusive Books in Cape Town? The answer is compelling, particularly given the questions facing intercultural and multifaith democracies today, though, as you might expect, it is far from straightforward, in part because the novel's status in the South Africa of 2006 was inseparable from the legacies of the past.

Just how *The Satanic Verses* fell into the hands of the apartheid censors is itself a knotty question. As it was not submitted by customs officials, the usual conduit for imported books, Nadine Gordimer suspected direct political interference. In an article, which appeared in the *New York Times* for 22 February 1989 and London's *Evening Standard* a week later, she speculated that the local 'Muslim extremists', as she called them, who campaigned for the ban were aided by 'a member of the Muslim community with influence in the House of Delegates' (Gordimer 1989: 27). This, as she explained, was 'the segregated "house" of South African Indian collaborators in our apartheid tricameral parliament, which excludes Africans'. In the same article she also claimed that the censors banned the novel without reviewing it, as she had the only copy in the country at the time—proofs sent to her by Rushdie's American publisher. The chief censor, Abraham Coetzee, refuted both these claims at the time, but the fact that he scribbled a note to his colleagues saying that 'certain things' on the censorship file 'must be removed' suggests that his public version of events was at best partial.³ Based on the surviving documentary evidence, it is possible to say that the censors received a copy of the book, that it is extremely unlikely that they read it, and that the circumstances surrounding its submission were more convoluted than Gordimer's simple, and narrowly local, story of 'Muslim extremists' and apartheid collaborators allowed.

Following the chain of correspondence in the archives, we can reconstruct the following sequence of events. For reasons that will become apparent in a moment I have to be precise about the dates:

* The novel is officially published in the UK on 26 September 1988.
* On 21 October the well-established Islamic Foundation in Leicester (UK), which has been co-ordinating an international protest since the beginning of the month, sends a fax to the African Muslim Agency in South Africa, which contains the foundation's general statement against the novel as well as annotated copies of the pages which it regards as especially offensive. The highly charged protest statement, which was also published in *Impact International*, an independent Muslim news magazine, for 14 to 27 October, states that 'this work, thinly disguised as a piece of literature, not only grossly distorts Islamic history in general, but also portrays in the worst possible colours the very characters of the prophet Ibrahim and the Prophet Muhammad (peace be on them)'. The annotations focus on thirteen passages from the novel. Many of these refer to the poet Salman's subversive commentaries on, and manipulation of, Mahound's teachings, the interpolated 'satanic verses', which, as Rushdie himself repeatedly insisted in his own defence, belong to the 'dreams of a man [Gibreel] who is losing his mind' as depicted in a work of fiction (Rushdie 2005). Rushdie's various defences, some more convincing than others, require careful and detailed analysis. For now I shall simply note that his appeal to the novel's literariness, and fictionality in particular, is both indispensable and inadequate in part because it underestimates the inherent frailty of literary writing, as a discursive category, from which, paradoxically, so much of its power to intervene in the public domain derives.
* On 24 and 25 October prominent, mainstream Muslim organisations in South Africa, including the Muslim Judicial Council and the Council of Muslim Theologians, write to the censors demanding that the book be banned, giving detailed reasons and

---

³ Censorship file for *The Satanic Verses*: P88/10/144, Western Cape Provincial Archives, Cape Town, South Africa.

including the passages with the Leicester Foundation's marginal annotations. Importantly, the latter include a reference to M. M. Ashan's scholarly article 'The "Satanic" Verses and the Orientalists', which appeared in *Hamdard Islamicus*, V.1 (1982), 27–36. Ashan challenged the 'unsympathetic and often hostile' responses to the Qur'an by 'scholars of the Occident' who treated it 'as the writing of the Prophet and not, as Muslims regard it, the word of God revealed through the angel Gabriel' (27). The various local organisations also say they will shortly be able to make a copy of the novel available.

* On 26 October A. M. Bhorat sends a handwritten report, on one of the censors' official forms, to the chief censor recommending that the novel be banned because it is 'detrimental to the religious beliefs and convictions of the Muslim community'. His 'expert's report', as the censors call it, is, for the most part, a verbatim transcript of the Islamic Foundation's general statement. Bohrat, a South African Muslim who works as a film censor, also appears to have submitted a copy of the novel at this point, which the chief censor returns on 2 November.

* On 28 October the chief censor, following the usual procedure, convenes an *ad hoc* committee chaired, in this case, by J. P. Jansen, an Afrikaans professor of politics and one of the main security censors during the late apartheid era. Significantly, there are no literary censors among the members of this committee. It unanimously endorses Bohrat's recommendation, and, in its own final report, it simply reproduces his version of the Islamic Foundation's general statement and adds the more detailed remarks contained in the protest letters from local organisations. The only comments the committee itself adds focus on the novel's status as literature:

> In reaching its decision, the Committee has taken due consideration of the literary merit of the publication and of the author's previously acclaimed works, literary distinctions, etc. It is however felt that these considerations do not outweigh the obvious offence which his latest work is likely to give to the strongly protesting Muslim community in South Africa who clearly regard the book as offensive to their religious convictions or feelings, and likely to bring them as a section of the inhabitants of the Republic into ridicule or contempt, a point of view with which the Committee concurs.

The legalistic final sentence incorporates phrasing from the provisions, covering blasphemy and community relations, of the relevant

Publications Act 1974. The committee's decision not to treat the literariness of the novel as a trumping value was consistent with apartheid censorship legislation, which never formally protected literature, and with the censors' own highly equivocal practice. Throughout the apartheid era their capricious and often politically expedient literary judgements made decisions either for or against a specific publication particularly unpredictable. I detailed this history in *The Literature Police: Apartheid Censorship and its Cultural Consequences* (2009). In this case, they agreed with the Islamic Foundation's view that the novel was the 'grossest sacrilege', which was at best 'thinly disguised as a piece of literature'.

* Consequently, *The Satanic Verses* is officially banned on 28 October 1988.

This meant that the whole process from complaint to banning was completed in four days, which was something of a record, since, as exasperated local booksellers and authors frequently noted, it generally took anything from a month to three months for a book to get through the apartheid censorship bureaucracy. Given the gaps in the record, it is not possible to say if this remarkable efficiency was a direct result of political interference, whether from the House of Delegates, as Gordimer thought, or any other branch of the apartheid state. Yet it is difficult not to infer from the timing and the wider circumstances that pressures of some kind were brought to bear on the censors to respond promptly to genuine protests by respected Muslim organisations. After all, as the local press reported throughout that week, Rushdie was due to speak against censorship at a high-profile anti-apartheid literary festival in South Africa on 31 October 1988 at the invitation of the Congress of South African Writers, which was affiliated to the United Democratic Front and the ANC. At that moment, then, the government had obvious political reasons for ignoring its official commitment to the idea of South Africa as an exclusively Christian state, which was written into the terms of the Publications Act of 1974, and for being especially concerned about the depths of Muslim feeling. Rushdie, in the end, decided to cancel his trip—but that is another complex story.

* * *

Whatever the truth about the precise extent to which the murky political manoeuvrings of the last apartheid government lay behind the banning of *The Satanic Verses* in 1988, the significance of the

21-OCT-88 FRI 14:15 ISLAMIC

The Satanic Verses

[Margin annotation: Satiric description of the contents of the Quran — the Holy Book of Muslims]

left unregulated, free. The revelation — the *recitation* — told the faithful how much to eat, how deeply they should sleep, and which sexual positions had received divine sanction, so that they learned that sodomy and the missionary position were approved of by the archangel, whereas the forbidden postures included all those in which the female was on top. Gibreel further listed the permitted and forbidden subjects of conversation, and earmarked the parts of the body which could not be scratched no matter how unbearably they might itch. He vetoed the consumption of prawns, those bizarre other-worldly creatures which no member of the faithful had ever seen, and required animals to be killed slowly, by bleeding, so that by experiencing their deaths to the full they might arrive at an understanding of the meaning of their lives, for it is only at the moment of death that living creatures understand that life has been real, and not a sort of dream. And Gibreel the archangel specified the manner in which a man should be buried, and how his property should be divided, so that Salman the Persian got to wondering what manner of God this was that sounded so much like a businessman. This was when he had the idea that destroyed his faith, because he recalled that of course Mahound himself had been a businessman, and a damned successful one at that, a person to whom organization and rules came naturally, so how excessively convenient it was that he should have come up with such a very businesslike archangel, who handed down the management decisions of this highly corporate, if non-corporeal, God.

After that Salman began to notice how useful and well timed the angel's revelations tended to be, so that when the faithful were disputing Mahound's views on any subject, from the possibility of space travel to the permanence of Hell, the angel would turn up with an answer, and he always supported Mahound, stating beyond any shadow of a doubt that it was impossible that a man should ever walk upon the moon, and being equally positive on the transient nature of damnation: even the most evil of doers would eventually be cleansed by hellfire and find their way into the perfumed gardens, Gulistan and Bostan. It would have been different, Salman complained to Baal, if Mahound

[Margin annotation: It casts serious aspersions on the process — nature and process of the divine revelation sent down to the Prophet Muhammad (peace be upon him)]

364

Figure 9 Annotated page from the fax dated 21 Oct 1988. Sourced from public domain file in the Western Cape Provincial Archives and Records, Cape Town, South Africa.

decision remains merely local and now historical. The same cannot be said for the subsequent ruling in the post-apartheid era. This decision speaks to the future of literature and its relation to the state in our globalised, intercultural era.

The novel remained technically banned in South Africa until February 2002, when it was removed from the list of restricted publications in terms of the new Film and Publication Act 1996. At that point many of the same local Muslim organisations that had campaigned against Rushdie in the apartheid era wrote to the new Film and Publication Board objecting in the strongest possible terms and requesting that a ban be re-imposed. As the board, which classifies rather than censors—its motto is 'We inform you choose'—has an obligation under the act and the constitution to be 'attentive to the needs and values of every faith system and every cultural community in South Africa', it convened a committee of experts to reconsider the case in June 2002. Representatives from among the principal complainants were invited to participate in the deliberations but none turned up.

The committee recognised that it faced a problem. For one thing, the option of outright banning was no longer available, except in very limited cases mainly to do with child pornography; for another, as it noted in its report, 'it might be argued that in a secular state, questions of religious propriety have no place in governmental decision-making'.[4] Moreover, under the new constitution the committee was bound to uphold Rushdie's right to 'freedom of expression', specifically including 'freedom of artistic creation', as well as his and his publishers' property rights. True, the constitutional guarantees in the case of the right to free expression were not unlimited, as they did not extend to the 'incitement of imminent violence' or the 'advocacy of hatred that is based on race, ethnicity, gender or religion, and that constitutes incitement to cause harm'. Yet even these limitations did not apply to '*bona fide* literary publications', which were specifically and additionally protected under the terms of the new Publication Act 1996. None the less, the committee was 'sympathetic to the charge of blasphemy and of severe hurt to the religious sensibilities of the Muslim community' and felt an acute 'sense of responsibility to the complainants, and to the public at large, to take these issues seriously'.

---

[4] Thanks to Iyavar Chetty, then Senior Executive Officer of the Film and Publication Board, for giving me a copy of the committee's report in 2003. The report is in the public domain.

Summing up its three main findings, which were on this occasion based on a careful reading of the novel and its history, the committee noted that

> although *The Satanic Verses* is considered profoundly blasphemous and injurious by the Muslim community, it does not in fact advocate hatred against Islam or indeed against any other religion or faith system. The material which is found to be injurious is a parodic literary deconstruction of ancient Islamic lore and belief, which is an unpacking of tenets of faith by an author, who, in the novel, questions the basis of his own belief. Salman Rushdie's Rabelaisian scepticism may well be profoundly shocking and hurtful to many of the Islamic faith but it does not invite hatred towards Islam. It certainly does not argue, in its pages, any incitement to cause harm or civil violence. Third, *The Satanic Verses* is without argument a bona fide literary work by a leading international literary figure.

For these three reasons the committee felt it was not 'legally possible' to consider giving the novel an XX classification which would, in effect, ban it by 'restricting all public access or possession'. Instead, it opted for an X18 classification, thereby limiting its distribution to adults only, and it recommended that the novel 'should not be for sale *in public* in South African commercial booksellers or any other commercial outlet, nor should it be available for borrowing from any municipal or public library' (the latter restriction did not apply to legal deposit or university libraries).

This is why I could not take a copy of the novel off the shelves at Exclusive Books in Cape Town in 2006, though, as the committee insisted, these restrictions did not prevent me from asking a local bookseller to order one for me, or, 'given the transnational nature of the contemporary book trade', buying one for myself over the internet.

* * *

It could be argued that *The Satanic Verses* does not make a particularly good test case for the post-apartheid legal framework in South Africa. For one thing, somewhat like D. H. Lawrence's *Lady Chatterley's Lover* in the landmark trials of the 1960s, its status as a '*bona fide* literary work' was, like Rushdie's reputation, too securely established by 2002 (though it is, of course, still contested in some quarters). It is possible to imagine other kinds of writing, say, a parody of vicious racist thinking or of pornographic violence against children published by a previously unknown author on the internet or social media, about which it might, in principle, be impossible for any committee of literary experts to reach a consensus. As the British philosopher Bernard Williams argued on several occasions, this is an insuperable juridical difficulty for any law intended to 'protect creative activity' in so far as it 'makes the deeply scholastic assumption that the merit of a given work must be recognizable to experts at the time of its publication' (Williams 1979: 110). This kind of argument lay behind the recommendation, put forward by the 1979 UK Commission on censorship and obscenity, which Williams chaired, that all restrictions on the 'printed word' (what about the digital word today?) should be lifted, and, no doubt, similar arguments about the essentially contested nature of the literary, or of artistic merit more generally, could be made in defence of the abolition of blasphemy laws (see chapter 8). To this extent the *Satanic Verses* decision in 2002 does not expose the potential pitfalls of the 1996 Publication Act, which does not lift all restrictions on the printed or digital word and does indeed make 'deeply scholastic' assumptions, partly for the well-intentioned purpose of redressing the legacies of apartheid censorship laws which did not protect creative activity.

Any claims about the international relevance of the 2002 decision rest, however, on the fact that the board restricted the public display of the novel not under the Publications Act but under Section 36 of the 1996 Bill of Rights. This section, which raises the self-reflexive question about application of constitutionally guaranteed rights in unusually general terms, empowers the board to restrict any right—in this case primarily Rushdie's right to free expression—'to the extent that the limitation is reasonable and justifiable in an open and democratic society based on human dignity, equality and freedom' (Constitution 1996). Any such restriction was also dependent on other factors, including 'the nature of the right' and 'the importance of the purpose of the limitation'. The committee took the view that its recommendations regarding the public display of the novel, which allowed the board to 'satisfy the theological and religious concerns of the South African Muslim community while also allowing for the crucial principle of right of access and freedom of expression', represented a legitimate interpretation of this general constitutional provision. In the context of the controversies over the Danish cartoons in 2005, and the passing of the Racial and Religious Hatred Act 2006 in England and Wales, to say nothing of the controversies and violence surrounding *Charlie Hebdo* (2011–20), this decision, which did in fact appear to satisfy the complainants, unsettles the predictable positions that tend too quickly to dominate public debates about free expression. At the same time, it opens alternative, less Manichean ways of thinking about the future of literary writing today.

In response to Muslim calls for an apartheid-era ban to be reimposed, it offered not censorship (nor a reinstatement of blasphemy law) but recognition, at the level of the state, of the offence many law-abiding Muslims feel the novel has caused them and their faith. In response to secularist, libertarian or literary arguments against all forms of state censorship, it offers both a robust defence of Rushdie's commitment to literature as a space in which, as he put it in an interview in September 1988, 'there are no subjects which are off limits', and a practical way of acknowledging, again at the level of the state, that understood in these terms literature has the power to produce shattering real-world effects (Basu 1989: 41).

In short, like the constitution on which it is based, the SA Board's decision goes beyond the disablingly emphatic either/or, in which an absolutely autonomous public sphere seems to be the only alternative to state censorship, or vice versa, while recognising that, in today's unpredictable, connected and heterogeneous world, states are judged and defined not just by the rights they regard as indispensable but by the ways in which they decide to apply and uphold them in particular cases.

Taking down a copy of *The Satanic Verses* from the shelves in Waterstones in Oxford in 2006, I was powerfully reminded of the modern, specifically European history in which, as Jacques Derrida once put it, literature tied its 'destiny to a certain noncensure, to the space of democratic freedom' (Derrida 1995: 28). Asking for a copy to be ordered for me in Exclusive Books in Cape Town gave me a vividly visceral sense of just how valuable, fragile and potentially incendiary that linkage continues to be.

(*Coda*, December 2023: though the SA Board's 2002 decision is still technically in force, it appears local booksellers are no longer adhering to it, as the paperback edition of *The Satanic Verses* is now on display once again.)

Bibliography

Achebe, Chinua [1958] (1985), *Things Fall Apart*, London, Ibadan, Nairobi: Heinemann.
—— (1977), 'An Image of Africa', *The Massachusetts Review*, 18.4: 782–94.
Adams, Thomas and Nicolas Barker (1993), *A Potencie of Life: Books in Society*, London: British Library.
Advertisement (1889), *Scots Observer*, 18 May: 731.
Armah, Ayi Kwei [1969] (1975 and 1984), *The Beautyful Ones Are Not Yet Born*, London: Heinemann.
Arnold, Matthew (1962), *Lectures and Essays in Criticism*, ed. R. H. Super, Ann Arbor: University of Michigan Press.
—— [1867] (1993), *Culture and Anarchy and Other Writings*, ed. Stefan Collini, Cambridge: Cambridge University Press.
Arts Council (1986), *41st Annual Report and Accounts 1985/6*, London: Arts Council.
Attridge, Derek and Jane Elliott, eds. (2011), *Theory after 'Theory'*, London: Routledge.
Barnes, Douglas and R. F. Egford, eds. [1959] (1982), *Twentieth-century Short Stories*, London: Harrap.
Basu, Shrabani (1989), 'Of Satan, Archangels and Prophets', eds. Lisa Appignanesi and Sara Maitland, *The Rushdie File*, London: Fourth Estate.
Barthes, Roland [1953] (2001), *Writing Degree Zero*, trans. Annette Lavers and Colin Smith, New York: Hill and Wang.
—— [1957] (1973), *Mythologies*, trans. Annette Lavers, London: Paladin.
—— (2000), *A Roland Barthes Reader*, ed. Susan Sontag, 2nd ed., London: Vintage.
Beach, Clare (2004), 'Beckett and the Institution of Literature', unpublished doctoral thesis, University of Oxford.
Beckett, Samuel, et al. (1929), *Our Exagmination Round His Factification for Incamination of Work in Progress*, London: Faber and Faber.
——, et al. (1975), *The Signature Anthology*, London: Calder and Boyars.
—— (1983), *Disjecta*, ed. Ruby Cohn, London: John Calder.
—— (2009), *Watt*, London: Faber and Faber.
Bell, Bill (2001), 'English Studies and the Trouble with History', *SHARP News*, 11(1): 3.

Blanchot, Maurice [1955] (1982), *The Space of Literature*, trans. Ann Smock, Lincoln: University of Nebraska Press.
—— (1995), *The Blanchot Reader*, ed. Michael Holland, Oxford: Blackwells.
—— [1959] (2003), *The Book to Come*, trans. Charlotte Mandell, Stanford: Stanford University Press.
Bloom, Harold (1994), *The Western Canon*, London: Macmillan.
Bornstein, George (1991), 'Remaking Himself: Yeats's Revisions of His Early Canon', *Text: Transactions of the Society for Textual Scholarship*, 5: 339–58.
Bourdieu, Pierre (1993), *The Field of Cultural Production*, ed. Randal Johnson, Cambridge: Polity Press.
Brooke, Stopford A. (1893), *The Need and Use of Getting Irish Literature into the English Tongue*, London: T. Fisher Unwin.
Brooke, Stopford A. and T. W. Rolleston, eds. (1900), *A Treasury of Irish Poetry in the English Tongue*, London: Smith, Elder, & Co.
Brouillette, Sarah (2019), *Unesco and the Fate of the Literary*, Stanford: Stanford University Press.
Calder, John (1961), 'Place for Small Publishers', *The Times*, 3 June: 9.
—— (1967), 'Introduction', in *A Samuel Beckett Reader*, ed. John Calder, London: New English Library: 7–20.
—— (1981), 'Why access to the arts must get precedence over the run-of-the-mill "James Joyces"', *Guardian*, 1 May: 12.
—— (1999), 'The Three-Headed Hydra', in *In Defence of Literature*, Oakville: Mosaic Press: 11–20.
—— (2001), *Pursuit: The Uncensored Memoirs of John Calder*, London: Calder Publications.
——, et al. (1973), 'Censorship and Freedom', *The Times*, 30 January: 15.
Campbell, D. (2008), 'A victory for irony as Elton John loses Guardian libel Case', *Guardian*, 13 December: 1–2.
Carroll, D., ed. (1990), *The States of 'Theory'*, Stanford: Stanford University Press.
Carroll, Noël (1998), *A Philosophy of Mass Art*, Oxford: Clarendon Press.
Carroll, Robert and Stephen Prickett, eds. (1997), *The Bible: Authorized King James Version*, Oxford: Oxford University Press.
Casanova, Pascale (2005), *The World Republic of Letters*, trans. M.B. Debevoise, Cambridge: Harvard University Press.
Castles, A., K. Rastle and K. Nation (2018), 'Ending the Reading Wars: Reading Acquisition from Novice to Expert', *Psychological Science in the Public Interest*, 19(1): 5–51.
Chartier, Roger (1992), 'Labourers and Voyagers: From the text to the reader', *Diacritics*, 22(2): 49–61.
—— (1994), *The Order of Books*, trans. Lydia G. Cochrane, Stanford: Stanford University Press.
Chaudhuri, Supriya (2016), 'Singular Universals: Rabindranath Tagore on World Literature and Literature in the World', in *Tagore: The World*

as his Nest, eds. Subhoranjan Das Gupta and Sangeeta Datta, Kolkata: Jadavpur University Press: 74–88.
Cheah, Pheng (2016), *What is a World?*, Durham: Duke University Press.
Clegg, Cyndia (2001), 'History of the Book: An Undisciplined Discipline?', *Renaissance Quarterly*, 54(3): 221–45.
Coetzee, J. M. [1974] (1982), *Dusklands*, Braamfontein: Ravan Press.
—— (1977), *In the Heart of the Country*, London: Secker & Warburg.
—— (1978), *In the Heart of the Country*, Johannesburg: Ravan Press.
—— [1980] 'The Book in Africa' (Seminar), Amazwi, Makhanda, South Africa, 2002. 13:2.1.1.
—— (1986), *Foe*, Johannesburg: Ravan Press.
—— (1988), *White Writing*, New Haven: Yale University Press.
—— (1988), 'The Novel Today', *Upstream*, 6(1): 2–5.
—— (1992), *Doubling the Point*, ed. David Attwell, Cambridge: Harvard University Press.
—— (1999), *Disgrace*, London: Secker & Warburg.
—— (2002), *Youth*, London: Secker & Warburg.
—— and Paul Auster (2013), *Here and Now*, London: Faber and Harvill Secker.
—— (2015), *In the Heart of the Country*, London: Vintage.
Constitution (1996), *Constitution of the Republic of South Africa*, https://www.gov.za/documents/constitution-republic-south-africa-1996-preamble. Accessed 22 October 2022.
Coomaraswamy, A. K. (1949), *The Bugbear of Literacy*, London: Dennis Dobson.
Cornelissen, P. L. et al. (2009), 'Activation of the Left Inferior Frontal Gyrus in the First 200 ms of Reading: Evidence from Magnetoencephalography (MEG)', *PLoS ONE* 4(4): e5359.
Council (2017), *Council decides about the future of the name of Rhodes University*, 6 December, https://www.ru.ac.za/latestnews/archives/2017/councildecidesaboutthefutureofthenameofrhodesuniversity.html. Accessed 22 October 2022.
Currey, James (1993), 'The African Writers Series at 30', *Southern African Review of Books*, March–April: 4.
—— (2008), *Africa Writes Back*, Oxford: James Currey.
Damrosch, David (2003), *What Is World Literature?*, Princeton: Princeton University Press.
——, ed. (2014), *World Literature in Theory*, London: Routledge.
Danto, A. C. (1999), *Philosophizing Art*, Berkeley: University of California Press.
Darnton, Robert (1990), *The Kiss of Lamourette*, London: Faber and Faber.
—— (1996), *The Forbidden Best-sellers of Pre-Revolutionary France*, London: Harper Collins Publishers.
—— (2007), 'What is the history of books? Revisited', *Modern Intellectual History*, 4(3): 495–508.

Davis, Caroline (2013), *Creating Postcolonial Literature: African Writers and British Publishers*, London: Palgrave Macmillan.
Deakin, S. et al. (2013) *Tort Law*, Oxford: Oxford University Press.
DeCasper, Anthony J. and Melanie J. Spence (1986), 'Prenatal maternal speech influences newborns' perception of speech sounds', *Infant Behavior and Development*, 9(2): 133–50.
de Costa, René (1979), *The Poetry of Pablo Neruda*, Cambridge: Harvard University Press.
Dehaene, Stanislas (2009), *Reading in the Brain*, New York: Penguin.
Derrida, Jacques [1965] (1978), *Writing and Difference*, trans. Alan Bass, London: Routledge.
—— (1992), *Acts of Literature*, ed. Derek Attridge, London: Routledge.
—— (1995), *On the Name*, ed. Thomas Dutoit, Stanford: Stanford University Press.
—— (1994), 'Some Statements and Truisms about Neo-logisms, Newisms, Postisms, Parasitisms, and other small Seisisms', in *The States of 'Theory'*, ed. David Carroll, Stanford: Stanford University Press: 63–94.
—— [1976] (1997), *Of Grammatology*, trans. Gayatri Chakravorty Spivak, 2nd ed., Baltimore: The Johns Hopkins University Press.
de Villiers, G. E., ed. (1997), *Ravan Twenty-Five Years*, Johannesburg: Ravan Press.
Dilks, John (2006), 'Portraits of Beckett as a Famous Writer', *Journal of Modern Literature*, 29(4): 161–88.
Du Garde Peach, L. (1960), *David Livingstone*, Loughborough: Wills & Hepworth.
Dugmore, Henry (1871), *The Reminiscences of an Albany Settler*, Graham's Town: Richards, Glanville & Co.
Dutta, Krishna and Andrew Robinson (1995), *Rabindranath Tagore*, London: Bloomsbury.
Eagleton, Terry (1996), *Literary Theory: An Introduction*, 2nd ed, Oxford: Blackwell.
—— (2003), *After Theory*, London: Allen Lane.
English, James (2005), *The Economy of Prestige*, Cambridge: Harvard University Press.
Ferguson, M. et al. (1996), *The Norton Anthology of Poetry*, New York: W. W. Norton.
Figes, Eva (1981), 'The writers who won't be invited to patronage's masquerade', *Guardian*, 4 May: 8.
Fish, Stanley (1980), *Is There a Text in This Class? The Authority of Interpretive Communities*, Cambridge: Harvard University Press.
—— (1989), 'Being Interdisciplinary Is So Very Hard to Do', *Profession* 89: 15–22.
Foucault, Michel [1969] (1988), 'What is an Author?', in *Modern Criticism and Theory*, ed. David Lodge, London: Longman: 196–210.
Foundation, Grahamstown (2015), 'Change of name 1820 Settlers Monument invitation for public participation', https://uploads.strikinglycdn.com/files/

d7ebd792-7c79-4fe2-9a56-560cc29909cb/name%20change%20call.pdf. Accessed 22 October 2022.
F.R.A.I. (1913), 'The House of Commons', *The New Freewoman*, I/5 (15 August): 85–86.
Garber, Marjorie (2001), *Academic Instincts*, Princeton: Princeton University Press.
Genette, Gerard (1997), *Paratexts: Thresholds of Interpretation*, trans. Jane E. Lewin, Cambridge: Cambridge University Press.
Gibbons, Simon (2014), *The London Association for the Teaching of English, 1947–67*, London: IOE Press.
Girodias, Maurice ed. (1971), *The Obscenity Report*, London: The Olympia Press.
Gordimer, Nadine (1989), 'Surely a novel can't shake Islam', *New York Times*, 22 February: 27.
Gould, Warwick (1978), 'Yeats as Aborigine', *Four Decades of Poetry, 1890–1930*, 2(2): 65–76.
Grainger J. and P. J. Holcomb (2009), 'Watching the word go by: On the time-course of component processes in visual word recognition', *Language and Linguistics Compass*, 3(1): 128–56.
Grüttemeier, R. and Laros, T. (2013), 'Literature in Law: Exceptio Artis and the Emergence of Literary Fields', *Law and Humanities*, 7(2): 204–17.
Guillory, John (2022), *Professing Criticism*, Chicago: Chicago University Press.
Harris, Roy (1986), *The Origin of Writing*, London: Gerald Duckworth.
Heaney, Seamus (1998), *Opened Ground: Poems 1966–1996*, London: Faber and Faber.
[Henley, W. E.] (1889), 'A New Irish Poet', *Scots Observer*, 9 March: 446–47.
Hyde, Marina (2008a), 'A peek at the diary of Sir Elton John', *Guardian Weekend*, 5 July: 16. See also http://www.theguardian.com/music/2008/jul/05/popandrock. Accessed 9 November 2022.
—— (2008b), 'Comment', *Guardian*, 13 December: 2.
Jeppie, Shamil and Souleymane B. Diagne, eds. (2008), *The Meanings of Timbuktu*, Cape Town: HSRC Press.
Johns, Adrian (2023), *The Science of Reading*, Chicago: Chicago University Press.
Johnson, Lorraine (2009), *Ladybird Books: a study in social and economic history*, doctoral thesis, Loughborough University.
Joyce, James (1930), https://tseliot.com/editorials/finnegans-wake. Accessed 22 October 2022.
—— [1939] (1975), *Finnegans Wake*, London: Faber and Faber.
—— [1939] (1946), *Finnegans Wake*, London: Faber and Faber.
—— (1957) *Letters of James Joyce*, vol. 1, ed. Stuart Gilbert, London: Faber and Faber.
—— (2000), *A Portrait of the Artist as a Young Man*, Oxford: Oxford University Press.

—— (1966), *Letters of James Joyce*, vol. 3, ed. Richard Ellmann, London: Faber.
Kelly, Kevin (2006), 'Scan this Book!', *New York Times Magazine*, 14 May, https://www.nytimes.com/2006/05/14/magazine/14publishing.html. Accessed 8 November 2022.
Kennedy, Maeve (1977), 'Dusty Africa', *Irish Times*, 11 June: 8.
Kenner, Hugh (1963), 'The Sacred Book of the Arts', in *Yeats: A Collection of Critical Essays*, ed. John Unterecker, Englewood Cliffs, NJ: Prentice-Hall: 10–22.
Keyes, Frances Parkinson (1944), *Also the Hills*, London: Eyre & Spottiswoode.
Kiefer, Markus and Natalie M. Trumpp (2012), 'Embodiment theory and education: The foundations of cognition in perception and action', *Trends in Neuroscience and Education*, 1(1): 15–20.
Kuhl, Patricia K. (2004), 'Early Language Acquisition: Cracking the Speech Code', *Nature Review Neuroscience*, 5: 831–43.
Lanier, Jaron (2010), *You are not a gadget*, London: Penguin.
Latham, Sean (2009) *The Art of Scandal: Modernism, Libel Law, and the Roman á Clef*, Oxford: Oxford University Press.
Lawrence, D. H. (1932), *Lady Chatterley's Lover*, London: Martin Secker.
Levenson, Michael (1984), *A Genealogy of Modernism*, Cambridge: Cambridge University Press.
Limbrick, Sarah (2008), 'Elton John demands £150k over "offensive, nasty and snide" article', *Press Gazette*, 26 September, https://pressgazette.co.uk/elton-john-demands-150k-from-guardian-over-offensive-nasty-and-snide-article. Accessed 9 November 2022.
Livingstone, David [1857] (1899), *Missionary Travels and Researches in South Africa*, London: John Murray.
Malan, Robin, ed. (1969), *Inscapes: A Collection of Relevant Verse*, Cape Town: Oxford University Press.
—— (2005), 'Me and Publishing', *Cape Librarian*, January/February, 49(1): 13–16.
Mampe, Birgit, et al. (2009), 'Newborns' Cry Melody Is Shaped by Their Native Language', *Current Biology*, 19(23): 1994–97.
Marsden, Dora (1913), 'Thinking and Thought', *The New Freewoman*, I/5 (15 August): 81–83.
McDonald, Peter D. (1997), *British Literary Culture and Publishing Practice, 1880–1914*, Cambridge: Cambridge University Press.
—— (2008), 'Old Phrases and Great Obscenities: The Strange Afterlife of Two Victorian Anxieties', *Journal of Victorian Culture*, 13(2): 294–302.
—— (2009), *The Literature Police: Apartheid Censorship and its Cultural Consequences*, Oxford: Oxford University Press.
—— (2017), *Artefacts of Writing: Ideas of the State and Communities of Letters from Matthew Arnold to Xu Bing*, Oxford: Oxford University Press.

—— (2020), 'Beyond Professionalism: The Pasts and Futures of Creative Criticism', in *The Critic as Amateur*, eds. Saikat Majumdar and Aarthi Vadde, New York: Bloomsbury.

McGann, Jerome J. (1991), *The Textual Condition*, Princeton: Princeton University Press.

McGurl, Mark (2021), *Everything and Less: The Novel in the Age of Amazon*, London: Verso Books.

McKenzie, D. F. (1999), *Bibliography and the Sociology of Texts*, Cambridge: Cambridge University Press.

McLuhan, Marshall (1962), *The Gutenberg Galaxy*, Toronto: University of Toronto Press.

Menand, Louis (2002), 'Cat People', *The New Yorker*, 23 December, https://www.newyorker.com/magazine/2002/12/23/cat-people. Accessed 13 February 2024.

Montag, J. L., M. N. Jones and L. B. Smith (2015), 'The Words Children Hear: Picture Books and the Statistics for Language Learning', *Psychological Science*, 26(9): 1489–96.

Mphahlele, Es'kia (2002), *Es'kia*, Cape Town: Kwela Books.

Mqhayi, S. E. K. (2018), *The Lawsuit of the Twins*, trans. Thokozile Mabeqa, Cape Town: Oxford University Press.

Mthethwa, Nathi (2018), 'Minister of Arts and Culture Nathi Mthethwa gazettes the renaming of Grahamstown to Makhanda', 2 July, https://www.gov.za/speeches/minister-arts-and-culture-nathi-mthethwa-gazettes-renaming-grahamstown-makhanda-2-jul-2018#. Accessed 22 October 2022.

Murphy, Colin (2009), 'Beckett begins again', *Prospect*, 26 April: 58–59.

Murray, P. R. and C. Squires (2013), 'The Digital Publishing Communications Circuit', *Book 2.0*, 3(1): 3–23.

Murray, Simone (2021), *Introduction to Contemporary Print Culture*, Abingdon: Routledge.

Murray, William and J. McNally (1962), *Key Words to Literacy*, London: Schoolmaster Publishing.

—— (1964), *1a: Play with us*, Loughborough: Wills & Hepworth.

Ndebele, Njabulo (1991), *Rediscovery of the Ordinary*, Johannesburg: COSAW.

Nelson, James G. (1971), *The Early Nineties: A View from the Bodley Head*, Cambridge: Harvard University Press.

Neville, Thelma (1974), 'Settlers' Commemoration', *South African Panorama*, October, 19(10): 10–15.

—— (1991), *More Lasting than Bronze: A story of the 1820 Settlers National Monument*, Pietermaritzburg: Natal Witness Printing and Publishing.

OED, https://www.oed.com/. Accessed 28 October 2022.

Ong, Walter J. [1982] (1988), *Orality and Literacy: The Technologizing of the Word*. London: Routledge.

Openshaw, Jeanne (2002), *Seeking the Bāuls of Bengal*, Cambridge: Cambridge University Press.

Opland, Jeff (2012), 'The Image of the Book in Xhosa Oral Poetry', in *Print, Text and Book Cultures in South Africa*, ed. Andrew van der Vlies, Johannesburg: Wits University Press.

Ortony, Andrew, ed. [1979] (1993), *Metaphor and Thought*, Cambridge: Cambridge University Press.

'Overview' (2016), *Journal of World Literature*, https://brill.com/view/journals/jwl/jwl-overview.xml#:~:text=The%20Journal%20of%20World%20Literature,all%20the%20world's%20literary%20traditions. Accessed 10 November 2022.

Payne, M. and J. Schad, eds. (2003), *life.after.theory*, London: Continuum.

Pethica, James, ed. (1996), *Lady Gregory's Diaries 1892–1902*, Gerrards Cross: Colin Smythe.

Pitman, Isaac (1843), *The Phonotypic Journal*, 1.

Pound, Ezra (1913), 'Contemporania', *The New Freewoman*, I/5 (15 August): 87–88.

—— (1951), *The Letters of Ezra Pound, 1907–1941*, ed. D. D. Paige, London: Faber & Faber.

Price, Leah and Matthew Rubery, eds. (2015), *Further Reading*, Oxford: Oxford University Press.

Price, Leah (2019), *What We Talk about When We Talk about Books*, New York: Basic Books.

Pringle, Thomas (1835), *Narrative of a Residence in South Africa*, London: Edward Moxon.

—— (1989), *African Poems of Thomas Pringle*, eds. Michael Chapman and Ernest Pereira, Pietermaritzburg: University of Natal Press.

Rainey, Lawrence (1998), *Institutions of Modernism: Literary Elites and Public Culture*, New Haven: Yale University Press.

Rée, Jonathan (1999), *I See a Voice*, London: Harper Collins Publishers.

Ricks, Christopher (1968), 'Mr Artesian', *The Listener*, 3 August: 148.

Rose, Jonathan (2001), 'From Book History to Book Studies', *American Printing History Association*, https://printinghistory.org/awards/society-history-authorship-reading-publishing-sharp/. Accessed 7 November 2022.

—— and Ezra Greenspan, (1998) 'An Introduction to *Book History*', *Book History*, 1: ix–xi.

Rushdie, Salman (2006), *The Satanic Verses*, London: Vintage.

—— (1988), *The Satanic Verses*, London: Viking.

—— (2005), 'Fiction of incitement law', *Guardian*, 19 February, https://www.theguardian.com/world/2005/feb/19/terrorism.religion. Accessed 16 December 2022.

Russell, Bertrand [1912] (1967), *The Problems of Philosophy*, Oxford: Oxford University Press.

—— [1918] (2010), *The Philosophy of Logical Atomism*, London: Routledge.

Sacks, Oliver (1984), *A Leg to Stand On*, London: Duckworth.

Sandwith, Corinne (2014), *A World of Letters: Reading Communities and Cultural Debates in Early Apartheid South Africa*, Pietermaritzburg: University of KwaZulu-Natal Press.

Sapiro, Gisèle (2016), 'How Do Literary Works Cross Borders (or Not)?', *Journal of World Literature*, 1(1): 81–96.
Schonell, Fred J. (1945), *The Psychology and Teaching of Reading*, Edinburgh: Oliver and Boyd.
Scott, James C. (2009), *The Art of Not Being Governed: An Anarchist History of Upland Southeast Asia*, New Haven: Yale University Press.
Selden, Raman, ed. (1995), *The Cambridge History of Literary Criticism: From Formalism to Poststructuralism*, Cambridge: Cambridge University Press.
Seuss, Dr (1958), *The Cat in the Hat*, London: Collins.
Sharp, Elizabeth, ed. [1896] (1910), *Lyra Celtica: An Anthology of Representative Celtic Poetry*, Edinburgh: Patrick Geddes and Colleagues.
—— (1910), *William Sharp (Fiona Macleod): A Memoir*, London: Heinemann.
SHARP (2008), *Conference Programme*, 1–40.
Sherry, Vincent (1993), *Ezra Pound, Wyndham Lewis, and Radical Modernism*, Oxford: Oxford University Press.
Slaughter, Joseph R. (2014), 'World Literature as Property / أدب العالم بوصفه ملكية', *Alif: Journal of Comparative Poetics* 34: 39–73.
Smallwood, Christine (2023), 'Misreading the Cues', *New York Review of Books*, 9 February: 6–8.
Stevenson, Randall (2004), *The Last of England?*, Oxford: Oxford University Press.
Stoddard, Roger (1987), 'Morphology and the Book from an American Perspective', *Printing History*, 9: 2–14.
Sun, Y., B. Sahakian, et al. (2023), 'Early-initiated childhood reading for pleasure: Associations with better cognitive performance, mental well-being and brain structure in young adolescence', *Psychological Medicine*, 1–15.
Tagore, Rabindranath (1961), *Rabindra Rachanabali* (Collected works of Rabindranath Tagore), 13, Calcutta: West Bengal Government.
—— (2001), *Selected Writings on Literature and Language*, eds. Sisir Kumar Das and Sukanta Chaudhuri, New Delhi: Oxford University Press.
Taylor, M. and D. Hill (2008), 'Johnson forced to remove his deputy mayor after magistrate claim proves false', *Guardian*, 5 July: 2.
Thompson, John B. (2010), *The Merchants of Culture*, Cambridge: Polity.
Tindall, William York (1969), *A Reader's Guide to Finnegans Wake*, New York: Farrar, Straus and Giroux.
Toynbee, Philip (1966), 'Order out of chaos', *Observer*, 2 January: 24.
Tugendhat, J. (2008), *Sir Elton John v. Guardian News and Media Limited*, EWHC 3066 (QB), 5 December: 1–47. See also http://www.bailii.org/ew/cases/EWHC/QB/2008/3066.html. Accessed 22 November 2022.
Unsigned (1889a), 'The Scot in Ulster', *Scots Observer*, 2 March: 402.
Unsigned (1889b), 'Irish Land Legislation', *Scots Observer*, 31 August: 397.
Unsigned (1890a), 'Thorough', *Scots Observer*, 10 May: 692.

Unsigned (1890b), 'National Types: In Ireland', *Scots Observer*, 27 September: 485–86.
Unsigned (1890c), 'Notes', *National Observer*, 22 November: 1.
Unsigned (1890d), 'A Word to Mr. Balfour', *National Observer*, 22 November: 4–5.
Unsigned (1892), 'Minors', *National Observer*, 7 May: 646.
Unsigned (1894), 'ΨAYMA ΨEASΨAI', *National Observer*, 21 April: 588–89.
van der Vlies, Andrew (2007), *South African Textual Cultures: White, black, read all over*, Manchester: Manchester University Press.
Vendler, Helen (1981), 'Presidential Address 1980', *PMLA*, 96(3): 344–50.
Watt, Ian and Jack Goody (1963), 'The Consequences of Literacy', *Comparative Studies in Society and History*, 5(3): 304–45.
West, Rebecca (1913), 'Imagisme', *The New Freewoman*, I/5 (15 August): 86–87.
Wicomb, Zoë (2020), *Still Life*, New York: New Press.
Williams, B. et al. (1979), *Report of the Committee on Obscenity and Film Censorship*, London: Her Majesty's Stationery Office.
Wilson, Duncan (1987), *Gilbert Murray*, Oxford: Oxford University Press.
Wittenberg, Hermann (2008), 'The Taint of the Censor: J. M. Coetzee and the Making of *In the Heart of the Country*', *English in Africa*, 35(2): 133–50.
Wittgenstein, Ludwig (1969), *The Blue and Brown Books*, Oxford: Blackwells.
Wolf, Maryanne (2018), *Reader, Come Home: The Reading Brain in a Digital World*, New York: Harper.
Woolf, Virginia [1927] (1977), *To the Lighthouse*, London: Grafton Books.
Yeats, J. B. (1972), *Letters from Bedford Park: A Selection from the Correspondence (1890–1901) of John Butler Yeats*, ed. William M. Murphy, Dublin: Cuala Press.
Yeats, W. B. (1889a), 'Village Ghosts', *Scots Observer*, 11 May: 692.
—— (1889b), 'Kidnappers', *Scots Observer*, 15 June: 100–01.
—— (1889c), 'Columkille and Rosses', *Scots Observer*, 5 October: 550.
—— (1890a), 'Tales from the Twilight', *Scots Observer*, 1 March: 409.
—— (1890b), 'Father Gilligan', *Scots Observer*, 5 July: 174–75.
—— (1892), 'The White Birds', *National Observer*, 7 May: 641.
——, et al. (1892), *The Book of the Rhymers' Club*, London: Elkin Mathews.
—— (1895), *Poems*, London: T. Fisher Unwin.
—— (1922), *The Trembling of the Veil*, London: T. Werner Laurie.
——, ed. (1936), *The Oxford Book of Modern Verse*, Oxford: Clarendon Press.
—— (1955a), *Autobiographies*, London: Macmillan.
—— (1955b), *Essays and Introductions*, London: Macmillan.
—— (1957), *The Variorum Edition of the Poems of W. B. Yeats*, eds. Peter Allt and Russel K. Alspach, New York: Macmillan.
—— (1970), *Uncollected Prose*, ed. John P. Frayne, 1, London: Macmillan.
—— (1972), *Memoirs*, ed. Denis Donoghue, London and Basingstoke: Macmillan.

—— (1975), *Uncollected Prose*, eds. John P. Frayne and Colton Johnson, 2, London: Macmillan.
—— (1986), *The Collected Letters of W.B. Yeats*, ed. John Kelly, 1, Oxford: Clarendon Press.
—— (1989), *Letters to the New Island*, eds. George Bornstein and Hugh Witemeyer, Basingstoke: Macmillan.
—— [1891] (1990), *John Sherman & Dhoya*, Dublin: Lilliput Press.
—— (1994), *The Collected Letters of W. B. Yeats*, John Kelly, et al. eds., 3, Oxford: Clarendon Press.
—— (1997), *The Collected Letters of W. B. Yeats*, John Kelly, et al. eds., 2, Oxford: Clarendon Press.

Index

Achebe, Chinua, 38–9, 42–4, 54, 104, 109, 112
Adams, Thomas, 20–2, 24–5, 30, 38, 51
Armah, Ayi Kwei, 111–12, 137
Arnold, Matthew, 85, 158, 173–5, 181, 186, 210–11, 215, 217
Arts Council, UK, 206, 208–9, 211–13, 220
Attridge, Derek, 80, 93

Barker, Nicolas, 20–2, 24–5, 30, 38, 51
Barnes, Douglas, 31–4
Barthes, Roland, 80–1, 83, 87–90
Beckett, Samuel, 50–1, 90, 203–21
Blanchot, Maurice, 76, 83, 89–91, 94, 144
Bloom, Harold, 87–8
Bourdieu, Pierre, 20, 80, 86, 90, 96–9, 115, 118, 137
Brooke, Stopford A., 151, 153, 167–8, 176–9
Brouillette, Sarah, 20, 22–4, 27

Calder, John, 203–21
Casanova, Pascale, 97, 135, 137
Chartier, Roger, 94, 102, 104, 133, 182, 192
Coetzee, J. M., 38–9, 43–4, 49, 54, 66–7, 94–6, 103–9, 111–12, 115, 128–41, 146–7, 221
Coomaraswamy, A. K., 29
Currey, James, 108–12

Damrosch, David, 138–9, 142
Danto, A. C., 114
Darnton, Robert, 4–5, 7–8, 10, 14, 20, 22, 38, 51–2, 73–5, 100–4, 107–9, 111, 133, 182
Dehaene, Stanislas, 10–11
Derrida, Jacques, 80–1, 83, 89, 90–1, 93–5, 97–8, 183, 192–3, 235

Eagleton, Terry, 80–3, 85–6, 88–90, 92, 97, 184
Egford, R. F., 31–4
English, James, 137

Fish, Stanley, 72, 85–6, 89–90, 97, 126
Foucault, Michel, 80, 94

Garber, Marjorie, 71–3
Genette, Gerard, 152, 161
Goody, Jack, 8, 10, 104
Gordimer, Nadine, 54, 137, 223, 227–8, 230

Harris, Roy, 142
Heaney, Seamus, 61
Henley, W. E., 154–61, 163–5, 170, 188
Hyde, Marina, 119–27

Johns, Adrian, 16
Joyce, James, 3, 49–51, 53–68, 77, 91, 93–5, 118, 121, 152, 187–9, 207, 213, 218

Keyes, Frances Parkinson, 45, 47–9
Kuhl, Patricia K., 16

Lanier, Jaron, 98–9
Lawrence, D. H., 32–4, 118, 190, 233
Livingstone, David, 28–9, 36–7, 41

McGann, Jerome J. 38, 46, 96, 182, 192
McKenzie, D. F., 44–50, 73, 92, 94, 102, 182, 192
McLuhan, Marshall, 8–12, 14, 25, 104
Malan, Robin, 34–6
Marsden, Dora, 193, 198–201
Menand, Louis, 17, 22, 26
Mphahlele, Es'kia, 30, 61, 104, 137
Mqhayi, S. E. K., 67–8

Ndebele, Njabulo, 61

Ong, Walter J., 8–13, 15–16, 30, 51, 104

Pitman, Isaac, 25
Pitman, James, 25
Pound, Ezra, 182–202
Pringle, Thomas, 59, 63–4, 66

Rée, Jonathan, 8
Rose, Jonathan, 75–7
Rosenbach, A. S. W., 3–4, 7, 49, 51

Rushdie, Salman, 61, 222–35
Russell, Bertrand, 38–42, 44–8, 50–2

Sacks, Oliver, 12
Sapiro, Gisèle, 139
Schonell, Fred J., 25–7, 29–30, 35, 37, 41, 52
Scott, James C., 23
Seuss, Dr, 14–17, 22, 26, 50, 52
Sharp, Elizabeth, 166, 174
Sharp, William, 166–7, 172–5

Tagore, Rabindranath, 53, 83, 142–7
Thompson, John B., 112
Tindall, William York, 56–7, 64

Vendler, Helen, 72

Watt, Ian, 8
West, Rebecca, 197–201
Wicomb, Zoë, 66
Williams, Bernard, 115–16, 127, 234
Wittgenstein, Ludwig, 4, 82, 131–2
Wolf, Maryanne, 10–12
Woolf, Virginia, 38, 42–3, 50, 190, 213

Xu, Bing, 2, 19

Yeats, W. B., 112, 151–81, 193, 205

EU representative:
Easy Access System Europe
Mustamäe tee 50, 10621 Tallinn, Estonia
Gpsr.requests@easproject.com